The Romantic Sublime
and Representations of Technology

Romantic Reconfigurations:
Studies in Literature and Culture 1780–1850

Series Editors:
Professor Tim Fulford, De Montfort University
Professor Alan Vardy, Hunter College and the Graduate Center, CUNY

As befits a series published in the city of Roscoe and Rushton, a city that linked Britain to the transatlantic trade in cotton, in sugar, and in people, *Romantic Reconfigurations* reconfigures the literary and cultural geographies and histories of Romanticism. Topics featured include, but are by no means confined to, provincial and labouring-class writing, diasporic and colonial writing, natural history and other scientific discourse, journalism, popular culture, music and theatre, landscape and nature, cosmopolitanism and travel, poetics and form.

The Romantic Sublime
and Representations of Technology

Michele Speitz

LIVERPOOL UNIVERSITY PRESS

First published 2024 by
Liverpool University Press
4 Cambridge Street
Liverpool
L69 7ZU

Copyright © 2024 Michele Speitz

Michele Speitz has asserted the right to be identified as the author of this book in
accordance with the Copyright, Designs and Patents Act 1988.

All rights reserved. No part of this book may be reproduced, stored in a retrieval
system, or transmitted, in any form or by any means, electronic, mechanical,
photocopying, recording, or otherwise, without the prior written permission
of the publisher.

British Library Cataloguing-in-Publication data
A British Library CIP record is available

ISBN 978-1-83553-670-4 cased

Typeset by Carnegie Book Production, Lancaster

Contents

Acknowledgments	vii
Introduction: Reinventing the Romantic Sublime, Nature, and Technology	1
1 Prometheus and Trophonius: Technological Myth and Sublime Scripts of Industry and Creativity	27
2 The Seismograph and a Keatsian "Material Sublime": On Sublime Worldbuilding and Unbuilding	63
3 Lyres, Levers, Boats, and Steam: Shelleyan Technologies of Sublime Correspondence	103
4 Suspension Bridges, Modern Canals, and the Infrastructural Sublime: Robert Southey, Thomas Telford, and the Traffic of Empire	135
Conclusion: An Aesthetic of Intimate Relations: Romanticism's Child of Sublime Nature and Technology—the Material Sublime	163
Bibliography	181
Index	195

for Jeff and Charlotte

Acknowledgments

This book's existence bespeaks many debts, just as any technology of the material sublime does. Among those kind and openhanded human beings who have contributed to its making, I must first name Professor Jeffrey N. Cox. He has always supported me as well as this book project, even though, when I first pitched it to him, he looked at me and said that whenever he reads of the sublime, he typically wants to throw any book containing such references out the window. Stalwart support also came from Jillian Heydt-Stevenson, Sue Zemka, Jordan Stein, David Clark, David Ferris, Padma Rangarajan, Devoney Looser, Adam Potkay, Orrin Wang, Tilar Mazzeo, Michael Gamer, Tim Fulford, Alan Vardy, Anahid Nersessian, Alexander Regier, Nancy Yousef, Billy Galprin, Dan White, Mark Lussier, Devin Griffiths, David Sigler, Kate Singer, Ron Broglio, Thora Brylowe, Kurtis Hessel, Scott Hagele, Terry F. Robinson, Dana Van Kooy, Devon Parks, Grace Rexroth, Rebecca Schneider, Greg Ellermann, Aaron J. Ottinger, John C. Leffel, Lindsay Thomas, and Mary Caton Lingold.

Vital help during the research stages of this project came from Huntington Library's Munger Research Center, the Furman Humanities Center, the National Humanities Center, the National Archives of Scotland, Jerwood Centre and the Wordsworth Trust, the British Library, as well as both the University of Colorado at Boulder and Furman University, with the latter two granting me not only necessary space but also time.

My colleagues and students at Furman have provided generous amounts of feedback on various ideas and chapters; they have inspired me, rooted me, and rooted for me whenever I most needed one or the other. For commenting on chapter drafts I offer special thanks to Nick Radel, Jeanne Provost, Laura Morris, Gregg Hecimovich, Shane Herron, Camille Lewis, Brandon Inabinet,

The Romantic Sublime and Representations of Technology

and Nadia Kanagawa. Joni Tevis has been a unique source of support and inspiration—ever ready to celebrate the book's arrival in printed, handleable form.

Family are the stuff that makes us and breaks us. And some of the family that have most helped me to spirit on from the start include my late great aunt Jean Fagan Yellin and my great aunt Ann Fagan Ginger, founder of the Meiklejohn Civil Liberties Institute of my home state, California—Berkeley, no less. Mary Fagan Bates, my grandmother, seeded teachings that have borne fruit and will continue to do so—not just through me but further, through my daughter. My grandfather, Paul Bates, was a barking man, taking me to Shakespeare before I could ever know what any of it meant. My grandmother, Shirley Speitz, is and was all that anyone good ever could be. My father, Charles John Speitz, is always with me wherever I go. My siblings have made me what I am. I thank you all.

Introduction

Reinventing the Romantic Sublime, Nature, and Technology

This book offers the first full-length study of the sublime stories British Romantic writers told about technology. Embracing a broad, capacious understanding of technology more at home today than during the long Romantic period (1750–1850), this project examines representations of Romantic machines and tools both aged and new: old standbys such as the lever or the teacup and modern marvels including the steam engine and the seismograph. Surveyed, in addition, are built environments and vast mechanical and infrastructural systems: mines, canal works, roadways, modern suspension bridges.[1] By grouping together this set of ancient and novel inventions, mechanisms, and systems—sourced from accounts penned by Anna Seward, Erasmus Darwin, John Keats, Robert Southey, Mary Godwin Shelley, Percy Bysshe Shelley and more—this book uncovers how each technology is linked to Romantic poetry through the discourse of the sublime. Moreover, this project demonstrates how a comparative study of these technologies relative to their aesthetic presentation and reception uncovers an overlooked iteration of the Romantic sublime, one that surfaces fresh accounts of Romantic nature that have bearing on twenty-first-century debates and concerns about the environment.

Building on landmark studies and a growing body of scholarship examining Romantic-era representations of technology, media, machines, and tools, *The Romantic Sublime and Representations of Technology* investigates how

---

[1] As Jon Klancher observes, "[i]n the long eighteenth century, a technology was something to read—a printed treatise or manual of skills that encompassed the whole range of what were then called the mechanical arts. The *OED* marks this meaning of the word as obsolete after 1860 (sense 1), but it flourished far and wide before then." "Scale and Skill in British Print Culture: Reading the Technologies, 1680–1820," *Studies in Eighteenth-Century Culture* 47 (2018): 89, https://doi.org/10.1353/sec.2018.0008.

The Romantic Sublime and Representations of Technology

technological aesthetics can deepen or foreshorten understandings of the natural world.[2] While literature comprises the primary source material for this project, beyond interceding in debates central to literary history, literary studies, and cultural studies, also at stake are the extra-literary actions and ideas informed by what we write and read. We need only look to literature's vast archive of sublime representations of technologies to begin to gauge just how much technological aesthetics can teach us about human–nature relations and valuations. Reaching back to Leo Marx's classic study of the American pastoral and nineteenth-century technological aesthetics, *The Machine in the Garden*, there we find Marx arguing that "to understand [Nathaniel Hawthorne's] response to the machine we must appreciate the intensity of his feeling for its opposite, the landscape."[3] Flipping such logic on its head, in what follows I explore how the reverse is true for authors of British Romanticism: to grasp their responses to the natural world we must inquire into the intensity of their feelings for inventions, technologies, machines, and tools. A core premise driving this book is that deeper understandings of technological aesthetics grant access to deeper understandings of humanity's relationships with nature. In other words, technological thinking frequently arrives enfolded with thinking about nature, such that how technologies are represented, valued, judged, and how they are felt or experienced often influences how nature comes to be known or imagined, and consequently, treated.

Three driving concerns animate this book: how the aesthetic of the sublime can clarify or contort our understandings of making, invention, and world-building; how sublime representations of poetry and technology ground our conceptualizations of human and natural agency; and how key Romantic-era stories of sublime technologies challenge fantasies of techno-utopia and myths of techno-salvation by instead insisting upon our technological *and* natural contingency. As aesthetic theorist Dominic McIver Lopes reminds readers, "A vast abyss has come to separate our best understanding of aesthetic value from the plain fact of its place in our lives."[4] *The Romantic Sublime and*

---

[2] See, for example, J. David Black, *The Politics of Enchantment: Romanticism, Media, and Cultural Studies* (Waterloo, Canada: Wilfrid Laurier University Press, 2002); Mark Coeckelbergh, *New Romantic Cyborgs: Romanticism, Information Technology, and the End of the Machine* (Cambridge, MA: The MIT Press, 2017); Jocelyn Holland, "From Romantic Tools to Technics: Heideggerian Questions in Novalis's Anthropology," *Configurations* 18, no. 3 (Fall 2010): 291–307, https://doi.org/10.1353/con.2010.0021; Allison Muri, *The Enlightenment Cyborg: A History of Communications and Control in the Human Machine, 1660–1830* (Toronto: University of Toronto Press, 2007); John Tresch, *The Romantic Machine: Utopian Science and Technology After Napoleon* (Chicago, IL: University of Chicago Press, 2012).

[3] Leo Marx, *The Machine in the Garden: Technology and the Pastoral Ideal in America* (Oxford: Oxford University Press, 2000; 1964), 32.

[4] Dominic McIver Lopes, *Being for Beauty: Aesthetic Agency and Value* (Oxford University Press, 2018), 1.

Introduction

Representations of Technology studies British literature's early industrial-era representations of technē (Greek for craft, technique, method, skill, making and doing), technology, and worldbuilding to expose the place of sublime aesthetics and sublime values in our lives.

Most students are taught that nature is the subject of Romantic poetry, but what about the lever or the modern canal? These technologies were of acute interest to poets and theorists grappling with the relationship between humanity and the natural world. An array of different technologies—from ancient lyres and levers to modern bridges, canals, seismographs, and steam-ships—are figured sublime across Romantic-era pages marked by Britain's growing industrial and imperial pursuits. It should come as no surprise that writers from this period would activate the logic and language of the sublime to ponder the creative powers of technology. As one of Romanticism's hallmark aesthetic categories, the sublime is known for framing the period's pressing debates about power, and especially about what has the power to change us: forces of nature, poetry, the poet, revolutionary politics, even the reach of the human mind. When we add sublime accounts of technology to the list, British Romanticism's engagement with built objects and built environs offers important lessons for today's readers. Rather than casting inventions, machines, and artificial systems in terms of humanity's technological mastery over nature, Romanticism's tales of technological wonder can drive home two important insights: first, if there is a master here, it is nature working jointly with humanity and technology; second, we alone do not determine what our made things might make of us.

This book reveals how the logic and language of the sublime underwrite and indeed underpin how we think about the worlds we build and unbuild in narrative, as well as the worlds we build and unbuild within the natural world. Rather than settling who has power over what, or what has control over whom, at its best the Romantic sublime indexes abiding ambivalences toward agencies of the mind and the natural world—as well as cultural artifacts large and small created by way of a union of the two. As Jocelyn Holland's work on Romantic technology and epistemology reveals, threads of Romantic-era thinking began to unravel the "view of man as an originally 'a-technical being,'" suggesting instead "that culture, including technology, is a part of human nature, not simply an extension of it."[5] Never quite settling debates it raises about human or natural agency, a largely unremarked catalog of Romanticism's sublime technologies of worldmaking and unmaking proves especially useful in thinking about the shared possibilities, limitations, potencies, and vulnerabilities that arise when nature and humanity work together—harmoniously and otherwise.

---

[5] Jocelyn Holland, *Lever as Instrument of Reason: Technological Constructions of Knowledge around 1800* (London: Bloomsbury, 2019), 1.

The Romantic Sublime and Representations of Technology

Works of famed British Romantic authors such as Mary Godwin Shelley or Robert Southey chronicle a historical moment that prized not just revolutionaries, war heroes, and genius poets, but likewise valorized genius scientists and inventors—with each coming to prominence on a stage set by intersecting histories of imperialism and industrialization that would alter thinking about nature on a conceptual level and change how people interacted with the natural world in daily life. For example, Mary Godwin Shelley's story of inventor-protagonist Victor Frankenstein is framed by narratives of imperial expansion before he takes up his scientific instruments with the aim of uncovering nature's darkest secrets. Poet Laureate Robert Southey befriended, traveled with, and styled sublime the acclaimed engineer Thomas Telford while the latter worked to expand networks of commerce for internal and imperial trade by overcoming great engineering challenges posed by the natural world. What linked the aesthetic characterization of the genius poet or the famed radical with Godwin Shelley's anti-hero scientist or Southey's acclaimed engineer? Across these examples and others addressed here, the logic of the sublime provided the ground upon which the Romantic period's lionized inventors and inventions stood—just as the discourse of the sublime framed Romanticism's perhaps more familiar accounts of much-vaunted poets, glorified generals, and heroized revolutionaries.

Authoritative accounts of the rise of the inventor in the eighteenth and nineteenth century have noted the role of the discourse of the genius at play in the inventor's ascendency but have yet to fully or explicitly recognize the role that sublime discourse played in their rise. Yet stock sublime language, logic, and tropes underpinned fictional and first-hand accounts that helped to bring to prominence the period's inventors and their storied creations. For example, in *Heroes of Invention*, Christine MacLeod notes that "in the libraries and salons of Europe the stock of the inventor was indubitably rising. The Enlightenment discourse of 'genius,' while focusing primarily on literature and natural philosophy, was to have important implications for all aspects of human creativity, including mechanical invention."[6] MacLeod goes on to discuss how inherited thinking about the figure of the genius would both "give philosophical sanction to the concept of the proactive inventor whose ideas were his own and independent of divine scheme, [and] it would also provide the grounds for seeing him in a more positive light ... [but] there remained, nonetheless, a strong current of thought which identified any human attempt to imitate the godly Creator with rebellion, disharmony and disaster."[7] Adding to MacLeod's findings about the rising figure of the genius inventor, and as the

---

[6] MacLeod, *Heroes of Invention: Technology, Liberalism and British Identity, 1750–1914* (Cambridge: Cambridge University Press, 2007), 45.

[7] MacLeod, *Heroes of Invention*, 45.

Introduction

chapters in this book demonstrate, we can see how Romantic-era accounts of the genius inventor arrive with the rubrics and politics of the sublime already baked into them. Sublime accounts of the storied inventor, poet, hero, and so on, all hinge upon narratives of striking creation and destruction long home to sublime discourse. At the same time, they also extend established thinking about sublime nature and narrative.

Across the eighteenth and nineteenth centuries, a pivotal connection binding representations of Romantic nature to those of Romanticism's genius creators and inventors was the aesthetic discourse of sublime. Those familiar with the sublime as an aesthetic category likely recognize some of its telltale tropes in the above references to an awe-inspiring nature that is at once dark or daunting, or in reference to an equally dark yet inspiring stripe of inventor. Afterall, by simply turning to two of the most frequently referenced expository works on the Romantic sublime, those of Immanuel Kant and Edmund Burke, we find period-specific discussions of sublime humanity and nature. Burke's sublime typology suggests that "the passion caused by the great and sublime in *nature*" prompts in the beholder "astonishment" coupled with "some degree of horror" (original emphasis).[8] Gesturing back to Longinus's ancient treatise on sublime rhetoric and writing (*On the Sublime* [*Perì Hýpsous*], c. 1st century CE), Burke alludes to "poets and orators which owe their sublimity to a richness and profusion of images."[9] Burke's treatment of such prized wordsmiths provides a telling example of how the sublime status of the creator often spills over onto the works they create and vice versa. In the above account from Burke, poets gain "their sublimity" because of the quality and quantity of the literary images they produce. The same was often the case for inventors and their inventions, with the sublimity of the one (human creator) reflexively playing off the sublimity of the other (human creation) to intensifying effect.

On the other hand, within Kant's *Critique of Judgement*, "nature is ... called sublime [*erhaben*] merely because it elevates [*erhebt*] our imagination," crucially allowing for "those cases where the mind can come to feel its own sublimity."[10] Kant's argument challenges Burke's typology of sublime things found in the world because Kant ultimately locates sublimity in the human mind rather than in any supposed sublime entity or force of nature or culture. Yet as Sianne Ngai's influential inquiries into aesthetic theory point out, "Aesthetics is a discourse not just of pleasure and evaluation, but of justification. How we talk about pleasure and displeasure turns out to be a very rhetorically tricky and

---

[8] Edmund Burke, *A Philosophical Enquiry into the Origin of Our Ideas of the Sublime and Beautiful*, ed. Adam Phillips, Oxford World's Classics (Oxford: Oxford University Press, 1990), 53.

[9] Burke, *A Philosophical Enquiry*, 72.

[10] Immanuel Kant, *Critique of Judgment*, trans. Werner S. Pluhar (Indianapolis and Cambridge: Hackett, 1987), 121.

5

socially complicated thing." And "the justification of aesthetic judgments ... will always involve an appeal to extra-aesthetic judgments—political, moral, historical, cognitive, and so on."[11] One such complicating factor for Kant was that to arrive at his argument, he had to first acknowledge a social and historical consensus which did indeed assume intimidating forces of nature, culture, and the divine to be sublime. In paragraphs just prior to locating sublimity in the mind rather than in the external world, Kant invites readers to "consider bold, overhanging and, as it were, threatening rocks, thunderclouds piling up in the sky ... volcanoes with all their destructive power ... the boundless ocean heaved up, the high waterfall of a mighty river."[12] Once more, directly following his claim about the mind experiencing its own sublimity rather than the natural world possessing sublimity in and of itself, Kant turns to examples of the work of sublime "war ... generals" and "tempests, storms, earthquakes, and so on – [wherein] we usually present God as showing himself in his wrath but also his sublimity."[13] Whether Kant agreed with it or not, according to the words that many people thought or read, and in the words that leapt from their tongues, the sublime resided in corporal and cultural forms, in natural and supernatural bodies.

It is worthwhile to pause here to bear in mind that in some circles the Romantic sublime can be understood to be nearly synonymous with Romantic nature, with the Romantic sublime often standing as a kind of shorthand for Romantic nature. But this view overlooks how Romantic writers and artists also worked in the vein of the picturesque, the pastoral, the georgic, the beautiful (a likewise complicated aesthetic category with ancient origins), and more. Shallow understandings of Romanticism or Romantic nature, as Mark S. Cladis recognizes, often lead to "'Romantic Nature' [being] understood as escapist, fanciful art focused on the sublime or the picturesque."[14] In *Natures in Translation*, Alan Bewell trades such reductive understandings for more historically sound treatments of the period's literature, ultimately countering any singular definition of Romantic nature. Bewell acknowledges various Romantic natures (plural) borne of differing cultural and natural circumstances and co-determinacies.

Working in similar spirit, this project engages with a constellation of Romantic sublime natures and cultures and their requisite histories to widen thinking about the sublime. In this sense, my project embraces Cian Duffy

[11] Adam Jasper and Sianne Ngai, "Our Aesthetic Categories: An Interview with Sianne Ngai," *Cabinet*, Issue 43: Forensics (Fall 2011), accessed 1 May 2018, http://cabinet magazine.org/issues/43/jasper_ngai.php.

[12] Kant, *Critique of Judgment*, 120.

[13] Kant, *Critique of Judgment*, 122.

[14] Mark S. Cladis, "Romantic Nature," in *Nature and Literary Studies*, eds. Peter Remien and Scott Slovic (Cambridge: Cambridge University Press, 2002), 153.

Introduction

and Peter Howell's analysis which recognizes how "many academic studies of the discourse of the sublime have granted" two sweeping assumptions: "first, that it is possible to produce a complete and objective definition of the sublime, which transcends specific historical or cultural circumstances (an assumption shared by Kant's 'analytic'); second that Kant's work constitutes this definition."[15] Duffy and Howell point out how most influential studies of the Romantic-era sublime, as divergent as their arguments and areas of focus might be, "share a core argument" that the Kantian analytic of disinterested aesthetic judgement "offers the definitive paradigm for the experience of the sublime."[16] My attention to British Romanticism's historically and culturally contingent representations of sublime poetry and technology marks a strategic departure from this trend.

Key iterations of the Romantic sublime offer more than we might assume, particularly those showcasing technologies—because much like poetry and other literary works—machines, tools, infrastructural systems all arrive only through a necessary conjuncture of human and natural forces. And just as Romantic nature "is not always particularly romantic (in the sentimental sense)" and therefore is not necessarily nostalgic nor escapist, nor is the Romantic sublime reducible to Kant or Burke, William Wordsworth or John Keats. When sublime nature counts as little more than "narcissistic reports of the individual's private gaze on the sublime landscape,"[17] we blunt the radical ecological and social potential of the Romantic sublime. Worse, we risk perpetuating fantasies of nature that paint the natural world as one more docile body in a fashion akin to what we find in still extant discourses of the picturesque, pastoral, and watered-down versions of the beautiful, all of which also functioned as standing Romantic aesthetic registers authors used to imagine idealized, nonthreatening accounts of Romantic nature, although by varying degrees.

As we have already begun to see in the above examples from Burke and Kant, in contrast with the bulk of aesthetic framings of nature found among the picturesque, the pastoral, and the beautiful, sublime nature typically casts the natural world as astonishing, challenging, and wonderous—yet ambivalently so since sublime nature provokes mixed feelings of both awe

---

[15] Cian Duffy and Peter Howell, *Cultures of the Sublime: Selected Readings, 1750–1830* (London and New York: Palgrave Macmillan, 2011), 2.

[16] See Frances Ferguson, *Solitude and the Sublime: Romanticism and the Aesthetics of Individuation* (New York and London: Routledge, 1992); Samuel H. Monk, *The Sublime* (Ann Arbor, MI: University of Michigan Press, 1960); Philip Shaw, *The Sublime* (New York and London: Routledge, 2006); Thomas Weiskel, *The Romantic Sublime: Studies in the Structure and Psychology of Transcendence* (Baltimore, MD: Johns Hopkins University Press, 1976).

[17] Cladis, "Romantic Nature," 156.

and terror in the observer. A key question then entails how the sublime resolves or not the tensions and conflicts it provokes. Ngai's thinking on the aesthetic category of the sublime is particularly helpful here. Rightly observing that "the sublime is still western philosophy's most prestigious example of an aesthetic category that derives its specificity from mixed or conflicting feelings," Ngai neatly characterizes the affective charge of the sublime as "a powerful response to sheer power."[18] Rather than pacify nature by figuring it as an easy Eden ripe for ready use (as with the pastoral) or as a manipulable landscape primed to accommodate a tasteful view (as with the picturesque), the sublime elevates and intensifies powers of nature. In accounts of sublime nature, the natural world both captivates and unnerves, both attracts and repels (to loosely paraphrase Kant). Commonplace Romantic-era accounts of sublime nature included references to beholding or encountering the vast and powerful Alps, Mont Blanc, or closer to home, Mount Snowdon and Ben Nevis—even simply imagining the great volcanic eruption of Mount Tambora in 1815.[19]

Marjorie Hope Nicolson's classic inquiry into the shifting aesthetic status of mountain ranges, *Mountain Gloom and Mountain Glory*, documents how, in the eighteenth century, peaks and pinnacles that had long been granted abject status came to be classed sublime. Here again Godwin Shelley and Southey provide helpful shorthand examples. Godwin Shelley's narrative has Victor traveling to an awe-inspiring yet perilously inaccessible Glacier Montanvert not as something only to be feared or dreaded but also as a prescribed restorative event. Southey's Telford is dubbed the "Father of Engineering" for inventing infrastructural works qualifying as wondrously sublime not least because they seem to triumph over the sublime landscapes that preceded them, such as the Menai Strait of Wales or the Great Glen Fault of the Northern Scottish Highlands. Noting how culture shapes what we see and sense in nature, Nicolson outlines how, "Like [people] of every age, we see in Nature what we have been taught to look for, we feel what we have been prepared to feel."[20] Of course, the same could be said for what we see and feel in response to what we have been taught to look for relative to people and culture, and during the Romantic period the sublime served as the aesthetic equivalent of a lodestar, guiding thinking and feeling about powerful forces of nature, technology, and

---

[18] Jasper and Ngai, "Our Aesthetic Categories: An Interview with Sianne Ngai."

[19] Representations of sublime nature also carried over into representations of culture, with an iconic example being Edmund Burke's *Reflections on the Revolution in France* where war and cultural revolution appear as a sublime mix of equal parts environmental destruction, cultural upheaval, and aesthetic wonder, with such wonder made possible by virtue of Britain's distance from France.

[20] Marjorie Hope Nicolson, *Mountain Gloom and Mountain Glory: The Development of the Aesthetics of the Infinite* (Ithaca, NY: Cornell University Press, 1959), 1.

Introduction

humanity—all the while connecting these categories more than severing them through lines of shared aesthetic discourse.

An evolving conversation emerges, one staged across various sublime figurations of nature and culture. This is in essence a conversation evaluating the greatest agencies of the natural world, the built environment, and humankind, including humanity's most powerful creations and inventions. In other words, the aesthetic category of the sublime has long been applied to more than landscapes or the natural world, more than divine creation or the rhetorical force of written words, and we stand to benefit from a comparative study of what falls into a given culture's sublime aesthetic categories. The diffusiveness of sublime discourse adds a layer of complexity that can prove daunting as the sublime can at times seem to be running all over the place.[21] But this capaciousness and complexity also manifests interpretive opportunity.

The sublime has applied and still applies to a wide range ideas and things; thus, to study comparatively the sublime's array of objects and concepts, feelings and judgments is to pave the way to determining key points of overlap and contact running across any given sublime sample set—both during a particular moment in history and across the longer history of the term. Philip Shaw reminds readers that the word *sublime* "has many applications: a cathedral or a mountain may be sublime, as may a thought, a heroic deed, or a mode of expression. But the definition of the sublime is not restricted to value judgements; it also describes a state of mind."[22] Historically the sublime applied to lofty states of mind and feeling, the horizon of human thought and expression, in addition to great works of nature and culture or the astonishing destruction thereof. The long arc of this aesthetic category reaches back to descriptions of an Old Testament God imbued with the force of fiat, where a godhead need only speak, need only turn to the power of utterance to instantly create worlds *ex nihilo*, or just as instantly destroy them. Given the sublime's status as an aesthetic discourse closely associated with the creative and destructive powers of gods or great poets, national heroes, or storied inventors, as well as great yet terrible forces of nature, the sublime proved a popular aesthetic home for Romantic writers seeking to reconcile, or at the very least, record the frightening agency and allure of humanity's technological inventions.[23]

---

[21] A familiar historical anecdote attests to the slipperiness of the sublime while also marking how the aesthetic categories of the sublime and the beautiful sometimes overlapped in the period. In Dorothy Wordsworth's journal from the tour she, William Wordsworth, and Samuel Taylor Coleridge took to Scotland in 1803, a frustrated Coleridge breaks from conversing with a couple he encounters at the foot of the Falls of the River Clyde at Cora Linn after one of them deems the site to be "sublime and beautiful."

[22] Shaw, *The Sublime*, 1.

[23] While scholarship on British Romantic representations of sublime technology is still relatively rare, critics of United States literature, culture, and history have produced a

The Romantic Sublime and Representations of Technology

Scholarly and popular explorations of British Romantic technology have done much to correct the once pervading assumption that either British Romantic literature rejected new technologies outright or at least ignored them in favor of celebrating an idealized rustic past. British Romanticism's longstanding associations with Marxist thought, the Luddite rebellion, counterenclosure movements—not to mention often being taken as necessarily or wholly counter to Enlightenment rationalism—all stood in the way of righting the historical record to acknowledge the extent to which Romantic authors welcomed modern machines and technologies, not just the occasional old tool or lost technical tradition of previous times.

According to current secondary literature on the period, Romanticism and technology have never been closer bedfellows. J. David Black remarks how "the antithesis of technology and romanticism is illusory, and the assumption that this opposition exists is a conceit with dire consequences for theory's critical effectiveness."[24] Black goes on to remind readers of Walter J. Ong's earlier work, "Romantic Difference and the Poetics of Technology," where Ong likewise suggests that Romantic thought in fact aligned with technological thought.[25] More recently, John Tresch's celebrated monograph, *The Romantic Machine: Utopian Science and Technology After Napoleon*, boldly pronounces that "both romanticism and mechanism have defined the modern world."[26] Mark Coeckelbergh's *New Romantic Cyborgs: Romanticism, Technology and the End of the Machine* intersects with and yet departs markedly from Black and Tresch. Underscoring British Romanticism's industrial backdrop, Coeckelbergh argues for a long historical arc framed by a "surprising marriage of Enlightenment rationalism and Romanticism" that influences "how people today,

number of classic studies on this topic. See notable contributions on US technological aesthetics and the politics thereof in Leo Marx's *The Machine in the Garden* and his student David E. Nye's *American Technological Sublime* (Cambridge, MA: MIT Press, 1994). Perry Miller is often cited as the one to coin the phrase "technological sublime" in *The Life of the Mind in America: From the Revolution to the Civil War* (London: Victor Gollancz Ltd., 1966). While Miller's book claims to study a universalizing ideal of the "American mind," his sample set includes only New England authors such as Emerson and Thoreau, Hawthorne and Melville, and Walt Whitman. But the logic surveyed by Miller does chime with that of some, but importantly, not all British writers. As noted by Elizabeth W. Miller in the Foreword to *The Life of the Mind in America*, "For those Americans who figure in this [book's] story, two considerations were always present to their vision: the challenge of the vast territory, its limitless prairies, its great rivers, its sublime mountains, all waiting to be explored, to be mastered, to be mined" (vii).

[24] Black, *Romanticism, Media, and Cultural Studies*, 133.

[25] Black, *Romanticism, Media, and Cultural Studies*, 133; Walter J. Ong, "Romantic Difference and the Poetics of Technology," in *Rhetoric, Romance, and Technology: Studies in the Interaction of Expression and Culture* (Ithaca, NY: Cornell University Press, 2013), 255–83.

[26] Tresch, *The Romantic Machine*, 1.

Introduction

albeit unintentionally, try to realize their romantic craving for freedom, self-expression, spirituality, utopia, and authenticity by electronic means and how companies unscrupulously respond to these romantic desires with electronic gadgets ... what [he calls] romantic technologies."[27] Because he identifies Romantic ideologies residing at the core of today's most harmful techno-cultural practices and patterns, Coeckelbergh's larger project stands as a critique of Romanticism, one marking "how difficult it is to escape from modern and Romantic thinking when dealing with technology and otherwise."[28]

Turning to questions of closer concern to the chapters that follow, in *The Enlightenment Cyborg: A History of Communications and Control in the Human Machine, 1660–1830*, a work that folds the Romantic period into the long span of the Enlightenment, Allison Muri examines mechanist and materialist philosophies of the seventeenth and eighteenth century. Muri shows how philosophical questions pertaining to the mind, machines, and matter grounded thinking about the Enlightenment concept of the man-machine in ways that chime with contemporary postmodern thinking about the cyborg. "Of course," writes Muri, "no unbroken lineage exists to be traced from an ancestor man-machine to its offspring cyborgs; what demands our attention, however, are the shared assumptions concerning the perceived relationships of human to mechanism, material embodiment to human spirit, and mind to matter in both the early modern and postmodern conceptions of the human machine."[29] As Muri takes stock of these shared assumptions she cannot help but turn to the logic and history of the sublime, rightly observing that prior to and across the Romantic era (1660–1830) the "rise of the 'sublime' did not replace mechanism, but reincorporated it and redeemed it."[30]

Then in terms of the popular imagination, from Richard Holmes's bestseller *The Age of Wonder: How the Romantic Generation Discovered the Beauty and Terror of Science* to Humphrey Jennings's *Pandæmonium 1660–1886: The Coming of the Machine as Seen by Contemporary Observers*, recent Anglo-phone reading publics have begun to understand how British Romanticism's historical scene was set against an influx of exciting yet discomfiting techno-logical marvels such as Herschel's telescope, Lunardi's flying air balloons, Davy's experiments with bags of laughing gas, or the lamp Davy invented for miners working in dangerously dark spaces, to name a few. But Jennings and Holmes move beyond offering historical accounts of novel inventions capti-vating past and current audiences. Their works draw upon examples of the British Romantic technological sublime at its worst, where the natural world is

---

[27] Coeckelbergh, *New Romantic Cyborgs*, 3, 4.
[28] Coeckelbergh, *New Romantic Cyborgs*, 3.
[29] Muri, *The Enlightenment Cyborg*, 5.
[30] Muri, *The Enlightenment Cyborg*, 155.

The Romantic Sublime and Representations of Technology

disregarded or presumed to be defeated by humankind, and at its best, where the natural world is deemed essential yet fearsomely inescapable and where even the most wondrous of human inventions bear out ambivalent forces and ethically freighted costs. Nonetheless, while these books may foreground sublime technologies of both poles within their pages, neither author investigates the larger implications of British Romanticism's representational range of sublime technologies.

Although they do not address the stakes of Romantic-era representations of sublime technologies, widely read works by the likes of Holmes and Jennings nevertheless capitalize on the tension and ambivalence borne out by the language and logic of sublime aesthetics. That is, their narratives cash in on how sublime experience relates to what is held in high esteem while also conjuring strongly conflicting feelings—provoking both pleasure and displeasure (for Kant), both terror and delight (for Burke). Take Jennings for example. He includes excerpts such as the following from B. R. Haydon. Haydon's account skirts a line between repulsion and attraction, and plays with the sublime push and pull of a cityscape mantled in smoke.

> So far from the smoke of London being offensive to me, it has always been to my imagination the sublime canopy that shrouds the City of the World ... the sight of it always filled my mind with feelings of energy such as no other spectacle could inspire.
> "Be Gode," said Fuseli to me one day, "it's like de smoke of de Israelites making bricks." "It is grander," said I, "for it is the smoke of a people who have made the Egyptians make bricks for them." "Well done, John Bull," replied Fuseli.[31]

Haydon's words demonstrate how the technological sublime can lend itself to an imperial chauvinism grounded not only by an ethos of dehumanization but grounded first in a necessary forgetting that without nature there is no nation. Here sublime inventors created sublime inventions and vice versa, prompting a new category of national hero, and for Britain, a new class of imperial hero. According to the logic ascribed to this sublime scene, the lives and livelihoods of Egyptian laborers are of no true concern and garner scant mention. The toll taken on the natural world to uphold the "City of the World," let alone the ecological cost of its smoke or smog, matters not at all, never even factors into the stated equation.

A more environmentally sensitive account of sublime technology is found in Jennings's excerpt taken from Dorothy Wordsworth's *Recollections of a Tour*

---

[31] Jennings, *Pandæmonium 1660–1886: The Coming of the Machine as Seen by Contemporary Observers* (London: Icon Books, 2012), 125.

Introduction

made in Scotland. In this case, Wordsworth also fashions the built environment to be sublime, but here byproducts of imperialism are less at issue than are the physical forces and notable agencies of sublime structures, tools, or mechanisms:

> Our road turned to the right, and we saw, at a distance of less than a mile, a tall upright building of grey stone, with several men standing upon the roof, as if they were looking out over battlements. It stood beyond the village, upon higher ground, as if presiding over it, - a kind of enchanter's castle, which it might have been, a place which Don Quixote would have gloried in. When we drew nearer we saw, coming out of the side of the building, a large machine or lever, in appearance like a great forge-hammer, as we supposed for raising water out of the mines. It heaved upwards once in half a minute with a slow motion, and seemed to rest to take a breath at the bottom, its motion being accompanied with a sound between a groan and "jike." There would have been something in this object very striking in any place, as it was impossible not to invest the machine with some faculty of intellect; it seemed to have made the first step from brute matter to life and purpose, showing its progress by great power. William made a remark to this effect, and Coleridge observed that it was like a giant with one idea. At all events, the object produced a striking effect in that place, where everything was in unison with it - particularly the building itself, which was turret-shaped, and with the figures upon it resembled much one of the fortresses in the wooden cuts of Bunyan's *Holy War*.[32]

For Wordsworth these sublime technologies (first, the built structure itself, next the machine or lever coming out of the building's side that is reminiscent of a forge-hammer) prove striking not simply because they (like sublime things of nature) appear to have a life or mind of their own. In addition, they appear to be almost divine or supernatural, otherworldly, something beyond nature's regular course—something surpassing earthly law in their ability to manifest a "great power" and possess a "purpose" seemingly all their own. Counterpoising the logic conveyed by Haydon's imperial and anthropocentric version of cultural sublimity, Wordsworth's narrative reveals how the aesthetic of the sublime can espouse a logic that honors tremendous agencies of technology and human labor alike—all without any baseline reassurance of imperious human control over the lives of others, the natural world, even the technologies they invent.

Jennings's collection of largely anecdotal accounts of sublime technologies tends toward sensationalizing a given invention, whereas Holmes's chapters on specific technologies go beyond simply showcasing the sublime receptions

---

[32] Jennings, *Pandæmonium 1660–1886*, 121.

The Romantic Sublime and Representations of Technology

that enflamed a given technology's mass appeal. Holmes further gestures toward what justified an invention's sublime reception. Holmes comes much closer to making explicit connections between the sublime and how it indexes human confrontations with unexpected or unfathomed power. In his chapter on the air balloon of Montgolfier fame, for example, Holmes writes of how "Ballooning produced a new, and wholly unexpected, vision of the earth. It had been imagined that it would reveal the secrets of the heavens above, but in fact showed the secrets of the world beneath."[33] Holmes closes the chapter by observing how "ballooning proved to have extraordinary theatrical power to attract crowds, embody longing, and mix terror and the sublime with farce."[34] Even when interfused with a sense of the farcical, the balloon promised secret knowledge, and by extension, secret power—because in this case—with sublime invention comes sublime revelation.

Then, in discussing Herschel's telescope, Holmes closes with a consideration of Keats's "On First Looking into Chapman's Homer," which allows Holmes to associate Hershel's invention with the trope of sublime fiat (instantaneous powers of creation and destruction) as well as Romantic characterizations of the "explorer, the scientific observer, the literary reader, [as they] experience the Sublime: a moment of revelation into the idea of the unbounded, the infinite."[35] Laying the groundwork for *The Age of Wonder*, Holmes marks how narratives of "Romantic science created, or crystallised, several … crucial conceptions – or misconceptions – which are still with us. First, the dazzling idea of the solitary scientific 'genius,' thirsting and reckless for knowledge."[36] Then "closely connected with this is the idea of the 'Eureka moment,' the intuitive inspired instant of invention or discovery."[37] To round out this historical sketch, Holmes points to technology: "Scientific instruments played an increasingly important role in this process of revelation, allowing man not merely to extend his senses passively – using the telescope, the microscope, the barometer – but to intervene actively, using the voltaic battery, the electrical generator, the scalpel or the air pump."[38]

For Jennings and Holmes alike, the technological sublime advances questions of human agency, or the lack thereof, just as sublime nature had. The key difference is that all too often narratives of sublime nature seem to contrive a battle of good and evil played out by two contradictory forces, with humanity on the one hand, and the natural world on the other. In many cases, especially

---

[33] Holmes, *The Age of Wonder: How the Romantic Generation Discovered the Beauty and Terror of Science* (New York: Pantheon, 2009), 161.

[34] Holmes, *The Age of Wonder*, 161.

[35] Holmes, *The Age of Wonder*, 207.

[36] Holmes, *The Age of Wonder*, xvii.

[37] Holmes, *The Age of Wonder*, xvii.

[38] Holmes, *The Age of Wonder*, xviii.

Introduction

within those narratives of the more sensationalizing sort, the technological sublime can merely reproduce such logic and stakes, with humanity on one side and the natural world on the other. But, crucially, in narratives espousing more agentic models of nature and technology as in Dorothy Wordsworth's account, the technological sublime can helpfully complicate stories that would reduce humanity and nature to sheer rivals. Accounts like Wordsworth's blur distinctions between sublime forces of nature and culture such that the stage is not one we watch from a safe distance as one giant masters the other. Rather, the role of ultimate winner or loser is shooed offstage, leaving audiences to confront a discomfiting scene wherein sublime forces of humanity, nature, and technology are all jointly, all ineluctably arrayed together.

The Romantic Sublime and Representations of Technology uncovers forgotten stories of technological wonder that reconceive humanity's relationship with nature. If we can grasp how Romantic-era writers characterize not only nature, but also technology as sublime—that is, as being simultaneously awe-inspiring and unnerving—presumed gulfs between nature and culture shrink, and fantasies of humanity's self-reliance dissolve. Each chapter charts how this era's literary figures (such as John Keats, Percy Shelley, Anna Seward, Robert Southey) as well as scientific writers and engineers (such as Erasmus Darwin and Thomas Telford) cut against hyperbolic accounts of humanity's creative agency that still permeate narratives of technological invention, innovation, even salvation. Renderings of sublime steam engines and suspension bridges showcase a world built upon stories of relational agency and collective potential. Crucial to both ecological thought and Romanticism, these stories stress the limits of making as well as the limits of repair. These authors dethrone the Romantic figure of the lone, godlike, genius creator. They tear down easy techno-utopic fantasies suggesting that we can build anything, repair whatever we break, our earthly world included.

Ironically, by granting due agency to technology—to the artificial, the fabricated, the unnatural—authors offer a less reductive understanding of the material world, where earthly scenes are not populated simply by dyads of protagonists and antagonists, but by a more complicated set of actors bearing out intersecting and overlapping agencies, contingencies, and aggregates.[39] The term *sublime* itself is born of relation, joining two Latin root words, with the latter root word pertaining to the built environment: *sub* (up to) joins *limen* (lintel, literally meaning the top piece of a door).[40] The term *sublime*

---

[39] For a book-length exploration of combinatory agencies running through and across human and nonhuman bodies see Jane Bennett, *Vibrant Matter: A Political Ecology of Things* (Durham, NC: Duke University Press, 2010).

[40] *Oxford English Dictionary*, s.v. "sublime (*adj.* & *n.*)," 18 December 2020, https://doi.org/10.1093/OED/1040109669 (accessed 20 February 2023); *Perseus Morphology Tool*, s. v.

The Romantic Sublime and Representations of Technology

has long prompted not singular but multiple meanings, with even traditional usage referring to value judgments as well as states of mind.[41] Moreover, we find sublime relationality and multiplicity all the way down to the fine-grain level of syntax. For example, when Longinus describes the powers of sublime rhetoric and language, by his account even sublime phrases often require aggregate syntactical arrangements whereby a distributed network of words suggest collectively what otherwise might be communicated by one word alone.[42] The key point here is how expressions of ambivalence proceed from various aggregate and distributed energies at play in sublime narratives. While the sublime has always been about questions of power, safety, and vulnerability in one form or another, Romanticism's sublime discourse catalogs concerns not only of humanity or nature but of fabricated things born of humanity and nature: poetry's blend of pen and page, thought and breath; the steam engine's mix of water and coal, imagination and metal. Overturning conventional readings of British Romantic literature, I argue that common understandings of Romantic sublimity, particularly those grounded in a simple human–nature dyad of oppositional actors, fuel misconceptions of human indebtedness to technology, which in turn perilously miscasts humanity's fragile dependence upon nature.

This project thinks capaciously about technology, its relationship to poetry, its relationship with nature. Tools, technē, machines with moving parts, and larger technological systems of infrastructure all provide valuable opportunities to rethink poetry. In the same way, we can reconceive the cultural work and worth of various technologies by reading them in light of poetry

"limen," Perseus Digital Library, G. Crane, ed., 18 December 2022, www.perseus.tufts.edu/hopper/morph?l=limen&la=la#lexicon.

[41] See Andrew Ashfield and Peter de Bolla, *The Sublime: A Reader in British Eighteenth-Century Aesthetic Theory* (Cambridge: Cambridge University Press, 1996); Duffy and Howell, *Cultures of the Sublime*; Alan Richardson, *The Neural Sublime: Cognitive Theory and Romantic Texts* (Baltimore, MD: Johns Hopkins University Press, 2010).

[42] Longinus's *On the Sublime*, his ancient work of literary criticism and aesthetic theory, offers a typology of literary devices capable of creating verbal artistry's "sublime condition." His short list of literary devices that produce the sublime includes periphrasis, asyndeton, and hyperbaton—figures of speech pertaining to irregular or disorderly aggregates or unexpected conjunctions and arrangements. In some cases (periphrasis) multiple words come together to bear meanings otherwise implied by the prefixes or suffixes of just one word. Others (asyndeton) manifest forces of juxtaposed variation and irregularity, where in most cases *words would have followed one another as independent actors*. Still others (hyperbaton) playfully foreground unexpected or inverse word orders to bring import to ordinary meanings or to add style even when the substance of the song remains the same. The first two literary schemes depend on word relations rather than individuated words to generate meaning. The last produces a similar effect or meaning by other, unexpected means and by transposed or inverted means. Longinus, *On the Sublime*, in *The Loeb Classical Library*, 2nd ed. (Cambridge, MA and London: Harvard University Press, 1995), 159–307.

Introduction

and in particular in light of the poetics of worldbuilding. Even as this project welcomes the risk of thinking broadly about representations of technological, mechanical, and poetic invention, *The Romantic Sublime and Representations of Technology* still gives different technologies and poetries their due. As one might expect, regardless of a shared aesthetic frame of reference (the sublime), different technological forms or systems seed different discussions of poetry. So too, different dimensions of sublime poetry (for example, as a larger system and in terms of literary tools, devices, and mechanics) speak differently to sublime technologies distinct from poetry. Yet even with these distinctions in play, across sublime representations of poetic and technological creation and invention, Romanticism's sublime figurations of various technologies and poetries emphasize how we are transformed in their wake, often unwittingly or uncontrollably. The following chapters offer an investigation of the sublime value associations poetry shares with other made artifacts that assume great transformative potential. Further, each chapter chips away at models of human and cultural exceptionalism that minimize nature's making, producing, and reproducing by understanding the natural word as given. Nature evolves, people invent. So goes common logic that tempts us away from recognizing nature's constructedness, not simply as in cultures inventing certain ideas of nature but as in how the natural world is itself *co-constituted*—just as poetry and technology are. As this project makes clear, when the idea of a given or granted natural world serves as a baseline logic underlying the sublime reception of the products or process of human invention, gross misunderstandings arise over just how powerfully nature and technology stand united in remaking us in ways that profoundly exceed our control or our knowing.

The book's opening chapter, "Prometheus and Trophonius: Technological Myth and Sublime Scripts of Industry and Creativity," charts the long history of the phrase "ponderous metal," a phrase that functions as a litmus test for how authors make sense of humanity's relationships with technology, ecology, and distinct cultures. By starting here, the book opens with a core example of just how important representations of sublime technology come to be. One key trope, image, figure, or metaphor can sever or connect daunting forces of nature and culture, can either join or isolate the sublime creative outputs of one culture and another. This chapter extends recent work by theorists such Bernard Stiegler who have drawn attention to the technological myths we tell and who have compelled readers to examine the politics at stake in technological aesthetics. The chapter is anchored by a study of the technological myths and aesthetic philosophy on display in pro-imperial scientific poetry penned by Erasmus Darwin. In *Temple of Nature* (1803) and *Progress of Society* (c. 1798–1799), Darwin invites readers to consider a mythic history of humanity framed not by distant, Titanic gods or Promethean fire, but grounded instead in a human-turned-Apollonian-oracle, by the legendary

17

The Romantic Sublime and Representations of Technology

builder, maker, and stonesmith: Trophonius, Nourisher of Minds. Activating key questions of sublime technological aesthetics expressing how we value and understand processes of making, becoming, and undoing, for Darwin, intertwined histories and potentialities of art and technology may never be fixed but—in the best scenario—they might continuously play out a story of repair.

The chapter reconsiders the Romantic preoccupation with the Prometheus figure in light of Darwin's representation of Trophonius and a Drury Lane play, *The Cave of Trophonius* (1791), by minor playwright Prince Hoare. By doing so, the chapter repositions the Romantic era's most retold account of the Titanic god of culture, technē, forethought, and fire—Mary Godwin Shelley's *Frankenstein: Or, the Modern Prometheus* (1818), a story itself loosely based on Benjamin Franklin's quest to channel the electric charge of sublime nature's lightning. Building on the commonplace knowledge in the period about the Trophonius myth and its framework for a more realist rather than escapist technological sublime, here I show how Godwin Shelley's modern Prometheus, Victor Frankenstein, advances overblown estimations of the powers of human ingenuity and imagination based upon an assumed schism between sublime nature and culture. As its point of repose, this chapter leaves readers with the largely unsung myth of Trophonius, a myth which confronts the limits of making to advance an ethic of repair that is at once infinite, intimate, and imperfect. Therefore, the book's opening chapter gives the last word to myths worth revisiting for their refusal to sever humanity from nature and for the tempered technological ethics they introduce. In the Trophonius myth, sublime tools span the metaphoric (words and tongues) and the literal (built structures), but in each case in this myth readers encounter a model of a world forged upon shifting sands, where precarious grounds do not depart from but rather move in line with the uncertain brilliance of human futures, values, works, words, and dreams.

The following chapters offer a series of case studies, each engaging inventions and technologies of different type, scale, and significance. Chapter 2 stays underground to a degree, moving away from sublime caves and subterranean spaces central to the myths of Trophonius to now foreground the earth's surface in an investigation of the period's fascination with early seismometers and prototypes of the seismograph. Entitled "The Seismograph and a Keatsian 'Material Sublime': On Sublime Worldbuilding and Unbuilding," this chapter introduces an understudied iteration of the Romantic sublime: the material sublime. Striking resonances run across sublime representations of innovative technologies created to better read the earth's movements, early Kantian accounts of earthquakes and built environs as sublime human inventions, and both Keatsian and Shelleyan accounts of poetics as a type of sublime creative force. Kant, Keats, and Shelley all turn to the logic of the sublime to theorize powers of human invention, worldbuilding, and poiesis (or making)

18

Introduction

and each makes legible how material sublimity undergirds any manifestation of human or cultural sublimity. For each author, human agencies of creativity and ingenuity are underwritten by a natural and built environment itself endowed with sublime powers of reinvention, a changeling agency not to be fully harnessed nor corralled by human hands, a material sublime.

Rather than assuming strict divides between human and natural systems— as we find in some better-studied sublime narratives from this period—these accounts think together the natural and built environment by styling each with tropes aligning with Keats's formulation of the material sublime. Immanuel Kant's early responses to the devastating Lisbon earthquake of 1755 frame the built environment in ways that complicate his later and widely known critical work on disinterested judgement where sublime capacities of human imagination and reason outpace sublime forces of nature. Keats's letter to J. H. Reynolds (25 March 1818) echoes Kant's remarks on Lisbon's famed quake, as Keats likewise pens a sublime yet tempered account of human creative agency in thinking through the cultural role of poiesis. Percy Shelley would compose *A Defence of Poetry* (1822) shortly after becoming a financial backer of a proposed steamship and after working and writing in an engineer's workshop (discussed in full in the subsequent chapter). In *A Defence of Poetry*, Shelley responds to emerging debates over great powers of invention spanning from the mechanical to the poetical. Here Shelley offers searching accounts of poetry and the poet, as well as cultural creation and cultural destruction, connecting each by way of sublime discourse. By linking these three writers' accounts of sublime worldbuilding and unbuilding to one of the most prominent vehicles for rethinking the orders of life in the eighteenth century, the earthquake, I demonstrate how poetics as technē and seismological instruments as technology are key examples of a Romantic technological sublime that rests upon figurations of a material sublime.

Early Kantian representations of an assumed *terra firma* transforming into quaking, riven ground join various other examples of eighteenth-century earthquake literature. These accounts helped to inspire inventors attempting to better read and study the earth's dynamic tremors as some produced ever more sensitive instruments and machines—while others paired such delicate inventions with increasingly destructive devices and experiments. But in the end neither approach delivered anything close to definitive answers. Such open-endedness at times parallels Keats's late figurations of a material sublime that inspires poetic dreams in line with his famous thesis of "Negative Capability" that asserts true poets must be at home with uncertainty. So too, popular writing and the periodical presses figure astonishing seismographic machines bearing witness to a moving, terrifying, changeling planet that neither we, nor our technologies could ever fully know or control. In sum, this chapter uncovers how Keats's and Shelley's Romantic characterizations of sublime

The Romantic Sublime and Representations of Technology

poetics reflect their historical moments, placing them in conversation with the eighteenth-century discourses that inform early nineteenth-century thought on the natural sublime. The chapter then gestures forward to popular and scientific literature on proto-seismological instruments to chart a continuum of ideas on the question of our necessarily disturbed, disturbing, and compromising earthly foundation and its evolving sublime representations in literature and visual culture.

By linking the theories of Kant, Keats, and Shelley to popular literature on earthquakes and the devices created to read them, this chapter reveals the pivotal place of sublime technological aesthetics in shaping modern ecological imaginings. Here the cultural work of poetics as technē aligns with that of seismological instrumentation and interpretation—each converting what otherwise might only be felt into something seen or heard, both calling attention to the precarity and ultimate unknowability of our inherited and imagined foundations. Vital is how in each account humanity is responsible and held accountable, not just technē or technics, not just nature. Whatever agency humanity does possess (creative, inventive, or otherwise) arises only in aggregate, only alongside forces and processes of making that are distributed throughout our built and natural worlds and which are conveyed by tropes of the material sublime. In this way nothing is presumed as given or granted but instead is presented as aggregately built, ambivalently born: things of human invention conjure the sublime's coincident terror tinged with wonder relative to what we cannot fully know or control. Kant, Keats, and Shelley relinquish overblown notions of human agency that would prop up fantasies of human chauvinism and exceptionalism. The technological aesthetics on display in their works replace combative sublime dyads (nature opposite culture) with constitutive sublime aggregates (inescapably interlinked human and natural systems).

The third chapter, "Lyres, Levers, Boats, and Steam: Shelleyan Technologies of Sublime Correspondence," takes to the skies to embark upon a comparative analysis of tales of sublime literary poiesis and stories of sublime technological genesis. Here I uncover a red thread of sublime discourse linking Romantic-era representations of pyrotechnic steam engines and steamships with Romantic literature's famed symbol for the inspired poet: the wind-driven Aeolian harp. The chapter holds fresh readings of Percy Shelley's familiar representations of the Aeolian lyre from *Ode to the West Wind* (1820) and *A Defence of Poetry* (1821). These central texts of Shelleyan studies are reread in light of the steamships and engineering equipment featured in his letters and neglected verse epistle, *Letter to Maria Gisborne* (1820). Across these works, all drafted late in Shelley's life as he resided in exile in Italy, the poet evokes technological objects and systems as figures for poetic process, social communion, even social regeneration. My comparative analysis reveals how Shelley's renderings of

20

Introduction

ancient devices and modern machines resonate with sublime tropes belonging to the English radical tradition of the 1790s, wherein Thomas Paine transformed the lever into a galvanizing symbol of political potential and the British abolition movement dubbed anti-slavery crusader Thomas Clarkson the "moral steam-engine."[43]

Shelleyan lyres work alongside transportation technologies such as sailboats and steamships to formulate a grounding logic of the Romantic technological sublime, offering a technologically and ecologically sensitive account of the more mundane built spaces within which poets and engineers conduct their work, and which inform the creative process in transformative ways. The wind harp or Aeolian lyre, then, joins a range of rousing inventions, and joins as well the animating forces of water, wind, and mind so central to Shelleyan scholarship, all to suggest that poetic inspiration originates outside of the poet, not only in the breath of the natural world but likewise in the machines and built environments that connect human communities. Contravening shallow thinking about a simple opposition between nature and technological progress, Shelley's view of entangled natural, poetic, and technological process pushes back against reductive ecological thought; so too, it challenges quixotic notions of the solitary Romantic poet.

The fourth chapter, "Suspension Bridges, Modern Canals, and the Infrastructural Sublime: Robert Southey, Thomas Telford, and the Traffic of Empire," turns to sublime inventions of grand scale and great imperial and industrial import. The chapter foregrounds Britain's growing network of modern bridges and canals, with particular emphasis paid to Robert Southey's sublime representations of Thomas Telford's vast infrastructural projects. Telford's famed engineering projects include not only Scotland's Caledonian Canal but also the first modern suspension bridge. The bridge appeared to be nothing short of magical to some, described by many as seeming to float over the turbulent Straits of Menai to instantiate a key link between Wales and Anglesey, and to expedite London to Dublin travel and transport. This chapter demonstrates how early nineteenth-century British bridges, byways, and canals all don the quasi-metaphysical dress of sublime discourse. In poetry and prose alike, structures rendering once-perilous straits newly navigable appeared as the mesmerizing technological answers to some of Britain's most impressive and impassible natural landmarks. Read through an antagonistic framing logic of sublime nature against sublime humanity, Britain's infrastructure all but rendered the impossible possible, and the stuff of dreams as attainable

---

[43] Thomas Clarkson was popularly dubbed the "Moral Steam-Engine" for authoring *An essay on the impolicy of the African slave trade* in 1788. See Tim May, "Coleridge's Slave Trade Lecture: Southey's Contribution and the Debt to Thomas Cooper," *Notes and Queries* (2008): 425–9.

The Romantic Sublime and Representations of Technology

inevitabilities. The chapter goes on to show how such competitive sublime frameworks were well primed to reinforce even the most speculative of colonial imaginings. I argue that, of all architectural forms, Britain's modern suspension bridge and advanced interlocking canals emblematized the intermixed material and imaginative urgencies of the period, imperial and beyond. Aside from accommodating trade lines and enabling human travel and communication, these infrastructural projects fueled a Romantic fascination with mobility, mutability, and mystery that went on to inform imperial ideologies, such that the stuff of colonial fantasy appeared to be anything but, and seemed as if it could follow suit to become suddenly real, tangible, not fantasy but fabric, manifested with ease.

The chapter closes with a counter to such reductive sublime ideologies. It turns to narratives that undercut those that would mystify and nationalize not just the work of the civil engineer, but also the work of the poet laureate, as well as the work of the technological artifact. Southey's *Letters from England* (1818) and some of his journals pair with Telford's *Memoirs* (1838) to project a baffling and unending fragility onto monuments and men. While this chapter does consider tangentially architectural and economic aspects of British Romantic bridges and canals, the bulk of the chapter demonstrates how Romantic representations of sublime landscapes in nature unfold in dialogue with representations of the infrastructural sublime. At issue in this unfolding dialogue is how British Romanticism's discourses of sublime nature and sublime technologies worked together both to undermine and reinforce the politics and aesthetics of empire.

The Romantic Sublime and Representations of Technology changes how we understand the afterlives of British Romantic literature in two key ways. First, it reorients the politics of the Romantic sublime in light of the sublimely made (or better: the sublimely co-constructed) instead of the sublimely given. This is a crucial intervention precisely because accounts of the sublimely given tend to isolate and naturalize whatever is written as holding great creative force or potential at a given moment. The great Romantic genius exists in the same breath as the looming Mont Blanc, even as the former had much more cultural shaping and support than the latter. But to place the powerful poet in conversation with not only intimidating forces of nature but also great and yet compromising creations of culture is to recognize the sublime for what it is: an aesthetic reckoning with the fact that human art and artifacts, technē and technics reveal not our independence but the troubling fact of our unending dependence, dependence upon first the natural world and second our cultural one. Reading the sublime as an aesthetic category concerning the more complicated realities and stories behind the world's most creative forces helps us to see the deep and abiding relationality at play in both the natural and cultural worlds, albeit occurring in different degrees and on differing levels.

22

Introduction

This first key point dovetails with the second: this project examines problems that transcend the page but which are shaped by Romanticism's literary aesthetics, such as how we understand human–nature relationships and how we understand human agency relative to our built and natural environments. This book stresses the fundamental role of technological aesthetics in modern understandings of human agency and the powers of nature. It reveals how figures of technological sublimity underpin Romanticism's vision of limited rather than limitless utopias by recording, announcing, and emphasizing accounts of sometimes transporting and sometimes suspended agencies of poiesis and technological genesis, powers that are far from autonomous and which routinely produce unforeseen if not unfortunate outcomes.

Literary theorists of the environment, and ecocritics in particular, have long turned to Romantic literature to challenge us to think deeply about how we aestheticize and mythologize the natural world. My project extends such efforts by unearthing the ways in which we aestheticize and mythologize our technologically co-built worlds. Historically, it has been the case that ecocritical scholars have taken aim at ecological aesthetics, exposing their human and earthly costs. To cite two influential ecocritics working within this vein of scholarship on Romanticism, Timothy Morton and Kate Rigby have made it nearly impossible for their readers to look innocently upon a sublime landscape, be it the Grand Canyon or Mont Blanc. The same goes for the beautiful, the pastoral, the rustic or picturesque in nature—from English gardens, the shepherd's pasture, to storied Edenic orchards—all easy paradise is lost, or never existed in the first place. Instead of the sublime or the beautiful, for example, Morton champions the natural abject prescribing an embrace of swamp and sludge as an ecocritical intervention of the aesthetic kind, suggesting an alternative aesthetic program that would not have us celebrate the mountain top as we forsake what lies below.[44] While Morton's work highlights the politics of hierarchized ecological aesthetics where naturalized, common, everyday aesthetic judgments train us to value certain landscapes over others, Rigby explores the politics of hierarchized accounts of nature and culture where traditions of art and aesthetics (culture) train us to feel that we stand apart from or transcend the external world (nature). Rigby's assessment of German Romantic nature philosophy provides a stark reminder that for the Jena School, nature was in fact always subordinate to art. However, she does not mean to point her finger at the Jena School alone, because writing, Rigby contends, is born of ecosocial rupture. She ultimately suggests that in "responding to the social and ecological brokenness of our world," literature must nonetheless move "beyond the opposition of naïve

---

[44] Timothy Morton, *Ecology Without Nature: Rethinking Environmental Aesthetics* (Cambridge, MA and London: Harvard University Press, 2007).

The Romantic Sublime and Representations of Technology

naturalism and sentimental yearning," and "be turned towards what, in the Jewish tradition, has been termed *tikkun olam*: 'repair of the world.'"[45] Rigby turns to myth to bring it all back together. But where writing and art (technē or craft) in her account are born of ecosocial rupture and thus culture is severed from nature, I turn to myth and the politics of sublime aesthetics to reframe technology's place in nature as sometimes occupying a delicate place of ecosocial repair.

When undergirded by a sublime plotline where nature precedes and necessarily conditions—even disturbs—humankind without prompting competition or violence, Romanticism's technological sublime provides readers opportunities to grapple with. and possibly accept or even embrace. the many checks upon individuated agency, human ingenuity, and creative potential. While the sublime always entertains questions of power and control, or the lack thereof, the aesthetic register of the sublime also marks our ambivalence toward our most profound and unchangeable relationships. Accounts of sublime technology, like representations of sublime nature, index our greatest debts and register our chief constraints, all to then script possible responses to such constraints. To trace the mark of the technological sublime is to chart a very startling but very real prospect—whatever empowers us also possesses power over us, delimits us. This book turns on its head the traditional myth of the Industrial Revolution and its concomitant parable of humankind's technological mastery by uncovering how authors repurpose the sublime's signature conflicted feelings of a higher order (a reverent ambivalence, a stunning vexation, a kind of cowed attraction or allure) to reframe poiesis, or making, as a necessarily fraught and uncertain collective endeavor.

Rethinking the Romantic sublime affords an opportunity to recognize the crucial relationship between technological aesthetics, assumptions about the reach of human agency, and modern perceptions of the environment. The payoff for studying Romanticism's overlapping sublime representations of the powers of the natural world, the technological world, and poetic world-building and invention, is that we see how the sublime indexes what most vexes us—that being our limitedness. Put another way, the Romantic sublime demarcates our unresolvable ambivalence toward what might be beyond us or might overpower us, toward what might determine or define us. It dramatizes states of unsettling, unresolved astonishment in poetic form, periodicals, novels, personal letters, and private journals, in essence providing an inventory of what we sense might have a life of its own and would at least appear to be able to live on without us. In Romantic literature, sublime representations of instruments and machines grant pronounced agency to fabricated artifacts

---

[45] Kate Rigby, "Writing After Nature," *Ecological Humanities* 39–40 (2006), https://australianhumanitiesreview.org/2006/09/01/writing-after-nature/.

Introduction

and built structures, admitting—sometimes indirectly or only tacitly—that our agency is often limited, if not in many cases foreshortened, by what we make and create.

Long associated with overwhelming powers of nature or transcendental powers of mind, eighteenth- and nineteenth-century accounts of sublime technologies index the forceful and unpredictable union of natural and human agency manifest within poetry and technology. Romanticism's sublime representations of technologies reroute the very same aesthetic terrain that gave rise to a radically different worldbuilding myth: that of the lone genius born of natural, innate talents, and endowed with godlike agency and control—one able to instantiate worlds on a whim or with the flick of a pen. Expanding sublime discourse to make room for more than individuated, instantaneous, and commanding models of creative force, British Romanticism's sublime portraits of long-storied technologies, like the lever, pair with outsized modern marvels like the modern suspension bridge to advance narratives of arduous construction and inescapable interdependence. Nothing is created in an instant. Most inventions and made things demand great revision, much repair, and alter us in the wake of their making, whether we know it or not. This book's chapters honor these truths by foregrounding a select sample of Romanticism's forgotten tales of technological wonder and sublime worldbuilding. In each case, those narratives that embrace the logic of a more material sublime replace the role of the rare sublime character fixated with a monomaniacal quest (*the creative genius or "mad" scientist*) with cast upon cast of everyday sublime communities, systems, and aggregates of human and nonhuman kind, creating together, running unwitting experiments, and writing uncertain futures.

Romanticism's sublime discourses embraced technological objects and systems, albeit ambivalently, and this ambivalence is paramount. The Romantic sublime brings to the fore an ambivalent stance toward all that we make, and in so doing, this aesthetic register proves crucial for chronicling our ongoing discomfort with the very idea of our creative contingency, of our limited autonomy. The Romantic sublime granted abiding agencies to technological objects and systems made possible by humanity and nature—working not quite in tandem but jointly to a degree. By foregrounding creative contingency and relentless relationality, Romanticism's sublime technologies provide readers with a sense that humanity does not simply control what it makes, but that we humans are remade in light of our creations and our collaborations. Regrettably, in leaving behind Romanticism's vexed representations of sublime technologies, we have forgotten a prime lesson of Romantic aesthetics. The Romantic sublime's telltale mixtures of terror and delight evoked by forces we cannot control point to abiding interconnections running across ourselves, across our natural and built environments—interconnections that we cannot transcend.

CHAPTER ONE

Prometheus and Trophonius

Technological Myth and Sublime Scripts of Industry and Creativity

There are two things essential to a technical treatise: the first is to define the subject; the second (I mean second in order, as it is by much the first in importance) to point out how and by what methods we may become masters of it ourselves.

[It] was not in nature's plan for us her chosen children to be creatures base and ignoble,—no, she brought us into life, and into the whole universe, as into some great field of contest, that we should be at once spectators and ambitious rivals of her mighty deeds, and from the first implanted in our souls an invincible yearning for all that is great, all that is diviner than ourselves. Therefore even the whole world is not wide enough for the soaring range of human thought, but man's mind often overleaps the very bounds of space.

—Longinus, *On the Sublime* (c. 1st century CE)

Invention, it must be humbly admitted, does not consist in creating out of void, but out of chaos; the materials must, in the first place, be afforded: it can give form to dark, shapeless substances, but cannot bring into being the substance itself.

—Mary Godwin Shelley, "Preface," to *Frankenstein: Or, the Modern Prometheus* (1831)

The Romantic Sublime and Representations of Technology

By the time Mary Godwin Shelley set out to compose *Frankenstein: Or, the Modern Prometheus* (1818) and had dreamed up the fictional character of Victor Frankenstein, genius inventor, the historical figure Benjamin Franklin had already been dubbed a modern day "Prometheus" by the likes of Immanuel Kant and others thanks to his celebrated experiments with electricity.[1] As scholars of Romanticism note, the moniker Prometheus was associated not only with the work of Romantic-era scientists and inventors but also with the work and aspirations of British Romantic poets.[2] That inventors and writers of the Romantic period, both fictional and actual, would be granted this godlike, deifying epithet is of course an explicit testament to the evolving cultural currency of the ancient Prometheus myth. At the same time the prominence of the myth of Prometheus is also an implicit testament to the evolving force of the logic of the technological sublime. The logic of this aesthetic category is on full display in the fictional worlds built within Romantic literature and historical accounts of the worlds created in part by Romantic-era scientists and engineers. The pendulum of this aesthetic category swings from staging great feats of human ingenuity as proof of an elite, exclusive mastery (human sublimity), to disproving fantasies of human and cultural exceptionalism, laying bear a shared fragility fueled by pervading forces of the natural world (material sublimity). The epigraphs opening this chapter speak to this range: Longinus's ancient treatise on sublimity opens with reference to the technical and the aim of mastery, and naturalizes the case of humankind as being *contra* and ultimately above even sublime nature; in contrast Godwin Shelley's prefatory remarks stress humility and a necessary human indebtedness to the natural world, upon which all invention depends.

As an offshoot of the sublime, the technological sublime applies to threshold events of wondrous creation or destruction, invention or demolition, to forging new narratives, techniques, structures, or worlds that prompt authors to run out of words, to feel amazed, if not also alarmed. In the Introduction to this book, I address how the traditional aesthetic category of the sublime is itself

---

[1] See Nick Groom, "Introduction" to Mary Shelley, *Frankenstein: Or, the Modern Prometheus*, 1818 Text (Oxford: Oxford University Press, 2018), xxx–xxxii; Brett M. Rogers and Benjamin Stevens, "Classical Receptions in Science Fiction," *Classical Receptions Journal* 4, no. 1 (May 2012): 127–47; Susan J. Wolfson, "'*This* is *my* Lightning' or; Sparks in the Air," *SEL Studies in English Literature 1500–1900* 55, no. 4 (Autumn 2015): 751–86.

[2] See, for example, Suzanne L. Barnett, "Romantic Prometheis and the Molding of *Frankenstein*," in *Frankenstein and Its Classics: The Modern Prometheus from Antiquity to Science Fiction*, eds. Jesse Weiner, Benjamin Eldon Stevens, and Brett M., Rogers (London: Bloomsbury, 2018), 76–90; Anne Mellor, "Promethean Politics," in *Mary Shelley: Her Life, Her Fiction, Her Monsters* (New York: Methuen, 1988), 70–88; Martin Priestman, "Prometheus and Dr. Darwin's Vermicelli: Another Stir to the *Frankenstein* Broth," in *Frankenstein and Its Classics*, 42–58.

Prometheus and Trophonius

notoriously complex and multifaceted, with the term *sublime* holding "many applications: a cathedral or a mountain may be sublime, as may a thought, a heroic deed, or a mode of expression … not restricted to value judgements; [the sublime] also describes a state of mind."[3] The technological sublime likewise bears many faces. The technological sublime aestheticizes, and thus values and judges, impressive examples of what is or can be built, crafted, constructed, and created (from the language arts and mechanical arts to natural and built environments) and frames the reception of whatever powerful forces or entities precipitate and generate such notable inventions, systems, and creations (from divine or natural causes to poets and their pens or engineers and their plans). A child of western philosophy's exalted category of the sublime, a category "mark[ing] the limits of reason and expression" as well as "what might lie beyond these limits," the technological sublime indexes technological and creative ambiguity, uncertainty, wonder, reverence, and awe.[4] In short, the technological sublime is a powerful response to agents and forces powerful enough to rewrite and radically reshape the worlds we build in narrative as well as those we build with and out of the natural the world.

The environmental implications of our aesthetic categories are hard to ignore in the technological sublime's Promethean plotlines. Such narratives in essence take Longinus at his word, when, in his ancient treatise, *On the Sublime*, he claims it is "nature's plan" for us to be ushered "into life, and into the whole universe, as into some great field of contest, that we should be at once spectators and ambitious rivals of her [nature's] mighty deeds." Anticipating Kantian thought on the sublime, if this much-vaunted rivalry between human beings and the natural world proves anything for Longinus, it is the triumphant reach of a sublime human mind: "Therefore even the whole world is not wide enough for the soaring range of human thought, but man's mind often overleaps the very bounds of space." The human mind leaps, soars, ranges, enjoys pervading license, boundlessness, and while the "whole world is not wide enough," even the sublime bounds of space cannot rise to the occasion of matching the sublimity of human thought. Promethean inventors of the Romantic period might be touched by sublime nature as would other astonished "spectators" trained to stand agape at nature's greatest wonders, but that is not all. They are further moved to assume their rightful place as nature's "ambitious rivals," ready to act bravely in "some great field of contest," a contest staged—conveniently enough for Longinus—by the natural world itself.

As if driving toward the logical conclusion of Longinus's words, whether recognized for first molding humankind out of clay or forming humanity from elemental parts of chaos (*Prometheus plasticator*) or bringing fire to humanity

---

[3] Shaw, *The Sublime*, 1.
[4] Shaw, *The Sublime*, 2.

by stealing lightning from Jupiter in the heavens (*Prometheus pyrphoros*)—or both—during the Romantic period Prometheus's sublime story makes gods out of humankind and their tools of invention by appropriating sublime powers of nature. Prometheus is the godlike inventor of a new species or he brings to humanity godlike means of invention symbolized by his gift of lightning or fire. Each character arc resonated powerfully with popular aesthetic discourse on the sublime. A leading example is found in Longinus's treatise, a genre itself emerging in the name of human mastery. "Longinian sublimity," as Micha Lazarus suggests, "offered a conceptual framework in which 'sublimity' attended the representation of divine power and acts." Lazarus reminds us how "Longinus is unique among Greek rhetorical theorists for quoting from Scripture, specifically the passage in Genesis 1:3 in which God declares 'let there be light.'" In addition, "as a valued ancient witness to the truth and the stylistic excellence of sacred Scripture, *On the Sublime* featured widely among English and European sermons, works of divinity, and rhetorical manuals from the early seventeenth century onward."[5]

By citing Old Testament narratives and bringing together in the same text various sublime storylines and exemplars, Longinus reinforced a close aesthetic association between the divine invention of worlds, the trope of divine fiat, and nearly instantaneous, godlike forces of creation and destruction brought about by nature—such as the lightning Prometheus mythically stole from Jupiter above. Then primarily as a treatise on high or lofty rhetoric and writing, *On the Sublime* lavishes attention on the transcendent force of humanity's well-wrought words. While Nicolas Boileau is typically credited with popularizing this text in England with his influential Anglophone translation of *On the Sublime* (1674), Longinus's accounts of sublimity had already reached a variety of English-speaking audiences. From the pulpit to the page, Longinus yoked together competing narratives of cultural, natural, and divine invention and creation under the sign of the sublime.

Godwin Shelley's modern Prometheus activates ramifying legacies of Longinian sublimity. Victor Frankenstein directly competes with nature, wields the very "instruments of life," and "pursue[s] nature to her hiding places," hoping to supplant nature's creative prowess and to single-handedly bring forth "a new species [who] would bless [him] as its creator and source; many happy and excellent natures would owe their being to [him]."[6] This version of the technological sublime scripts a zero-sum game. Humankind and their

---

[5] Micha Lazarus, "Sublimity by Fiat: New Light on the English Longinus," in *The Places of Early Modern Criticism*, eds. Gavin Alexander, Emma Gilby, and Alexander Marr (Oxford: Oxford University Press, 2021), 195.

[6] Mary Godwin Shelley, *Frankenstein: Or, the Modern Prometheus*, 3 vols (London: Lackington, Hughes, Harding, Mavor, & Jones, 1818), I:3, 2, 3.

Prometheus and Trophonius

inventions climb the ladder of western aesthetics and achieve sublime standing; sublime nature—even with its vast forces and incalculable processes—falls to the status of mere obstacle or inspiration, sheer vehicle, or instrument. Under the auspices of the Prometheus myth, the technological sublime dresses up the story of the instrumentalization of nature in the guise of a human destiny rightly and finally fulfilled. By these lights, even powerful forces of sublime nature ultimately withdraw into the background as standing reserve: to put it in Heidegger's terms, ready and waiting to be put to good use by Promethean minds eager to give form to some new sublime creation.

Nature and humanity are staged here as antagonistic binary forces playing against one another. The novel centers around the social cost and requisite death toll accrued by the lone creator figure of Victor Frankenstein, who "pursued nature to her hiding-places."[7] Shelley's isolated Byronic hero turns to science and technology to follow in the footsteps of those who had "penetrate[d] into the recesses of nature."[8] Thus, her modern Prometheus pits himself against nature and aims for both subduing and unseating sublime nature with this own unique, human sublimity, wishing to join the ranks of those scientists who ultimately "ascend into the heavens; they have discovered how the blood circulates, and the nature of the air we breathe. They have acquired new and almost unlimited powers; they can command the thunders of heaven, mimic the earthquake, and even mock the invisible world with its own shadows."[9]

Frankenstein famously abandons the creature he creates and his pursuit is framed in terms of a fear of death. Working under an egotistical god complex, Frankenstein suggests "No father could claim the gratitude of his child so completely as I should deserve their's [sic]. Pursuing these reflections, I thought, that if I could bestow animation upon lifeless matter, I might in process of time (although I now found it impossible) renew life where death had apparently devoted the body to corruption."[10] Rather than working with others and being committed to caring, nurturing, or nourishing, Shelley's modern Prometheus assumes the role of the technological sublime's lone genius creator and fancies himself a godlike prime mover. Detached from what he creates, Frankenstein mistakes himself for nature's great rival and seeks to usurp single-handedly nature's creative, life-bestowing and life-taking forces. Romanticism's most well-remembered modern Prometheus wishes to eschew death and yet in striving to transcend nature's life-giving and life-taking agencies only hastens the demise of those family and friends who cared for him.

---

[7] Shelley, *Frankenstein: Or, the Modern Prometheus*, I:2.
[8] Shelley, *Frankenstein: Or, the Modern Prometheus*, I:2.
[9] Shelley, *Frankenstein: Or, the Modern Prometheus*, I:2.
[10] Shelley, *Frankenstein: Or, the Modern Prometheus*, I:3.

The Romantic Sublime and Representations of Technology

To understand the place of the technological sublime at the heart of the Prometheus myth is to grasp how technological aesthetics play a key part in shading and shaping our imagined and lived relationships with the natural world. In this case we find the Prometheus myth painting the natural world as a, if not the, sublime challenger of humankind, a competitor worthy of domestication and subjugation by way of sublime technology and invention. When we appreciate the influence of the technological sublime in Romantic literature, key studies of Romanticism gain renewed purchase. Susan Wolfson, for one, all but recognizes the technological sublime by name in a recent article that takes for its point of departure Byron's "aesthetics of lightning" and which keys into a post-Benjamin Franklin, post-Enlightenment "electrical sublime" running throughout the Romantic period.[11] Tacitly cuing the Promethean technological sublime, which lionizes the mind of the genius inventor or creator titled toward mastery, Wolfson hands her opening lines to Lord Byron's "tormented, transgressive scientist Manfred."[12] Manfred claims for himself a Promethean genealogy shaded by Franklin's sublime rise into the ranks of modern myth, with Manfred announcing, "'The mind, the spirit, the Promethean spark, / The lightning of my being."[13] Like Franklin and the Titanic Prometheus before him, Manfred lays claim to lightning—sublime nature's great fire starter, a force once taken to be held exclusively by the gods. Quickly following Byron's words, Wolfson's own arrive to offer grounding historical context: "When in 1752 Franklin's kite captured lightning for popular and applied science, the fame of his experiment became a symbol for the age, the Promethean spark of philosophical and revolutionary agenda."[14] Wolfson's richly historicized essay, with its generative assessment of sublime renderings of lightning, electricity, and galvanism does much to unearth the literary and metaphorical significance of the era's electrical experiments and their inventors but leaves room for readers to surmise what such representational trends might cost relative to the natural worlds, not to mention the human cultures, that gave rise to them.

As is typical for Promethean versions of the technological sublime and following Longinus's move to cast human beings as nature's sublime rivals, Byron's lines and Wolfson's language both author sublime nature, metaphorized in the form of lightning or electricity, as a sublime thing possessed by godlike, sublime human handlers. First Byron's scientist Manfred names "the Promethean spark" as the "lightning of my being," with the possessive pronoun *my* signaling how powerfully Manfred identifies with the

[11] Wolfson, "'*This* is *my* Lightning,'" 751, 773.
[12] Wolfson, "'*This* is *my* Lightning,'" 751.
[13] Wolfson, "'*This* is *my* Lightning,'" 751.
[14] Wolfson, "'*This* is *my* Lightning,'" 751.

Prometheus and Trophonius

Titanic figure of Prometheus and how easily he equates forces of lightning with powers of his own. Wolfson's language registers the possessive posture of the Romantic poet's lines as she points to what is a key trope of the technological sublime, with "Franklin's kite captur[ing] lightning for popular and applied science." Sublime nature, here appearing as lightning, is contained as ready fodder for the needs of the populace, for scientific research, for future experiments, for what Longinus calls the "soaring range of human thought." Even the article's title stages humanity's relationship with the natural world in terms of aestheticized competition and control: "'*This* is *my* Lightning' or; Sparks in the Air." Borrowing more of Byron's emphatically possessive vocabulary, Manfred here owns lightning, and after Manfred, lightning—a signature force of sublime nature—may still be airborne but is now reduced to a spark.

Reading Romantic literature in light of the environmental politics of the technological sublime, that is, in light of the technological sublime's place as an aesthetic category that presses us to revision nature and ourselves, likewise extends scholarly inquiries penned by those less interested in histories of technology and science. In a classic chapter entitled "Promethean Politics" from *Mary Shelley: Her Life, Her Fiction, Her Monsters* (1988), Anne K. Mellor notes that "when Mary Shelley subtitled her novel 'The Modern Prometheus,' she forcefully directed our attention to the book's critique both of the promethean poets she knew best, Byron and Percy Shelley, and of the entire Romantic ideology as she understood it."[15] Mellor goes on to argue that "Victor Frankenstein's quest is nothing less than the conquest of death itself. ... In his attempt to transform human beings into deities by eliminating mortality, Victor Frankenstein is himself participating in the mythopoeic vision that inspired the first generation of Romantic poets and thinkers."[16] As Mellor suggests, Godwin Shelley's narrative invites readers to identify a through line linking the myth-engendering projects of seemingly disparate types of Modern Promethean inventors: natural philosophers and experimental scientists such as Franklin and Frankenstein; authors and experimental poets such as Percy Shelley and Lord Byron. Godwin Shelley's novel takes aim at those whose creative agencies, aspirations, and expertise would render them vulnerable to fantasies of Promethean license, a kind of wholly justified and unquestionable creative control. Mellor stresses that "Mary Shelley's critique of romantic Prometheanism thus has direct social and political ramifications. Encoded in the Romantic poets' use of the Promethean myth is an affirmation of revolution, of rebellion against the established social order."[17] I would add

[15] Mellor, "Promethean Politics," 70.
[16] Mellor, "Promethean Politics," 70.
[17] Mellor, "Promethean Politics," 80.

The Romantic Sublime and Representations of Technology

to this claim that such references to the Prometheus myth endorse where they do not outright excuse human beings taking full license of presumed orders and forces extant in the natural world, such that even life's sublime cessation in death is not beyond bounds.

When the novel is read for its sublime technological aesthetics, Godwin Shelley enlarges her critique beyond social and cultural politics to include the direct ecological ramifications of Romantic Prometheanism. While it is the case that technological myths and aesthetics register and influence humanity's social, cultural, and political dimensions in accord with Mellor's compelling analysis, they also participate in something larger: they index and contour humanity's relationships with nature. As we have seen with the case of anti-hero Victor Frankenstein, the technological sublime can easily be folded into the story of humanity's great conquest of the natural world, even to the extent of striving to surmount death. Yet in rare but important cases, the technological sublime also cuts against such logic, instead powerfully reaffirming humanity's unfathomable indebtedness and ineluctable bondedness to the natural world.

While the Prometheus myth appears across many pages of Romantic literature including historical documents detailing newsworthy inventors and inventions, another sublime myth about technology was well known and frequently cited in the period. The myth of Trophonius likewise throws into question the overlap between sublime forces of nature, poetry, and technology. But in contradistinction to the still familiar myths of Prometheus, the now little remembered Trophonius myth scripts sublime technology, creativity, and invention in less heroic, less reductive, less techno-utopian terms, in effect staging more honest but often more difficult, more ambiguous representations of the natural world. The model of the technological sublime stemming from the myth of Trophonius complicates the role of humanity and technology relative to nature. According to the myths of Trophonius, humanity and technology stand indebted to a sublime natural world that is not meant to be countered, possessed, or outdone. Characteristic formulations of Romantic Trophonianism convey a sense of sublime realism rather than Promethean sublime escapism. For example, in his 1796 political correspondence, Edmund Burke dresses Britain's precarious relationship with France's revolutionary leadership in not so many Trophonian terms: "there is great danger that they who enter smiling into this Trophonian Cave, will come out of it sad and serious conspirators."[18] John Fitzgerald Pennie's epic poem, *The Royal Minstrel*

---

[18] Edmund Burke, *Two letters addressed to a member of the present Parliament, on the proposals for peace with the regicide directory of France* (Dublin: William Porter, for P. Wogan, P. Byrne, H. Colbert, W. Porter, J. Moore, J. Rice, H. Fitzpatrick, and G. Folingsby, 1796), 25.

Prometheus and Trophonius

(1817), includes verses not just underscoring the myth's central narrative of sublime transformation but also stressing the grim realities found at the heart of the Trophonius myth: "More gloomy than that grim Trophonian cave, / Within whose portal he that enter'd once, / Was never seen again to wear a smile!"[19] At best, the lives lived within the worlds Trophonius helps to build are to be starkly faced and soberly embraced for the limitations and constraints they pose, while at the same time, within the myth's rubrics of the technological sublime, the natural and built environments stand as exemplars of what cannot, or ought not to be, instrumentalized.

The Problem of Prometheus

Scholars of United States literature have long discussed the aesthetic category of the technological sublime, but this body of scholarship has tended to frame the technological sublime as uniquely "American."[20] Or, it has concentrated on studying only those instances of the technological sublime deemed to be "distinctive[ly] American" in religious affiliation and popular reception.[21] The long history of the technological sublime and its larger stakes are less at issue than how the technological sublime takes shape in the United States. Yet by drawing these studies into a broader conversation, we find their accounts of technological sublimity often resemble Promethean narratives that funnel forces of sublime nature into human hands. They also harbor Longinian notions of sublime rivalries of invention and contests of creation that heroize the mind more than matter. Perry Miller is often cited as the first literary critic to examine sublime representations of technology. His work is limited to canonical white male authors of early New England such as Ralph Waldo Emerson and Henry David Thoreau, Nathaniel Hawthorne and Herman Melville, and Walt Whitman. While he does not mention Kant as a guiding influence, Miller nonetheless espouses a Kantian version of the sublime that ultimately champions agencies of the human mind. Miller addresses sublime technology and nature to make his case, but in the end, suggests that "technological triumph is [a] demonstration of triumph of mind over matter."[22] As with Longinus's account of the place of sublime nature relative to the human creative impulse and the Prometheus myth, where sublime technologies evince the sublimity of the human mind, a sublime contest here again emerges between humanity and nature with the United

---

[19] John Fitzgerald Pennie, *The Royal Minstrel; Or, The Witcheries of Endor, An Epic Poem, In Eleven Books* (Dorchester and London: G. Clark; Longman, 1817), 7.

[20] Elizabeth W. Miller, Foreword to Miller, *The Life of the Mind in America*, viii.

[21] Nye, *American Technological Sublime*, 17.

[22] Miller, *The Life of the Mind in America*, 319.

The Romantic Sublime and Representations of Technology

States arising uniquely triumphant: "America, led by Science out of Colonial isolation into National magnificence, has discovered, more than anybody else, the TRUE SUBLIME behind the obvious SUBLIME of the immense pageant of Technology. This is MIND itself."[23]

Proceeding with a greater emphasis on historical documents and sources, David E. Nye's landmark work, *The American Technological Sublime* (1994) charts how the "American sublime embraced technology" and likewise was "not limited to [sublime] nature."[24] Nye argues that as "technological achievements became central to July Fourth [celebrations of US independence], the American sublime fused with religion, nationalism and technology, diverging in practice significantly from European theory. It ceased to be a philosophical idea and became submerged in practice."[25] Mounting a case for US national exceptionalism relative to sublime aesthetics grounded in technological aesthetics, Nye distinguishes between how "Kant [as a stand-in for a singular European sublime] had reasoned that the awe inspired by a sublime object made men aware of their moral worth," while "the American sublime transformed the individual's experience of immensity and awe into a belief in national greatness."[26] While Miller and Nye foreground the politics of aesthetics—especially concerning the relationship between technological aesthetics and national identities or mythologies—these projects nonetheless overlook what is not particular to the United States and the technological sublime. Miller and Nye do not acknowledge how the technological sublime likewise became a practice, not just a philosophy, outside of the United States. Nor do they register how easy it is for narratives of cultural exceptionalism to be propped up by the broader logic and narrative structure of the technological sublime, which routinely reduces the relationship between humanity and the natural world to an epic battle between two giants.

Promethean versions of the technological sublime tend to run on a Longinian logic of contest, risk, and reward. Inventors gain sublime status by conquering iterations of sublime nature that they dare to work upon or channel. The stakes of such patterns of thought are well trod. Although famed Frankfurt School thinkers Max Horkheimer and Theodor W. Adorno do not directly consider how sublime aesthetics play a hand in (post) Enlightenment models of human mastery over nature, in *Dialectic of Enlightenment* they address the costs of narratives like that of the modern Prometheus. In their framing remarks, Horkheimer and Adorno argue that the "Enlightenment, understood in the widest sense as the advance of thought, has always aimed at liberating

---

[23] Miller, *The Life of the Mind in America*, 321.
[24] Nye, *The American Technological Sublime*, 43.
[25] Nye, *The American Technological Sublime*, 43.
[26] Nye, *The American Technological Sublime*, 43.

Prometheus and Trophonius

human beings from fear and installing them as masters."[27] For their opening evidence, they include the following from Francis Bacon: "'Therefore, no doubt, the sovereignty of man lieth hid in knowledge ... now we govern nature in opinions, but we are in thrall unto her in necessity: but if we would be led by her in invention, we should command her by action.'"[28] With these opening moves, Horkheimer and Adorno link the cause of instantiating hierarchical human sovereignty to "liberating human beings from fear," a goal achieved by governing, mastering, or commanding nature through acts and thoughts of human "invention" inspired first and foremost by nature's own great powers and processes of invention. Humanity goes on the offensive by way of invention. This is the very same logic that grounds the technological sublime after Prometheus and Longinus—sublime inventors craft sublime inventions able to put down or tame humanity's original opponents: great and fearsome forces of a sublime natural world.

The prominence and staying power of the Prometheus myth matters because it suggests the story of human technology is fundamentally a story of heroic efforts marked by forward progress, one invention after the next. As we know, references to the Titanic god Prometheus (Greek for forethought or foresight), and to a lesser extent to his likewise Titanic brother, Epimetheus (Greek for afterthought, memory, or forgetting), recur throughout the Romantic period, a period that witnessed no shortage of celebrated inventions or inventors. Prometheus's name signals forward thinking, forward mindedness, suggesting that technological development marches along in linear, historically progressive lines. Bernard Stiegler's influential critique of Heideggerian thought on technology and his larger assessment of the Prometheus and Epimetheus myths relative to western philosophy, *Technics and Time, 1*, laments the lopsided thinking about technology that arises from remembering Prometheus but forgetting Epimetheus. Stiegler holds that the "figure of Prometheus ... *makes no sense by itself*. It is only consistent through its doubling by Epimetheus ... the intertwining of the two figures of prométheia and épimétheia [forgetting, afterthought, reflection] yields the major elements of the structure of temporality" (original emphasis).[29] It is safe to say that literary works of Romanticism exacerbate the problem as Prometheus overshadows his brother to near oblivion. A story of the Modern Epimetheus was certainly nowhere to be found. Even as the Prometheus myth ostensibly admits regress in rare instances where Epimetheus is included (with the latter at times being showcased as a

---

[27] Max Horkheimer and Theodor W. Adorno, *Dialectic of Enlightenment: Philosophical Fragment*, ed. Gunzelin Schmid Noerr, trans. Edmund Jephcott (Redwood City, CA: Stanford University Press, 2002), 1.

[28] Bacon quoted in Horkheimer and Adorno, *Dialectic of Enlightenment*, 1.

[29] Bernard Stiegler, *Technics and Time, 1: The Fault of Epimetheus*, trans. Richard Beardsworth and George Collins (Stanford, CA: Stanford University Press, 1998), 186.

The Romantic Sublime and Representations of Technology

dim-witted buffoon, but generally positioned aside wife Pandora rather than brother Prometheus), it ultimately assumes a linear temporality of advance—only occasionally misfiring and moving backward in the spirit of Epimetheus where there is a failure to remember or reflect, but generally moving forward by way of one sublime Promethean invention after the other.

The word history of the adjective *promethean* corresponds with the myth's sublime narratives, pertaining alike to the figure of the inventor, what comes to be invented, and legacies of coopting agencies long ascribed to sublime nature. During the Romantic period, *prometheans* referred to those resembling Prometheus in their revolutionary if not reckless spirit, frightful punishment, or groundbreaking work. But what constituted a groundbreaking achievement was of course historically contingent and in the eye of the beholder, as is always the case with aesthetic judgments, regardless of how universal people might mean their aesthetic judgments to be when they assert them. Point in case, *prometheans* also referred to an early type of match invented in the first quarter of the nineteenth century and heralded by Charles Darwin, among others, for "produc[ing] instantaneous light."[30] Sublime aesthetics of invention often privilege temporal models of immediate action and impact, partly because of the longstanding prominence within sublime discourse of the story of godlike fiat, a narrative of nearly effortless and instantaneous creation where gods create or destroy worlds in no more than the time it takes to utter a few words. Notably in this case, time once again resides at the heart of an invention's sublime reception, with the temporal models of explosive spectacle and forward progress both helping an artifact as small as a match to qualify as an ingenious artifact.

A pattern emerges within sublime aesthetics that marks the march of technological progress not as painstaking process but nearly instantaneous—or compressed epiphanic moments of genesis or apocalypse. Sublime events of ingenious creation arise seemingly out of nowhere, as in the case of fashioning entire worlds through sheer powers of utterance. This aesthetic of unlabored invention and creation, unmoored from process, downplays where it does not erase questions of arduous labor and realties of the long creative durée, both from a human perspective and when considering material processes of the natural world. The longer, more extensive temporalities required by human hands and the natural world to produce whatever comprises a given sublime invention either go unnarrated, uncelebrated, or unrecorded. Even when arriving in the small form of a match, *prometheans* create sublime marvels seemingly at the blink of an eye, at wonderous little cost—all while true costs are nonetheless extracted offstage. The Promethean model of the technological sublime displaces realities of joint human and environmental sacrifice as it

---

[30] "Promethean, adj. and n.," *OED Online*, December 2022, Oxford University Press, https://doi.org/10.1093/OED/9700155679 (accessed 5 February 2023).

Prometheus and Trophonius

shifts attention from processes of making to instead lavish narrative attention on the bestower of invention and the invention itself.

The Promise of Trophonius

Much less well known today is that British Romanticism's inherited technological pantheon included another set of fabled brothers: legendary architects and stonemasons of ancient Greece, Trophonius (Nourisher of Minds) and Agamedes (Cunning of Mind or the Mindful One). This second pairing runs parallel to Prometheus and Epimetheus in the historical receptions and literary afterlives the brothers received: Agamedes's story tends to fall by the wayside while Trophonius garners such regular reference that his name would, like Prometheus, inspire an adjectival epithet: *trophonian*, meaning grave, grim, or solemn in character. As the *OED* records, those described in *trophonian* terms bear some resemblance or relation to "Trophonius, the deified legendary builder of the original temple of Apollo at Delphi, whose oracle in a Boeotian cave was said to affect those who entered with such awe that they never smiled again. Hence (figurative): gloomy, saturnine."[31] The mark of a *trophonian* is a tempered if not dampened spirit. As legend has it, a *trophonian* is a changed person, one who aquires solemnity and the tinge of grimness from facing death; they are transformed by learning too much as they honestly confront humanity's inevitable future—the finitude of human being, death. While Mary Godwin Shelley's novel interrogates the dark side of Prometheus, as we shall see, other Romantic authors would uncover the lighter side of Trophonius, revealing a technological sublime guided less by individual agency, ego, and competition and more by creative material process, abiding togetherness, and unavoidable transformation.

For the fabled Trophonius and Agamedes, the central questions concerning technology involve whether technologies are or will be nourishing, how they alter us, how they frame processes of becoming and making as well as those of ending and undoing. In addition, the Trophonius script for technology keys directly into technological thought and belief, questioning our technological faith and ethics. Here both the material and metaphysical sublimity of humanity's entanglement with what it builds and unbuilds takes center stage, a sublimity anchored in solemn practices of mental and physical work and ongoing care. In stark contrast to the Promethean technological aesthetic, the narrative of Trophonius is grounded by the unambiguous recognition that even the most crafty, wily, and inventive among us cannot escape our fates, cannot like Frankenstein, the Modern Prometheus, circumvent death.

---

[31] "Trophonian, adj.," *OED Online*, December 2022, Oxford University Press, https://doi.org/10.1093/OED/5347874060 (accessed 7 February 2023).

The Romantic Sublime and Representations of Technology

Romanticism's engagement with the ancient Greek Trophonius myth foregrounds a material sublime wherein technologies are created interdependently—in concert. In turn, and in one way or another, technologies of the material sublime do not obey human commands or ends. Instead, they commonly bring about vexed outcomes mirrored by and indeed indexed by the sublime's telltale emotive cross: those highly charged positive and negative feelings generated as a response to what we revere and fear because of its great presence or power. In the case of Trophonius, humanity's works of immaterial and material worldbuilding and unbuilding always emerge in conjunction with nonhuman creative agencies. Worlds are built together, lived together, loved together, weathered together, undone together. Crucially, co-built worlds of the material sublime cannot be put to reductive, assured, foreseeable ends. They are not invented by figures of exceptionally empowered human genius (sublime humanity) in a fight against mighty natural cataclysms (sublime nature). Materially sensitive accounts of the technological sublime often envision a world built upon precarious grounds, positing an existence framed by the inexorable ambivalence and uncertain promise of human values and dreams. Indeed, the stripe of sublime technological aesthetics that repatterns the noncombative logics of the material sublime may not paint a prettier, safer, or more comfortable picture. Yet, in representations of technology that largely depart from the antagonistic logic of the Promethean technological sublime to instead feature collective and interdependent rubrics of the material sublime, at last we encounter a more honest aesthetic terrain within which to explore the nexus of human, natural, cultural, and technological invention and destruction.

Trophonian iterations of the technological sublime adopt the overarching narrative structure and logic of *sublime* in its verb form, activating material legacies arising from the root words of the term. The verb form allows for more temporal nuance than we expect. Referring to a seemingly sudden and surprising transformation from one physical state to another, linearly progressive models of material transformation that would change sequentially from solid to liquid to gas or vice versa appear to be overturned. Instead, the verb accommodates a timeline of gradual process, since *to sublime* a substance requires gradually heating it to cause the material to change directly from dense matter to gaseous form without first liquefying. Then, in a related but less ubiquitous usage of the verb, the act of subliming a substance refers to nearly the opposite process of transformation. In this case *to sublime* means "to subject (a substance) to the action of heat in a container so as to convert it into vapour, which is driven off and is deposited in a solid form on a cool surface."[32] As we shall see, a

---

[32] "sublime, v.," *OED Online*, March 2023, Oxford University Press, https://doi.org/10.1093/OED/5248396476 (accessed 17 March 2023).

40

Prometheus and Trophonius

close resonance with the Trophonius myth exists both in the sublime story of non-linear disjunctive transformation and, perhaps surprisingly, in reference to a necessary container or restrictive enclosure wherein such transformations take place. The Trophonius myth is known for two complementary transformative spaces: the magnificent built environs Trophonius and his brother helped create and the earthen, underground cave that pilgrims would visit when seeking the oracle of Trophonius.

Notably, the Prometheus myth includes the narrative of the Titan's enchainment not just as a form of punishment but also as containment or constraint; for humanity, however, that technological myth foregrounds unmoored creative license and liberty. The Trophonius myth, on the other hand, foregrounds scenes of inescapable creative limitation and restraint, echoing underacknowledged word histories of the sublime, "where the ambivalent, transformative, and uncontrollable aggregate agencies of nature are always all around us—building us up and breaking us down like everything else in the natural world."[33] As I have delineated elsewhere, "when read through the lens of the *longue durée*, the word's root meanings of *sub* and *limis* or *limin* erode antagonistic and individuated conceptualizations of agency ... point[ing] instead toward combinatory agencies, contingencies, and dependencies."[34] Relative to the term *sublime* in its verb form and as a noun, the word's roots allude to supporting structures of both organic bodies and built environments as well as to what stands beside, rises above, or runs below us:

> Partly a borrowing from the French *sublime* meaning "excellent, admirable, perfect," and partly from the Latin *sublīmus* meaning "elevated, high" or "shallow breath" or later "also designating a muscle lying near the surface," the English term arises out of a union of multiple senses: perhaps most intriguingly the Latin *sub* and *limis* or *limen*. While *sub* denotes the condition of being "under, below, beneath, underneath" or even behind, *limis* marks a sidelong position of being "askew" or "askance," while also referring to "slime, mud, mire." *Limen* adds to the mix more senses of positionality and locality, denoting the threshold of a doorway, the "cross-piece, head piece," the very top of a door as well as the sill beneath it or the "foot-piece of a doorway."[35]

The Trophonius myth as rendered in Romantic literature grants access to a transformative model of sublimity that does not shed the tensions

---

[33] Speitz, "The Sublime," in *Nature and Literary Studies*, eds. Peter Remien and Scott Slovic (Cambridge: Cambridge University Press, 2002), 175.
[34] Speitz, "The Sublime," 163.
[35] Speitz, "The Sublime," 163.

and conflicted feelings long associated with sublime rhetoric, affect and experience—honoring sublime etymologies tied as much to the elevated and the excellent as the mud underfoot, muscles under skin, a shallow breath, earthly slime. Retained as well are the sublime's associations with something askew and to the side as well as above and below, as in the structure of a doorway, a threshold, through which both spatial dislocation or relocation and transformation may take place. Instead of offering a lopsided technological sublime that chiefly draws out the wonder and grand spectacle of the inventor or the invention, the poet's revolution in words, the radical's new social order, the Trophonius myth bestows a sublime that relentlessly paints a fuller picture, not forgetting the mud, the slime, and registering a core adjacency of sublime experience borne of conflicted, unresolved if not unresolvable feelings and matters.

The second half of this chapter first contextualizes the understudied technological mythography and aesthetic philosophy alive in poetry penned by Erasmus Darwin and in a Drury Lane play by Prince Hoare and then examines each of those texts in light of that context. Both late eighteenth-century works invite us to consider a mythic technological history of humanity framed not by Titanic gods or Promethean fire, as commonly found in narratives aligning more squarely with Longinus's more antagonistic models of sublime invention and competition, but framed instead by a child of the always adjacent material sublime: the human-turned-Apollonian-oracle—a legendary builder, maker, and stonesmith: Trophonius, Nourisher of Minds.[36] For Hoare and Darwin, intertwined histories and potentialities of art and technology are ever involved with natural and cultural processes of making, becoming, and undoing, and while the worlds we build with culture and nature may never be fixed, in the best case scenario they might continuously play out stories of transformative, collaborative repair.

Romantic Myths of Trophonius: Or, an Ecological Technological Sublime

As the Prometheus story goes, humankind is born in light of lack, in light of what's missing, what's wanting, what's needed. Technology in the form of sublime Promethean fire resolves the problem of human vulnerability, undergirding the now entrenched idea that technology might save us. Under

---

[36] I am indebted to Scott McGill for directing me to relevant ancient Greek sources on this figure including the Homeric Hymn to Apollo where Trophonius was said to have built the temple to the oracle at Delphi; Pausanias's *Description of Greece*, 9.37.4 and 9.39.3–4, pertaining to the cave of Trophonius, and additional references to his cave in Strabo, *Geography*, 9.2.38; and Philostratus, *Life of Apollonius of Tyana*, 8.19.

Prometheus and Trophonius

this rubric, technology bestows upon us bolstered agency, heightened powers of creation, invention, innovation, and so on, so we can compete, survive, or perhaps even thrive against potent, aggressive others. And, as mentioned previously, Prometheus is eternally punished. The vulture, as predatory natural other, continually feeds on the liver of the humanistic god, who himself had to work antagonistically against his ruling other to steal the gift of fire in the first place to give humanity protection against everything else in the natural world. It is time to retell another technological tale, a tale where invention and technics are driven by something other than fear, antagonism, or skirting death. Where Prometheus saves us—propping up wish-fulfillment and desires of human exceptionalism *qua* technological salvation—Trophonius transforms us—making it hard to ignore realities of relation, of co-determining human, technological, and environmental contingency.

The ancient Trophonius myth envisions a world of technological relationality, human contingency, and transformative care. Always first circumscribed by the natural world, here technology also promotes and supports nature, and ultimately, points to humanity's rootedness to the earth. "Trophonius," as Clinton DeBevoise Corcoran notes, "plays a shaman-like role of a spiritual intermediary, connecting humans back to their own roots in the archaic powers of nature."[37] As Joan Connelly points out, "At the very core of Athenian solidarity and civic devotion was the awareness of a shared past, and part of that awareness for some was special pride in being earthborn, or gegenes (from the Greek Ge or Gaia, meaning 'Earth,' and genes, meaning 'born'). Gegenes denotes a literal springing up from the earth itself."[38] In the Trophonius myth, technology does not have us forget nature and would not have us set against it. Rather it asks us to remember our past and present places in nature. In similar spirit, the logic of the Trophonius myth makes technology nearly synonymous with terms mostly reserved today for natural growth and organic sustenance, or even familial upbringing.

As with most ancient Greek myths, there exist multiple versions of the Trophonius story. Plutarch and Pausanias both offer narratives about Trophonius, with Pausanias's *Description of Greece* offering a full account of his humble origins and later transformation into cave-dwelling oracle. In Pausanias, Trophonius and his brother Agamedes are either granted to a childless king named Ergins, or they both are sons of Apollo—god of sun, light, poetry, medicine, (social) order, rules, and structure. Pausanias assumes Apollo to be the father, admittedly based on hearsay and because the boys "proved clever at building sanctuaries for the gods and palaces for men," not

---

[37] Clinton DeBevoise Corcoran, *Topography and Deep Structure in Plato: The Construction of Place in the Dialogues* (Albany, NY: SUNY Press, 2016), 35.
[38] Joan Connelly, *The Parthenon Enigma* (New York: Knopf, 2014), 37.

43

The Romantic Sublime and Representations of Technology

least the famed temple for Apollo at Delphi.[39] Regardless of this disputed patrimony, Trophonius's name would become synonymous with the Apollonian temple at Delphi, home to the lights of medicine, structure, and poetry. Yet his legacy becomes bound up with descents into Dionysian darkness, disorder, and undoing. Building structures above ground and later occupying caves beneath the earth, the arc of the Trophonius myth runs in accord with sublime materiality as it hangs upon interfused lines of light and dark, order and chaos, stable structure and transformative dissolution.

As with the Prometheus myth, key to the Trophonius story are the roles of his brother as well as questions of order and disorder. But whereas Epimetheus's forgetting sets Prometheus into action to correct what appears as natural imbalance (Epimetheus bestows all other animals with tools of defense, forgetting to do so for humanity, and thus Prometheus steals fire for humankind to set the world aright), Agamedes gets into trouble alongside Trophonius as they both try to work around what appears as cultural imbalance (stealing from the rich man for whom they built a treasury by leaving one stone loose).[40] Trophonius and Agamedes both get punished, albeit in different ways, for secretly chipping away at a king's holdings. Upon noticing that the "keys and seals [of the treasury were] untampered with, while the treasure kept on getting less," the befuddled king sets snares and traps over his stores of silver and gold, which then leads to Agamedes's capture.[41] So "Trophonius cut off [Agamedes's] head, lest when day came his brother should be tortured, and he himself be informed of as being concerned in the crime."[42] Thus, Agamedes becomes trapped and dies within a structure that he himself has a hand in building; Trophonius must kill his brother within this same structure that he helped build. Trophonius must take his brother out of this co-built structure to keep him from being tortured into confession, to keep his brother from talking, and to keep himself out of another, larger structure of containment and confinement: the existing criminal, juridical system. Yet Trophonius's punishment does not stop with these cultural disciplinary measures, as next the "earth opened and swallowed up Trophonius at the point in the grove at Lebadeia where is what is called the pit of Agamedes, with a slab beside it."[43]

Once swallowed by the earth, Trophonius drops out of Pausanias's narrative, only to reappear later in another form—as an oracle visited by those who

---

[39] Pausanias, *Description of Greece*, trans. W. H. S. Jones, Litt.D. and H. A. Ormerod, M.A., 4 vols. (Cambridge, MA: Harvard University Press, 1966; London: William Heinemann Ltd., 1918), 9.37.5.

[40] Pausanias, *Description of Greece*, 9.37.5–7.

[41] Pausanias, *Description of Greece*, 9.37.5–6.

[42] Pausanias, *Description of Greece*, 9.37.6.

[43] Pausanias, *Description of Greece*, 9.37.7.

Prometheus and Trophonius

would descend into the Cave of Trophonius. Trophonius's trajectory takes him from human builder to oracular demigod. Romantic-era writers assumed readers would connect Trophonius to each of these legacies simultaneously. Trophonius's name alludes to the legendary master builder, architect, and stonesmith, who (with his brother) co-built the temple of Apollo at Delphi and who then becomes an oracle and spiritual intermediary to those visiting his cave.[44] Those entering Trophonius's cave and drinking from its waters inevitably emerge greatly changed. Visitors first drink from the waters of Lethe (forgetting) and then from Mnemosyne (memory), forgetting themselves only to gain a new sense of self marked both by a profound sense of loss and profound change.[45] They emerge from the Cave of Trophonius bearing new and different memories—that is, they become someone else, something else, because of a changed relationship to themselves and a transformed relationship to the past. A key element of a Trophonian transformation derives from the fact that when visitors drink from the waters of Lethe and shed their previous sense of self, they are said to face death; they must reckon with death as the ultimate loss of self. Here exists an important distinction between the Trophonius and Prometheus myths: the former case hinges upon facing death and being transformed in light of doing so, while, as we have seen, the latter case revolves around fleeing death or attempting to outwit death—as with Mary Godwin Shelley's Modern Prometheus, Victor Frankenstein.

Trophonius and those visiting his cave are transformed by becoming something other and this becoming is fraught and beyond knowing—in a word, this becoming takes shape as sublime transformation, where outcomes are unavoidably ambivalent and uncertain. This aesthetic of uncertainty has long been home to the sublime. As Burke's sublime typology notes, "there is a passage in the book of Job amazingly sublime and this sublimity is principally due to the terrible uncertainty of the thing described."[46] In this spirit, the Trophonius myth raises important open questions about technology. What happens after technology? What happens with technology? An answer the Trohponius myth provisionally offers is that technology leads to sublime transformation: change without escape, just as there's no escaping nature. That is, the Trophonius myth suggests a wider ethic of technological and environmental interdependence premised upon the combined and qualified agencies of humanity, nature, and technology: we bear change and death, never finding some techno-utopic or techno-salvation-type cure or antidote to them—and as we see from both Prometheus and Trophonius, as it turns out, our technological foresight tends to be extremely limited.

---

[44] Pausanias, *Description of Greece*, 9.39.5.
[45] Pausanias, *Description of Greece*, 9.39.7.
[46] Burke, *A Philosophical Enquiry*, 108.

The Romantic Sublime and Representations of Technology

Even with technological security proving oxymoronic and our (technological) futurity being ultimately unknowable, the fearsome faces of the Trophonius myth are tempered by offering a picture of a life worth living. As befitting a figure so closely associated with Apollo (god of medicine, sun and light, poetry and social structures), related root words of Trophonius's name refer to the maintaining or rearing of nurslings, to tending, cherishing, fostering (τρέφω [trephō]), and to nourishment, nurturement, education, sustenance, a way of life, a place in which animals are reared (τροφή [trophē]).[47] Trophonius's name weds the growth of the Grecian mind to physical care, provision, and upbringing. Furthermore, his name knits together the immaterial, ideational realms with the somatic and material, and these linkages coalese and play off of one another in the name of a rearing, a bringing up, a guiding and supporting, where growth figures less in terms of increase in size and more in terms of change over time. This tale of technological life, crime, and punishment foregrounds humanity's collective contingency in relation to one another and in relation to the external, natural world. Its logic pivots around necessary interrelationality and co-reliance. Human exceptionalism and heroic independence are absent.

Trophonius's technological tale foregrounds the relational politics of material sublime aesthetics, where intimate, transformative change is all but the only certainty, and where the biggest myths of all are those of purported autonomy, supposed self-reliance, so-called individuated agency. Different tellings of this myth reinforce etymological links that bind the figure of Trophonius the builder to notions of nourishment, support, and growth that come with change and transformation. Because the ancient Greek words comprising Trophonius's name denote a physical reality premised upon rearing, nursing, providing, here technological change and transformation arrive predominantly through economies of care. Routine patterns and practices of intimate care bring up the world. The abiding ethos is one of daily dynamic maintenance and support such that educational, transformative growth and change are possible; thus, it comes as little surprise that Trophonius's signature epithet suggests a fundamental spiritual and material interplay, translating as it does to nourisher of minds.

On this end of the spectrum of sublime technological aesthetics and ethics, is a lighthearted Drury Lane drama of loving repair and intimate

---

[47] I am indebted to Christopher W. Blackwell for directing me to authoritative translations of these Greek terms and associated etymologies. For more on τρέφω (trephō) and τροφή (trophē) see *A Greek–English Lexicon*, eds. Henry George Liddell and Robert Scott; revised and augmented throughout by Sir Henry Stuart Jones with the assistance of Roderick McKenzie (Oxford: Clarendon Press. 1940), http://folio2.furman.edu/lsj/?urn=urn:cite2:hmt:lsj.chicago_md:n104690 and http://folio2.furman.edu/lsj/?urn=urn:cite2:hmt:lsj.chicago_md:n105550 respectively.

Prometheus and Trophonius

transformation featuring none other than Trophonius. Prince Hoare's play, *The Cave of Trophonius* (1791),[48] posits interlinked sublime worlds of nature and culture wherein little is certain beyond the uncertain change and transformation all worldbuilding yields.[49] Hoare's play showcases interlinked built and natural environs all marked by the material sublime's signature formula of aggregate agencies, relational contingency, and uncontrollable alterations. While better known Prometheus myths tether human invention and technics to tales of humanity's separateness from nature, myths of Trophonius underwrite a grounding technological narrative bespeaking humanity's rootedness in nature. The Prometheus myth (along with its attendant plotlines related to his brother Epimetheus) yokes the inventive work of forethought and forgetting to divine orders of ongoing vengeance, punishment, injustice and to human realms of naturalized competition, antagonism, social hierarchy. Not erasing nor denying the existence of such realities, the Trophonius myth imagines another way: a humbler and more ambivalent path of ecosocial repair.

Linking sublime aesthetics to technē and technology, Hoare's play reprises the notion that language (as technē or craft) just might be humanity's prime tool. Whereas Holland and Strätling define the aesthetics of the tool as belonging to the aesthetic category of the beautiful, their appraisal runs into sublime territory when they designate tools as also belonging to realms of the alien, the foreign, the formless, the unknown or unknowable. As Holland and Strätling put it, "in a gray area between the aesthetic and technical, the tool leads a double existence: it participates in the discourse of the beautiful yet remains a foreign body. The tool therefore operates on the threshold of an unshaped thing and product and exists in the ambivalent zone of the 'becoming of the work' both as art and artifact."[50] This threshold effect and the tool's link to transformational becoming tie it to the politics of sublime aesthetics.

In the opening sequence of the play, the audience is introduced to a conflict between two sisters, with Phædra, the more loquacious of the two, chiding Daphne about a lost opportunity to use their tools of communication: "Now see the Consequences of your Silent ways, if we had spoken our minds to each

---

[48] Prince Hoare, *The Cave of Trophonius*, manuscript held in the Larpent Collection, Huntington Library, LA899.

[49] The play ran for two seasons, being performed three times during the season of 1790–1791 and four times in the 1791–1792 season. See Charles Beecher Hogan, ed., *The London Stage, 1660–1800: A Calendar of Plays, Entertainments & Afterpieces Together with Casts, Box-Receipts and Contemporary Comment* (Carbondale, SI: Southern Illinois University Press, 1968), 1275–9, 1377–80.

[50] Jocelyn Holland and Susanne Strätling, "Introduction: Aesthetics of the Tool—Technologies, Figures, and Instruments of Literature and Art," *Configurations* 18, no. 3 (2010): 203.

The Romantic Sublime and Representations of Technology

other sooner we shou'd have known better how to Answer my Father."[51] Without language, discourse, and dialogue the sisters are bereft of understanding and more. It is tempting to read speech and dialogue in this case as functioning akin to tools because they are understood to be ready and available for sure, instrumental use—precisely the type of overriding grantedness that Heidegger later critiques as it ignores elements of language that are not at our command, such as the air it takes to vocalize words, to cite just one example. However, according to the overriding logic of the play, language is akin to a tool more because of its profoundly conditional potentiality, for the way characters *could* have arrived at an alternative place or path with its use. In this instance, the play's characters fail to arrive at a different place, and indeed stay where they are, because of their relationships with language as technē and due to their relationships with one another and their father. Daphne's "shou'd" signals technology's conditionality and contingency which might have amounted to something, but that something is an outcome not settled, not yet known.

A later scene extends the sublime-tool-as-tongue metaphor when a transformed Daphne finds herself newly equipped and freshly empowered with words. Daphne's suitor compares her newfound verbal prowess to the sublime event of warfare: "What a Troop of Words you have disbanded since Yesterday!" (34). The sublime-tool-as-tongue trope and only that trope frames how Daphne emerges newly emboldened after her transformation in Trophonius's cave (39). While verging on farce, the trope nonetheless registers more complicated temporalities and contingencies than the Promethean brand of sublime fiat that emphasizes the nearly instantaneous power of one person's words. A day has passed in this case. And the force of her words is recognized as an aggregate force—inclusive of the speaker—and so pays homage to their collective agency, rather than being conflated with the agency of the speaker *qua* inventor or reduced to the more singular sounding "speech act." In response to her suitor's negative assessment of her newly acquired verbal agency (equating spoken words to igniting a war), Daphne revises the sublime-tool-as-tongue metaphor in light of the Trophonius myth where technē and technology are not necessarily ceded to violent or antagonistic ends: "Wou'd you prevent me from / talking, deny me the free use / of my tongue – the happiness of my life – the privilege of my Sex – the Air, food, Exercise / of a Woman – Monstrous! Would you have me a Mute / a Fish – a piece of Furniture" (39). The tongue-as-tool metaphor now highlights intersections between sublime, transformative technics and earthly elements that echo Trophonius's epithet denoting nourishment. In the same vein, fish

---

[51] Prince Hoare, *Cave of Trophonius* (London: Theatre Royal, Drury Lane, 1791), 12. Manuscript access curtesy of Huntington Library Munger Research Center. Hereafter citations are noted in-text by page number.

Prometheus and Trophonius

and furniture (earthly entity and technological invention) share common ground here, both signaling what Daphne does not want to become. In essence, she does not want to be rendered inert, akin to the Burkean beautiful in its well-known formulation as counterpoint to his untameable sublime. Daphne would prefer not to be controlled, instrumentalized, reduced to the rote existence left to her without access to the sublime's unknowable transformative agency. Sustenance in the form of food and more are here wedded to unpredictable, though limited, powers of sublime technē as Daphne presses her suitor: "Wou'd you prevent me from / talking, deny me the free use / of my tongue ... happiness ...the Air, food, Exercise."

Hoare's play foregrounds the uncertain promise of human invention in part by painting Trophonius's cave as a sublime landscape that exceeds human powers of expression. Aristo, father to Phædra and Daphne, begins to wonder if his daughters have visited Trophonius's cave against his wishes, and so he orders his servant, Dromo, to enter the cave, experience its transformative magic, and report back. Dromo recounts a traumatizing descent into the cavern's belly. Inside he reaches a lake, its bottom, then a handful of islands all aflame and accompanied by "Stars as big as / Mountains" (49). That is, Dromo encounters a sublime landscape replete with elemental fire, earth, air, and water, all pressing him to the very limits of mind, memory, and making sense. Even the stars seem out of order as they sound off and whirl about his head: "Whirl! Whirl! til they made such a noise in my Ears, that I could not tell if I was asleep or awake—Then there was such a Screaming, and such a Singing ... I cannot tell you what follows—I'm so terrified at the recollection" (49, 50). Here Dromo declares an inability to tell and so wades into familiar sublime territory with the trope of sublime-experience-induced aphasia. From Kant to Lyotard, philosophers note how sublime discourse acknowledges the limits of representation and language, and entails questions of the unpresentable. That is, sublime narratives commonly point to what transcends human tools of verbal expression and articulation, with sublime experiences or entities existing well beyond the ken of human communication, definition, and understanding. For Dromo, these screaming voices and songlike soundings prompt aphasia, an inability to narrate, demarcate, describe. The playwright incorporates numerous stock sublime tropes, from the unspeakable and unpresentable to ambivalent feelings and settings beyond human control, such that audiences could hardly miss that Trophonius's transformative cave exists squarely within the provenance of sublime aesthetics.

Across Trophonius's myths, sublime technics and poetics instantiate transformative programs of care and nourishment in support of ever-changing selves and others, premised first upon a double meaning of repair, with the term referring both to places of refuge and to tending to what is cracked, broken, and ruptured, such that it might exist in a new (repaired) form. The

The Romantic Sublime and Representations of Technology

dramatic climax of the play recalls the ancient myth as told by Pausanias, as it showcases a rigged, competitive political economy. While the moral universe of this play is uneven at best, it is nonetheless uniform in suggesting that the space and place of technics transforms us whether we like it or not. Each of the play's main characters, the sisters Daphne and Phædra, visits Trophonius's cave multiple times throughout their life and so neither represents any stable self, identity, or subjectivity (10). Aristo bids Daphne and Phædra to recall the following: "you can scarcely forget that when you were Infants in this place ... you were often led to the Temple of the Sage Trophonius" (10). Throughout their upbringing these two characters had been led to a place of repair wherein they would change and change again by visiting the cave that doubles as metonym for the sublime force of technological transformation.

In light of these characters' ongoing engagements with the mythical seat of technology in the play, Daphne and Phædra's always technologically contingent empowerments and disempowerments ebb and flow. Aristo's character explains to his daughters and thereby reminds audiences that Trophonius's cave alters all beings passing its threshold regardless of their motivation for entering into it: "Whatever Animal Enters it—either to procure refreshment from the fervid Sun, or Shelter from the driving Rain, appears to change it's [sic] nature – the fearful and innocent Lambs, become Savage, and make cruel War on each other – whilst the Wolf ... returns mild and harmless, and tamely Submits to the Crook of the Shepherd" (11). Aristo's statement suggests that, regardless of our technological intentions when we go to the place of technology, when we are with technology we cannot escape being profoundly changed by it in ways that depart from those initial intentions or goals. The play uses the sublime setting of Trophonius's cave to foreground the ambivalent fallout that springs from technology's unforeseen and unintended consequences.

Embracing the sublime promise of radical transformation leading to uncertain ends, Daphne takes Aristo's description of changing into otherness as a point of inspiration, almost as if it were an invitation to visit the cave once more. Daphne accepts and even seems to embrace the kinds of sudden transformations and manifestations that are part and parcel of the material sublime. While she welcomes the fact that the cave can transform those who enter, nonetheless she realizes that even these transformative powers run up against their own limits. As she argues with her more cautious and fearful sister that they should step inside, she insists that while the cave as cradle of technology will certainly make its undeniable impact, "It can neither turn us into Men, nor Monsters" (31). Here Phædra disagrees. Phædra questions Daphne's plan and disavows the sublime agencies of cave by consigning its "marvellous Effects" exclusively to the reach of nonhuman animals, therefore leaving humankind safely out of the danger brought about by the techno-logical change represented by Trophonius's cave. Here Phædra endorses a logic

50

Prometheus and Trophonius

of human exceptionalism, counting herself to be separate, to be lucky to be "neither Sheep nor Wolf" (11).

Yet by the play's end, Daphne joins a cadre of other characters entreating audiences to see Trophonius's transformative, aggregately co-constructed cave as representing the normative case of the work of art, technē, and technology, and the world from which all technics spring. The cave next becomes a metonym for a sweeping worldly norm rather than figuring as some rare and limited magical space of exception applicable only to some technē, certain technologies. Here humanity and the broader world are all staged as inescapably changed by and with technics. As mentioned, Daphne by this point has been radically changed various times by entering and reentering the Cave of Trophonius, a cave itself comprised of intermingled natural and built environments (and the same goes for her sister).[52] Because of Daphne's history of subjective instability and flux, she's far from acting out of character when she suggests we finally recognize how across the entire "World around / In Plains and Cities far and near / This wond'rous Cave is found ... the gaming Table's set ... Life, or Death hang on a Bet / And Reason shifts with Gold ... The World itself's a Magical Cave / Where spite of early Care / At Entrance all must taste the wave / And various Changes bear" (78). The only certainty here is change. What makes this seemingly pat cliché into a topic worth exploring is that here, regardless of self-serving rationalizations born of the play's corrupt political economy, the world co-built by Trophonius (culture), technology, humanity, and nature is on all accounts a collective endeavor, leaving none out, allowing for no escape, no exceptionalisms.

By showcasing the transformative power of technology in terms of sublime aesthetics, Hoare's play presents a less restrictive understanding of the material world. Such sublime narratives tell the story of powerful, sublime aggregates and so frustrate oversimplified protagonist-contra-antagonist plotlines found in reductive tellings of sublime humanity against sublime nature. Narratives of the material sublime index ambivalences engendered by combined sets of contingent actors in flux, registering humanity's desire for, but ultimate lack of, control. Victor Frankenstein seeks to gain control of nature by techno-scientific means, to bring the dead to life, to reduce the future to little more than an archconservative reliving of the past. But a wider cast of characters in *The Cave of Trophonius* together wrestle with an unconquerable world in flux where nature and technology unavoidably work together challenging humanity to face a present collectively rendered and pointed toward uncertain futures of transformational repair. Even in the scientific poetry of Erasmus Darwin, technologies of all sorts do not separate us from nature nor engineer freedom from restraint. Akin to Hoare's play, Darwin's verse invites readers to press

---

[52] See Pausanias, *Description of Greece*, 9.39.9.

The Romantic Sublime and Representations of Technology

against fantasies of creation and control that suggest that when we invent, we only unlock old stories of freedom, license, and power. For Hoare and Darwin humanity's technological agency not only stages untold uncertainties but also manifold constraints.

Darwin's Sublime Temple and the Cave of Trophonius

For all his love of plants, Erasmus Darwin, grandfather of Charles Darwin, was a strong advocate for technology and industry. In a work called *The Progress of Society* (1798–1799), an historical and allegorical poem which was an early version of his final poem, *Temple of Nature* (1803), the elder Darwin stresses the "technological impetus behind art, myth and poetry."[53] As Martin Priestman observes, in both poems Darwin calls attention to the relationship between technology and myth by setting nature's temple atop a fallen Eden. But whereas the published text frames human history under the aegis of evolutionary science, the earlier poem situates the story of humanity firmly within the provenance of technology. In the unfinished poem, *Progress of Society*, it is the work of art and technologies of all kinds that demarcate and define humanity, our mythologies, our histories. In either version of the poem, we find a mythology of technology not inspired by transcendent Promethean pyrotechnics but grounded in a Trophonian aesthetic of interconnected material sublimities. And if there are shades of technological determinism here, in this case the historical agency of the work of art shares its fate with that of the hand tool, weaponry, even large machinery.

Any joint consideration of technology and technē—or craft—might be especially hard to swallow today, particularly in light of compelling cases made for thinking about different kinds of technologies in regard to their specificity and particularity. Can we run the risk of assuming that what's true for Heidegger's hammer, for example, applies to Bentham's panopticon, or the Gutenberg press? Yet in *Progress of Society*, Darwin sacrifices a good degree of historical particularity in order to think broadly and mythologically about technology. Following Darwin, then, my aim in this book is to initiate a conversation that allows us to think in broad terms about the aesthetics of technology. Thus, unlike this book's other chapters which focus in on particular technologies such as the lyre or the lever, steamships or seismographs, or even facets of British infrastructure, this chapter considers how Darwin promiscuously attaches the term *ponderous* to various technologies

---

[53] Martin Priestman, "Introduction" to *The Progress of Society by Erasmus Darwin, Romantic Circles Scholarly Editions* (2006), para. 3, https://romantic-circles.org/editions/darwin_temple/progress/progress.html. Hereafter citations from the poem itself are noted in-text by line number.

52

Prometheus and Trophonius

and thereby invites their joint consideration. The word *ponderous* bears out a structural antagonism implicit within Darwin's technological mythography. For him *ponderous* rings ambivalently, resisting exclusively positive or negative connotations, just as it applies to overlapping notions of nature and culture that anticipate recent theoretical work by the likes of Donna Haraway, Bruno Latour, and Jane Bennett, among others, who all advance models of distributed agency in place of individuated agency.[54]

To provide a historical point of reference, Darwin's polyvalent use of *ponderous*, which resonates with logics of the material sublime, counterpoises how his friend and interlocutor Anna Seward leverages the term in her anti-industrial and anti-imperial poem, "Colebrook Dale" (1810), a poem that is simultaneously perspicacious and problematic.[55] "Colebrook Dale" is perspicacious for its delineation of various links between "environmental damage ... and processes of capitalism and technology."[56] Yet the poem proves problematic for its binarized conceptualizations reminiscent of the antagonistic logics of the Promethean technological sublime: of a nature severed from culture; of poetry and aesthetics existing apart from industry and commerce; of women necessarily existing *contra* men. Seward divorces the sublimity of poetry from that of technology and deploys *ponderous* in a wholly negative fashion to make her point. A dark, Burkean sublimity casts a pall over a nostalgic, pastoral landscape "invade[d]" by an ominous ironworks (7).[57] Cycloptic workers labor amid a din of "pond'rous engines" that overpower the songs of poetry (23). Seward's "sullied" English countryside is forced to yield "ponderous metal" from its leaden, "livid breast" (97, 101, 100). Contextualized by discourses of sexual violence and a vulnerable if not feminized landscape,[58] in these lines

[54] See Jane Bennett, *Vibrant Matter*; Donna J. Haraway, *Manifestly Haraway* (Minneapolis, MN: University of Minnesota Press, 2016); Bruno Latour, *Reassembling the Social: An Introduction to Actor-Network-Theory* (Oxford: Oxford University Press, 2007).

[55] Anna Seward, "Colebrooke Dale" in *Eighteenth-Century Poetry: An Annotated Anthology*, eds. David Fairer and Christine Gerrard, 3rd ed. (Hoboken, NJ: Wiley-Blackwell, 2014), 582–5. References cited in-text by line number.

[56] Donna Coffey, "Protecting the Botanic Garden: Seward, Darwin, and Colebrookdale," *Women's Studies* 31, no. 2 (2002): 159.

[57] See David Fairer, "Eighteenth-Century Poetic Landscapes," *The Coleridge Bulletin*, New Series 13 (Spring 1999): 1–18. Fairer likewise identifies Seward's poem as uniting nostalgic visions of pastoral landscapes with Miltonic and Burkean renditions of sublime landscapes (16–17). Burke famously advances a gendered account of aesthetics where men's bodies count as sublime for their assumed strength and imposing form and where he classifies women's bodies as beautiful on account of their assumed softness and weakness (see Burke, *A Philosophical Enquiry*).

[58] See Fairer, "Eighteenth-Century Poetic Landscapes," 17; Donna Coffey, "Protecting the Botanic Garden"; Sharon Setzer, "'Pondr'ous Engines' in 'Outraged Groves': The Environmental Argument of Anna Seward's 'Colebrook Dale,'" *European Romantic Review* 18, no. 1 (2007): 69–81.

ponderous helps to demonize metal and machine in the same manner that Seward's allusion to the mythic Cyclops figure vilifies laborers working in Coalbrookdale's mines. As Martin Priestman observes, "From Darwin's own period, a poem such as Seward's 'Colebrooke Dale' can easily be set up as the truer poetry, but I would finally argue that such moves are simply easier than Darwin's effort to bestow real imaginative ... vision on the world we actually inhabit, and to which we owe so much of our way of life."[59] Contrastingly, under the rubric of Seward's poem, ponderous metal is separate from us, is a sublimely alien and horrific heavy metal which opposes nature's poetry and overpowers nature's poet.

But the story is not that simple, nor has it ever been so dichotomous. While Seward rightly connects practices and politics of industrialization and imperialism to unjust, uneven, and inequitable ideologies and histories, her reliance on assumedly mutually exclusive gender binaries clouds the issue. These binaries reduce issues related to questionable if not wholly objectional uses of scientific or commercial invention to the problem of one rather than many; to the problem of one gender; to the problem of cultures, never natures, and most certainly not any union of the two. Donna Coffey argues similarly, noting in her discussion of this poem "the dangerous ground that ecofeminists [with whom she numbers Seward] continue to tread in envisioning a parallel between women and nature."[60] Coffey observes how "on the one hand, the flower/woman analogy provides Seward with a powerful tool with which to indict the oppression of both women and nature by men. The implicit image of a rape of nature shocks readers into awareness and a sense of outrage," as it should.[61] The resulting outrage should go without saying, but it's important not to sensationalize such violation nor blindly repeat scenes of aestheticized violence that collectively risk desensitizing audiences, such that rapes of women or men and violations of nature or environments and their respective cultures become normalized, naturalized, ordinary, permissible.[62] For, as Coffey points out, "on the other hand, the flower/woman analogy reinforces traditional gender roles ... [and] reinforces the image of women who are as ornamental and delicate as hothouse flowers and who are helpless

---

[59] Martin Priestman, *The Poetry of Erasmus Darwin: Enlightened Spaces, Romantic Times* (Abingdon and New York: Ashgate, 2016), 102.

[60] Coffey, "Protecting the Botanic Garden," 148.

[61] Coffey, "Protecting the Botanic Garden," 148.

[62] Saidiya Hartman and Fred Moten have written powerfully on the necropolitics of reproducing aesthetic violence in artistic and scholarly work. See Saidiya V. Hartman, *Scenes of Subjection: Terror, Slavery, and Self-Making in Nineteenth-Century America* (Oxford and New York: Oxford University Press, 1997); Fred Moten, "Resistance of the Object: Aunt Hester's Scream," in *In the Break: The Aesthetics of the Black Radical Tradition* (Minneapolis and London: University of Minnesota Press, 2003), 1–24.

Prometheus and Trophonius

and passive victims, engendering a similarly artificial and distorted view of nature."[63] Operating beyond antagonistic binaries and reductive parallels, the polysemous word *ponderous* more typically evokes a moral ambiguity and moral ambivalence rather than any simple moral dichotomy and it does so by evoking a sublime web of overlapping uncertainties, agencies, and intimacies.

By the close of the eighteenth century and when both Seward and Darwin were composing their respective poems, the term *ponderous* already enjoyed a broader range of meanings than are activated or accommodated by Seward's poem. By the 1790s *ponderous* had long borne cross-pollinating associations with deep thought and dense earth. Added to this joint sense of ideational and physical profundity was a newer meaning that applied to the heavenly bodies of the cosmos. This connotation became popularized when acclaimed astronomer William Herschel published on the gravitational pull of ponderous bodies transiting the starry skies. By this time commonplace phrases such as *terra ponderosa*, ponderous earth, or heavy spar were used interchangeably to refer to lead or barium extracted with great difficulty from English mines. Given these associations that knit together celestial movements, heavy earth, and hard work, it becomes easy to see how ponderous ideas could accrue a kind of intellectual dignity both by virtue of and in spite of their sheer laboriousness. By yoking nature's temple to this polysemous word, a term that binds together numerous stock images of sublime entities (the undeniable weight of this earth and its mysterious subterranean allure, an unseen gravity pulling on planetary bodies, arduous yet ambitious flights of mind), Darwin builds a mythological vocabulary that weds praxis to poiesis, that binds the technical to the aesthetic.

For example, the temple of nature that replaces Eden in Darwin's *The Progress of Society* has a ceiling formed of ponderous domes connecting heaven and earth even as it divides them. Here ponderous technologies, structures, and architectonics do not drive off worlds of art or nature, but instead unite them, indeed shelter them: "Unnumber'd ailes connect unnumber'd halls, / And sacred symbols crowd the pictur'd walls / With pencil rude forgotten days design, / And arts, or empires, live in every line" (73–6). These sprawling domes evoke the full range of connotations borne by the term *ponderous*, with Darwin making them seem at once "rude" and earthly while also being unending, "sacred," and celestial; they appear an amalgam of unknowable sublime nature, humanity's artistic cultures, and history's imperial projects. In addition, the poet relies on sublime figures of seeming physical paradox to signal the phenomenological capaciousness of nature's temple.

The stock image of material sublimity arising in the form of a disjunctive materiality here pushes the boundaries of how we understand the making of

---

[63] Coffey, "Protecting the Botanic Garden," 149.

The Romantic Sublime and Representations of Technology

technology and the production of the work of art. In Darwin's lines each is represented as being necessarily aggregate and everywhere contingent rather than being what we expect or at least fantasize: suggesting that what we create is more or less innocent, individual, instrumental, inspiring, predictable, and finally, escapable. Styled as a "vast" structure that exits almost acrobatically, first towering "high in [the] air," then "amid the desert soil," and next extending its vaults "deep [with]in the earth," Darwin's temple of nature—in other words, his central image of Haraway-esque natureculture—also tropes on the sublime for appearing to be "*un*wrought by mortal toil" (66, 65, 68, 66, emphasis added). One implication of Darwin's lines suggests that these ponderous domes could be a labor of the gods, as if nature's temple might link Hephaestus in the heavens to Hades deep below by the fiat-like force of divine intervention alone. But given Darwin's emphasis on a ponderousness derived in part from the temple's sublime mixture of aerial and subterranean features, Darwin tempers our ability to read these domes as being no more than the result of some facile *deus ex machina* trope. Instead, running across surface and soil, the temple retains an undeniable earthiness, a not-wholly-other-worldly quality allowing for the more mortal possibility that it might be undone, unbuilt, unwrought, and perhaps in part undone by the work of human hands ("unwrought by mortal toil"). In this sense Darwin's temple and his larger poetic project are necessarily both ecopoetic and technopoetic because, for him, nature gods have always been technological gods and therefore closely resemble the case of humankind. Darwin's use of *ponderous* here follows Lucretius and a broadly materialist Epicurean tradition that enables Darwin to advance a sublime vision, a vision of an external world comprised of interrelated aggregates working in conjunction—for better and worse—all of which foregrounds the related material origins of technology and the work of art.[64]

It is important to pause here to note that Darwin did not espouse any innocent or blindly optimistic view of the relationship between ecology, technology, and poetry. He replaces a laborless Eden with a temple grounded by a mythos of costly human and earthly loss. Darwin concludes his survey of the temple by revealing its sublime subterranean underworld that's awash in graves:

> Deep-whelm'd beneath, in rock-surrounded caves,
> *Oblivion* dwells, and labels all her graves;
> O'er each dark nich [*sic*] a ponderous stone is roll'd, (101–3)

---

[64] For more on Darwin's debt to Lucretian and Epicurean philosophical traditions, see Martin Priestman, "Introduction" to *The Temple of Nature by Erasmus Darwin*, *Romantic Circles Electronic Editions* (2003), paras. 6–8, http://romantic-circles.org/editions/darwin_temple.

Prometheus and Trophonius

Darwin's ponderous dome is echoed here in the ponderous stones laid by each grave, over "each dark nich." The allegorical and personified figure of Oblivion represents a kind of poiesis that links technics to poetics and nature to culture. Earthen stones write and unwrite cultural histories and legacies. Stones mark and leave traces of attenuating legibility where labeling and writing ultimately serve not remembrance, permeance, nor any depository or teleological accumulation of knowledge. Rather human technē serves Oblivion's rolling, ongoing program of forgetfulness and erasure. Whether located above ground or below, humankind everywhere exists with ponderous technics and poetics that never promise advancing lines of progress but that do guarantee epistemological losses and ontological change. Furthermore, the poet's repetition of ponderous knits together built environment and earthly *oikos* (Greek for home), stressing the tension that exists between our temporary building and our attenuated dwelling in the earth after life. Hovering overhead is always the weight of our technological way of being, a ponderous weight that presses us as the heavy earth will do, and as deep whelmed thought may do. Technological sublimity surrounds us, and together, with it, we each and all become changeling earthlings, children of joint agencies, limited authorship, and illusionary autonomy.

Deepening the significance of this ponderous stone, Darwin links it to the mythic cave of the master builder and stone worker, Trophonius. The poet trades sublime Promethean myths, of unbridled progress and competitive agencies, for Trophonian journeys of ponderous repair, care, and the unexpected, disjunctive transformations of the material sublime. The myth of Trophonius and his brother Agamedes may have had special purchase for Darwin as philosopher-poet for a number of reasons. First, Trophonius and Agamedes are less divine and more humanized figures who, as previously mentioned, co-build the foundation for Apollo's temple at Delphi. They and their legends provide a technological foundation grounding all things Apollonian and palliative—and so including poetry, music, and medicine. Second, the tragic myth associated with Trophonius's cave confronts inescapable truths and sorrows that we can neither talk, write, invent, nor build our way out of.

Darwin, known for his affinity for analogy, compares Oblivion's underground graveyard with its ponderous headstones to Trophonius's oracular cave, from which visitors emerge inescapably transformed. Just as in the variant of the myth detailed in Pausanias's *Description of Greece*, in Darwin's lines those daring to visit the Cave of Trophonius undergo a sublime experience, forgetting how to laugh, forfeiting their smiles:

> So in rude rocks, beside the Aegean wave,
> *Trophonius* scoop'd his sorrow-sacred cave;
> Unbarr'd to pilgrim feet the brazen door,
> And the sad sage returning smil'd no more. (113–16)

The Romantic Sublime and Representations of Technology

Akin to Hoare's play, Darwin's verse echoes Pausanias's ancient account. Here any pilgrims visiting the sacred cave emerge transformed, now bearing a different self and different knowledge. Visitors of the Cave of Trophonius assume a new aesthetic epistemology that makes them see, know, feel, and judge their world in alternate ways. This newfound "sage" wisdom banishes the ignorant smiles of the blithely unaware and the naïvely sentimental, of those only ever engaging with their world as if only from above and never below and thus, as the myth tells it, never see the world anew. The myth functions as a variation on the theme of the material sublime, its unavoidable costs and losses tied to the profound and transformative powers of technē, technics, poetics, and technology.

It is worth emphasizing that in his own origin story Trophonius himself is transformed irrevocably and ambivalently by the joint sublime operations of the natural and built environment. In other words, Trophonius is transformed in accord with narratives of the technological sublime informed by the material sublime where neither nature, humanity, nor technology is savior or destroyer but rather all work together and resound with one another to afford new possibilities and new uncertainties, always within a framework of limited creative capacities. Trophonius may have helped to lay the foundation for the Apollonian arts, but nonetheless, afterward he would lead an underground life as an oracular god whose unmediated consultations proved so awe-inspiring that they both caused a necessary forgetting and bestowed pilgrims with an irreversible gravity and solemnity. Even for Trophonius, there is no escaping earth as grave. Like this master builder and stonemason, we cannot simply engineer a way out. But we can do a better job of recognizing technology's place in the natural world and its non-escapist relation to human finitude.

By locating the Trophonius myth deep within the recesses of the temple of nature, Darwin exposes what for him exists at the very core of humankind's mythic history: the place of technology. Technology, like poetry, is not the fix but the place wherein we reside and the path upon which we have always trod, the place to which we return, the place we repair to and emerge from, often forgetting ourselves but sometimes remembered by stone and always surrounded by earth—as we are supported first and finally by the earth. Counterintuitively, Darwin's poem makes any artifact of technology or poetry into less of an individuated thing or innovative object and instead into a communal locale of ponderous ritual and tragic recognition. Darwin's gloss on Trophonius in the later version of the poem (*The Temple of Nature*) concludes with images of technologies that enswathe humanity from the start of life to its end, emphasizing processes of material transformation and core truths: "When we reflect on the perpetual destruction of organic life, we should also recollect, that it is perpetually renewed in other forms by the same materials, and thus

Prometheus and Trophonius

the sum total of the happiness of the world continues undiminished; and that a philosopher may thus smile again on turning his eyes from the coffins of nature to her cradles."[65] Spatializing his mythic history of technology, Darwin emphasizes our earthly dependence while delineating technology as a first and final home for humanity, just as the earth is. Technology, for Darwin, is foundation and frame, which exists first within earthly foundation and frame. Technology not only has the potential to repair but, crucially for Darwin, it is a place of repair—wherein people gather, go, assemble.[66] A place we repair to on the earth, of the earth, and ultimately within the earth. Technology in Darwinian longform plays out a kind of repair that Walter Scott depicts in *Guy Mannering*: "The footpath leading there was well beaten by the repair of those who frequented it for pastime."[67] Or that Byron refers to *Childe Harold's Pilgrimage*: "On sloping mounds, or in the vale beneath, / Are domes where whilome kings did make repair."[68] As Martin Priestman's careful engagement with Darwin reminds, "However rhetorically simple it may be to divorce … technology from 'Nature', Darwin … traces connective lines of force between the supposed opposites which make him a major poet of Nature in the larger, holistic sense of exploring all the connections of 'how things are' – or *De Rerum Natura*, as the title of his greatest model [Lucretius] puts it. The refusal of divisions which allows the elemental beings of a poem supposedly devoted to vegetation to spend so much of their time on machines and other matters, is fundamental to Darwin's vision of the physical world as a complex of interrelated forces."[69] Technological repair and ecosocial repair are nearly synonymous for Darwin, because for him technology is a form of *oikos*, not ever replacing or circumventing the earthly *oikos* but rather always affixed to it and dependent upon it.

Here we find that sublime characterizations of wondrous and often startling worldbuilding and unbuilding come in tandem with chronicling subsequent feelings of empowerment and disempowerment. Sublime narratives rehearse stories of creative and destructive spectacle, which smuggle within them key assumptions about humanity's creative agency and human agency more broadly conceived. Tales of sudden fabrication, unparalleled production, even dazzling dissolution underwrite estimations of human agency relative to assumptions

---

[65] Erasmus Darwin, *The Temple of Nature; Or, The Origin of Society: A Poem. With Philosophical Notes* (London: J. Johnson, T. Bensley, 1803), Canto I, line 126, note I.126.

[66] "repair, n.1.a.," *OED Online*, June 2018, Oxford University Press, https://doi.org/10.1093/OED/1755458862 (accessed 10 March 2020).

[67] Walter Scott, *Guy Mannering: or The Astrologer*, 2 vols. (Boston: Estes and Lauriat, 1893).

[68] Byron, *Childe Harold's Pilgrimage*, Cantos I & II, i.xxii.19; *The Complete Poetical Works*, eds. Jerome J. McGann and Berry Weller (Oxford: Clarendon Press, 1980).

[69] Priestman, *The Poetry of Erasmus Darwin*, 102.

about nature's capacities of worldbuilding and unbuilding. It was only fitting, then, that the sublime would become a leading aesthetic category shaping narratives of great technological force, where technology takes the stage alongside all-powerful nature, genius authors, and omnipotent gods in the sublime's common cast of prime movers.[70]

Running in accord with longstanding rubrics of sublime aesthetics, wherever technology assumes great powers and seemingly excessive agencies it likewise inspires the sublime's signature affective mixture of awe coupled with fear. This mixed reaction is important. These mixed feelings are what matters most in exploring how representations of sublime technologies can help us think differently about technology and nature as well as human relationships with each of these. In addition to aligning with common sublime judgments discussing whatever seems to carry supernatural, suprahuman, or extraordinary agency, sublime technological aesthetics chronicle our ambivalent reactions, our vexed judgments, our uncertain feelings emerging from sensing something that overrides human agency due to its vast and superseding powers, its undeniable forces—even or especially when that something is human made, or at least in part.

But these ambivalent responses do more than expose humanity's humbling reliance upon the technological. They reconfirm humanity's inescapable dependence upon the natural world precisely at a time of ramped up technological and industrial production. Yes, Anahid Nersessian is spot on in saying that there is "nothing new about labeling Romanticism a critique of political economy, or (in other language) a working-through of the 'trauma of industrialization.'"[71] But Romanticism's "working-through of the 'trauma of industrialization'" entails more than explicit or implicit critiques of political economy. It also involves Romanticism's wrestling with its own alignment with traumas of industrialization, its constitutive relationships with its contingent political economies. Quite often Romanticism's recognition of its ties, binds, and debts to differing waves of industrialization arise in the form of sublime tropes, languages, and logics—meaning that Romanticism's relationship with industrialization reads more ambivalently than perhaps we've been taught to believe or wanted to admit. As demonstrated in this chapter's engagement with sublime aesthetics and Romantic technological myths, Romanticism becomes tantamount to a working-through of the control we never had, either over our fabricated creations or over the fabric of the natural–cultural world from which they transpire and within which they operate. Overturning conventional readings of British Romantic literature, here we begin to see how common

---

[70] David E. Nye, *American Technological Sublime*.

[71] Anahid Nersessian, "Romantic Difficulty," *New Literary History* 49, no. 4 (Autumn 2018): 451–66.

Prometheus and Trophonius

understandings of Romantic sublimity, particularly those grounded in either a simple human–nature dyad or reductive distinctions between technology and nature, fuel misconceptions of human indebtedness to technology, which in turn perilously underplay humanity's fragile dependence upon nature. The politics of the aesthetic of the sublime in this case paves the way for us to imagine and therefore acknowledge humankind's interwoven and interdependent dangers, debts, and dreams.

CHAPTER TWO

The Seismograph and a Keatsian "Material Sublime"

On Sublime Worldbuilding and Unbuilding

The exemplary machines of the romantic era, powered by steam, electricity, and other subtle forces, could be seen to have their own motive force within them; they were presented as ambiguously alive. ... Unlike the classical machine, the romantic machine did not stand alone; it involved the active participation of the observer and articulated a spontaneous, living, and constantly developing nature; it produced aesthetic effects and emotional states. ... it was imbued with the aesthetics and the affects of the organic, the vital, and even the transcendent.

—John Tresch, *The Romantic Machine:*
Utopian Science and Technology after Napoleon (2012)

A related route is to rethink our relation to the environment. ... we could take the view that the environment should be understood as neither a dead realm of objects studied by science nor a blank slate onto which we project our romantic imagination; instead we are engaged and entangled with, and involved in, our environment. Such views could then lead to a different view of technology, for instance, not as machine but as praxis, which interweaves the material and the cultural.

—Mark Coeckelbergh, *New Romantic Cyborgs: Romanticism,*
Information Technology, and the End of the Machine (2017)

The Romantic Sublime and Representations of Technology

Introduction

The Romantic sublime and Romantic nature are regularly conflated, often understood as twin developments of Romanticism ultimately driving toward escapism or egotism or both.[1] A more accurate account would recognize the Romantic sublime and Romantic nature as distinct while acknowledging key points of overlap between the two, and between them and Romantic technology, with the latter featured not always as counterpoint but instead sometimes as kindred spirit. The Romantic sublime did not place the technological at arm's length, but rather held tight to it. The same applies for Romanticism's grounding notions of vitalism, organicism, nature, and cultural revolution. Conventional accounts once set machines and modern inventions apart from the Romantic movement or relegated technology only to Romanticism's periphery, deeming technology to be Romanticism's conceptual antithesis or imagined nemesis. But as rightly suggested by historian John Tresch in his celebrated monograph, *The Romantic Machine: Utopian Science and Technology after Napoleon*, "the romantic aim of integrating all aspects of humanity into a living synthesis depended upon technology."[2] In other words, Romanticism's envisioned organic whole contained a technological core. Confirming this view in *New Romantic Cyborgs: Romanticism, Information Technology, and the End of the Machine*, literary and cultural studies scholar Mark Coeckelbergh contends that the "romantics were not only fearful of but also fascinated by the new science and technology that delivered magic machines."[3] Put in terms of the aesthetic category underlying Coeckelbergh's claim, by finding technologies and their related sciences to be at once fearsome and fascinating, Romantic authors presented them as sublime. What follows chimes with recent work on Romanticism that recognizes the hand played by Romantic tools, technologies, and machines in shaping Romantic notions of nature, life, vitality, and agency. Building on this body of scholarship, this chapter initiates a series of case studies considering different Romantic technologies and technological discourses, broadly conceived. Each chapter charts how sublime aesthetics and discourse influenced and informed Romanticism's views of technology, which in turn shaped Romantic understandings of the natural world.

The epigraphs that open this chapter tacitly register how the sublime— how this paradigmatic aesthetic of the Romantic movement—helped to paint technologies as "hav[ing] their own motive force[s] within them," collectively comprising a "praxis, which interweaves the material and the cultural." While not directly inquiring into the relationship between the Romantic sublime and

---

[1] See Mark S. Cladis, "Romantic Nature," 152–3.
[2] John Tresch, *The Romantic Machine*, 22.
[3] Mark Coeckelbergh, *New Romantic Cyborgs*, 13.

The Seismograph and a Keatsian "Material Sublime"

the period's natural or technological aesthetics, politics, or ethics, each epigraph nonetheless bears the mark of the sublime. According to Tresch, "ambiguously alive" Romantic inventions were "imbued with the aesthetics and affects of the organic, the vital, and even the transcendent"—that is, Romantic technologies were imbued with the aesthetics and affects of the sublime. The language and logic of the sublime offered narrative frameworks that allowed authors to render Romantic tools and technologies as being at once organic and transcendent.

But Romanticism's sublime technologies amounted to more than portraits of vivified, agential tools or wondrous machines. As will see in the example of early seismological instruments and devices discussed in the period's earthquake literature, sublime technologies complement Romanticism's representations of sublime nature, everywhere auguring "a spontaneous, living, and constantly developing nature." Crucially, Romanticism's sublime technologies appear both as wondrous spectacles of creation and invention and as being part and parcel of stunning scenes of undoing and upheaval impossible to transcend. When the sublime's positive and negative dimensions are held in combination and in tension with one another they make possible a more nuanced, more tempered technological ethics. This note of sublime ambivalence is crucial, since, as Louise Economides warns, cultivating a sense of wonder or awe, as the sublime is known for, is no guarantee but "is rather a *potential* for ecological connection that is ever in play within technē" (original emphasis).[4] Following Heidegger, Economides rightly points out that "wonder's open-ended receptivity … can devolve to an enchantment with sublime technology which reduces [the natural world] to standing reserve."[5] In other words, sublime wonder alone is not enough to inspire understandings or representations of technologies that would do more than objectify and instrumentalize both the natural world as well as any inventions that might be made from it. Beyond simply lionizing new inventions and inventors, Romanticism's more ethically instructive examples of sublime technologies come to emblematize intermingled mysteries and agencies of nature and technology. These examples support ways of thinking about technology such that questions of human (technological) exceptionalism, ingenuity, and agency take a backseat to larger questions of human limits, indebtedness, and responsibility.

German philosopher Immanuel Kant and British Romantic poets John Keats and Percy Shelley all turn to the sublime as they write of powers of human invention, worldbuilding, and *poiesis* (Greek for making, as in to bring into being something that had not existed previously). And in key moments when these authors take up questions of human and more-than-human

---

[4] Louise Economides, *The Ecology of Wonder in Romantic and Postmodern Literature* (New York: Palgrave Macmillan, 2016), 165.
[5] Economides, *The Ecology of Wonder*, 164.

unbuilding, dismantling, and dissolution, the sublime again takes center stage. Their sublime stories of creation and invention never stray far from sublime stories of destruction, which in tandem scaffold a technological ethics that foregrounds humanity's debt to the natural world. I argue this is the case because the logic alive in their writing aligns with what I'm calling the material sublime, after Keats. In an 1818 verse epistle, discussed below, the poet introduces the phrase "material sublime" and only two lines later notes how "in the world / We jostle," with Keats's enjambed set of poetic lines serving as a nice shorthand for the unsettled, tenuous, trembling picture of human life that the material sublime paints. From beginning to end, not stopping at the end of a line of verse but instead spilling over to the start of another, Keats's material sublime promises more of an ongoing jostling movement, a life in flux, rather than life lived in a world of sure stability and predictability. This is a branch of sublime discourse conveying powerfully, and without question, the fragility and uncertainty of the immaterial worlds we build in narrative *and* the material worlds we build within the natural world.

As technological historians and literary critics such as Leo Marx and David E. Nye have noted, arts, artifacts, and technologies (from the poetry that writes human life to the seismographic instruments that narrate earthly change) might rank sublime for assuming a godlike place in our lives or might make us seem all the more sublime for inventing them in the first place.[6] But at their best, technologies can also be presented as sublime for their fundamental relationship with an unpredictable natural world and the likewise unpredictable landscapes of human cultures. These latter representations of technologies belong to the aesthetic of the material sublime. The sublime is western philosophy's most revered aesthetic category that trades in paradox and that prompts ambivalent feelings. Famously provoking "delightful horror" for Burke,[7] inspiring both attraction and repulsion for Kant,[8] and producing a simultaneous vexation and pleasure for Keats,[9] sublime paradox and ambivalence appear as defining features of the aesthetic of the material sublime. The heightened push and pull of the material sublime counterbalances other, more one-sided (sublime) narratives that celebrate the great creative promise and potency of poetics and technics at the cost of covering over either their darker, more destructive or their more vulnerable and dependent sides. When Romantic nature, technology, and sublimity work in concert, escape and ego give way to the radical realism of the material sublime.

---

[6] See Nye, *American Technological Sublime* and Marx, *The Machine in the Garden*.

[7] Edmund Burke, *A Philosophical Enquiry*.

[8] Immanuel Kant, *Critique of Judgement*.

[9] John Keats, "[Dear Reynolds, as last night I lay in bed,]" in *Keats's Poetry and Prose*, ed. Jeffrey N. Cox (New York and London: W. W. Norton & Company, 2008), 132–5.

The Seismograph and a Keatsian "Material Sublime"

By reading key thinkers and inventors from the Romantic century (1750–1850) in dialogue with one another we can trace lines of thought that anticipate a Heideggerian union of aesthetics and technics, poiesis and technē, where "*technē* is the name not only for the activities and skills of the craftsman but also for the arts of the mind and the fine arts."[10] While dominant discourse tends to think the sublime as either technological and mechanistic or naturalistic and humanistic, the authors studied in this chapter offer an opportunity to think past this dichotomy.[11] Their work gestures toward an alternate aesthetic rubric, that of the material sublime, which captures elements of both the technological sublime and the natural sublime while exceeding the bounds of each. By this logic, like poetry, "technology is a way of revealing" not reducible to "mere means" or ends, not reducible to the instrumental definition of technology that, for Heidegger, fuels illusions of a human "will to mastery" over both technology and the natural world.[12]

I advance that Kant, Keats, and Shelley all activate the language, logic, and affective charge of the material sublime wherever human agencies of invention are underwritten by a natural and built environment itself endowed with sublime powers of invention and mystery that defy fantasies of mastery. In these accounts, poetry and technology assume the ambivalent and uncontrollable force of the material sublime, a mercurial agency one might sense or feel but that is never fully harnessed nor corralled by human hands. Rather than assuming strict divides between human and natural systems, as we might expect to find in sublime narratives from this period, these accounts link the natural and built environment by styling each with tropes of paradox and ambivalence home to the material sublime.

Such narratives undercut sweeping notions of technological determinism or salvation that remain in play today. Technological determinism assumes that we have relinquished control and responsibility for the artifacts we make, thinking instead that we now live in the world that technology built rather than the worlds technology, humanity, and nature together have manifested, though in asymmetrical ways. Technological salvation, on the other hand, suggests that in the end we need not trouble ourselves over our behavior because we control what we make to such an extent that we can engineer a solution to any problem. Each framework rests upon normative logics of the technological sublime where human invention transcends sublime nature. Technology rules supreme over nature and is speciously separate from humanity in the former

[10] Martin Heidegger, "The Question Concerning Technology," in *Basic Writings: From "Being and Time" [1927] to "The Task of Thinking" [1964]*, trans. David Farrell Krell, rev. ed. (San Francisco, CA: Harper Collins, 1993), 318. See also "The Origin of the Work of Art" in *Basic Writings*, 139–212.

[11] See, for example, Nye and M. H. Abrams.

[12] Heidegger, "The Question Concerning Technology," 318, 313, 318.

The Romantic Sublime and Representations of Technology

case. In the latter, humanity reigns supreme over the natural world by virtue of the technology it wields.

The material sublime upends such habits of thought. This is the case because, for the material sublime, the natural world is not simply up for grabs, available for easy or straightforward use, and neither is it assumed to be ripe for dominion or any sort of willed or unwitting technological determination wrought by humankind. Instead, the material world from which poetry and technology are made is always already sublime and beyond the limits of human comprehension, instrumentalization, or possession. The rubric of the material sublime urges humankind to relinquish overblown notions of human agency that prop up fantasies of human chauvinism and exceptionalism. At the same time, the material sublime does not let humankind off the hook for the part we play in worlds jointly and aggregately built at the meeting points between nature and culture. The stripe of technological aesthetics on display in the material sublime replaces combative sublime dyads (nature opposite culture) with constitutive sublime aggregates (inescapably interlinked human and natural systems).

Regardless of, or perhaps due to, its great potential to present humanity as estranged from nature or to render humanity's relationship with nature as antagonistic, the Romantic sublime provides a crucial resource for thought. This is especially true when the larger category of sublime nature narrows to present examples of the material sublime. The former regularly foregrounds the always-ambivalent harm and help the natural world poses to us. The latter also stresses the ambivalent harm and help we might create for ourselves in any act of worldbuilding, in each creative endeavor. The material sublime is not about rationalization, suppression, sublimation, nor about consigning the world to contests of combative aggression. Contrarily, this sublime aesthetic works in the opposite vein entirely as it sources and senses humanity's most pressing and proximate problems. Cian Duffy and Peter Howell, authors of *Cultures of the Sublime*, rightly question two central assumptions grounding scholarship on eighteenth-century and Romantic-era sublime discourse: "first, that it is possible to produce a complete and objective definition of the sublime, which transcends specific historical or cultural circumstances (an assumption shared by Kant's analytic); second, that Kant's work constitutes this definition."[13] Duffy and Howell point to a number of influential works espousing these assumptions, such as Frances Ferguson's *Solitude and the Sublime*, Philip Shaw's *The Sublime*, and Thomas Weiskel's *The Romantic Sublime*, "all of which cast Kant's 'analytic of the sublime' as the culmination of eighteenth-century speculation."[14] Beyond the Kantian analytic, in the pre-critical Kantian

---

[13] Duffy and Howell, *Cultures of the Sublime*, 2.
[14] Duffy and Howell, *Cultures of the Sublime*, 2.

The Seismograph and a Keatsian "Material Sublime"

rendition of sublime nature addressed here in the form of Shelley's and Keats's work on intermingled sublime materiality and invention, Romantic sublime discourse expresses an instructive ambivalence toward our historically constitutive creative and created worlds, both natural and built. Here we encounter logics of the material sublime running throughout these authors' narratives of the technological sublime, where the technological sublime stands not as a testament to humanity's battle against or triumph over nature, but as a reminder of our surprisingly intimate, always inescapable technological and natural interdependencies.

A Critique of Infrastructural Hubris and a Seismographic Sublime

In the below passage, originally drafted the year after the devastating 1755 Lisbon earthquake, Kant attempts to write out of existence the darker side of the material sublime:

> I shall now begin from the history of the earthquake of 55 itself. I understand by it no history of the misfortunes, which men have suffered, no list of cities destroyed and inhabitants buried under their ruins. Everything horrible, which the imagination can represent to itself, must be collected, in order in some measure to figure one's self the consternation, in which it must be, when the earth under their feet moves and is torn with convulsions, when every thing around them falls to the ground, when the water put in violent motion completes the misfortune by overflowing, when the fear of death, the despair on account of the total loss of property, and finally the sight of others in misery discourage the most steadfast mind.[15]

Channeling precisely what he first disavows—"misery," "despair," "fear of death," and "[e]verything horrible"—Kant frames his early essay on Lisbon's famed earthquake by cataloging the emotional, environmental, and structural tolls wrought by the quake's dynamic tremors. The carnage left in the earthquake's wake is at once technological and cultural, human and natural. As evinced by Kant's translated language, here content and form reinforce one another, which is often the case for narratives of the material sublime. Accounts of material sublimity frequently rest upon sprawling, combinatory syntactical structures that allow authors to build tension by connecting and collecting awe-inspiring, anxiety-provoking horrors through housing them under the roof of just one sentence. Here Kant's sentences only grow—in a

---

[15] Immanuel Kant, "History and Physiography of the Most Remarkable Cases of the Earthquake Which Towards the End of 1755 Shook a Great Part of the Earth" (1799).

The Romantic Sublime and Representations of Technology

structural, formal homage to the extensive range and impact of a quake that so moved mind and matter, bodies and buildings. The second gathers together "misfortunes," "cities destroyed," people buried in ruins. The following lengthy sentence grammatically echoes the mounting anxieties that emerge "when the earth under [people's] feet moves and is torn with convulsions," as it goes on to include floods, properties reduced to rubble, death's undeniable nearness, then finally the "sight of others in misery" all pressing upon the mind. Such expansive sentences corroborate the sublime's longstanding associations with excess, as each arresting image and stunning idea crowds together and compounds upon the next to dizzying effect.

As an aesthetic that trades in paradox, material sublimity binds together fear and fascination while also undermining the safety proffered by aesthetic distance. In this case, aesthetic distance is undercut by a syntactic proximity that reinforces and redoubles each expression of shock, alarm, and disaster. Sentences densely populated with horror after horror offer an intensifying sense of closely knitted fates conveyed alike in content and sentence structure. Secondary literature on the sublime routinely notes that Kant, following Burke, insists in the *Critique of Judgement* that the aesthetic of the sublime depends upon a necessary distance, a safe distance, an aesthetic distance—otherwise, as Burke suggests, there is only terror without wonder, no room for fascination, only fear. I'd like to suggest that although the sublime is famous for requiring aesthetic distance, both in content and form the material sublime also requires and accrues its charged affective tensions by cultivating senses of proximity and shared experience, if not also shared vulnerability.

Appealing to the sympathetic imagination, Kant directs readers to orchestrate an imaginary show playing out escalating mental and physical losses produced by the planet's wrenching convulsions and surging waves. Reinforcing his call for imaginative empathy, the passage concludes with a concept that just one sentence earlier he forswears—the resulting discouragement of even the "most steadfast mind" in light of a history of "men [who] have suffered." Kant's essay manifests tensions that arise from horrors which we fear and shun in fact, but entertain from a certain kind of distance, mediated by things like printed accounts and at times costumed in scientific reports, but which nonetheless preserve a sense of pressing, impending closeness that lends these sublime narratives their telltale ambivalence, vexation, and overall fraught, if not frenzied, affective charge. As the literature and knowledge of the great quakes of the late eighteenth and early nineteenth centuries became so commonplace that one could, like Kant, knowingly refer to "55," a growing population drafted and consumed tales of disaster and discouragement from far away, and these sublime narratives did as much to chip away at guaranteed notions of *terra firma* as they did to deliver reassuring data—in turn bringing these concerns closer to home. With them went any granted notion of safe

The Seismograph and a Keatsian "Material Sublime"

hearth and home, even in more geographically protected areas like Britain and New England. This anxiety would rise as the built environment became more dense, as cities grew.

The storied journal *Philosophical Transactions of the Royal Society of London* afforded room for writers to take part in the type of consolatory sublime mythologizing Kant both enacts and resists in his essay. This journal spurred massive movements of information gathering and emotively charged reporting, generating narratives in which the planet plays a starring role, but humanity stands at the crux of it all, often framed both as the unfortunate victim falling prey to sublime nature and as a potential victor over it for inventing sublime technics. A cottage industry emerged, with eye-witness accounts of geological tremors written throughout Europe and places as far off as Siberia and the Americas leading up to the invention of the first true seismograph of 1875.[16] Produced sporadically, since they tended to be inspired by a given seismic event, these reports show how colonists, travelers, explorers, and theorists had to wait to be struck by the next "big one" to log their often heated accounts as one type of response and launch or test new technologies as responses of another sort. *Philosophical Transactions* became a popular medium for channeling harrowing tales of civilization under fire, captivating readers by registering not only human dismay and supporting the idea of a shared global threat, but also ushering forth a heroic supporting cast of "characters" in the guise of performative, animated instruments like the seismoscope and the seismograph. To cite a late example of this trend which framed inventors and inventions in sublime terms and thereby primarily defused the agency of sublime nature, a popular publication printed an article bearing the title, "The Earth Speaks." The sublime tension suggested by the title all but dissolves as the piece regales how, beyond graphically tracking the earth's movements, "Palmeri first observed that the seismograph, with the aid of a transmitting microphone and a receiving telephone, enable[d] the ear to hear the vibrations of the ground."[17]

Historical documents chronicle a parade of pendulums, clocks, tables, and maps, all deployed across the Romantic century to mark and guess the earth's next move. In these accounts an array of happenstance observers and skilled inventors rewrite the story of dreaded earthly devastation into a tale of enthralling, though fraught, planetary performance that would pave the way for groundbreaking geological discovery. Anxiety becomes the mother of invention and narratological reinvention, with technological artifacts working in concert with sublime narratives to sensationalize and—whether knowingly

---

[16] Mihailo D. Trifunac, "75th Anniversary of Strong Motion Observation: A Historical Review," *Soil Dynamics and Earthquake Engineering* 29, no. 4, (April 2009): 591–606, 593.

[17] "The Earth Speaks: Scientific Notes," *Friends' Review; a Religious, Literary and Miscellaneous Journal (1847–1894)* 32, issue 22 (11 January 1879): 351.

The Romantic Sublime and Representations of Technology

or not—misrecognize the earth. Kant falls prey to similar sensationalism as he catalogs Lisbon's sublime horrors. But later in the same work Kant goes on to offer a poignant corrective (discussed at the close of this section). As we shall see, the following accounts of earthquakes and seismological instruments serve as grounding examples of normative sublime narratives that evade the uncomfortable realities captured in narratives of the material sublime. Understanding the shortsighted logic of normative accounts of a sublime nature and a sublime technology always at odds with one another helps to expose the stark departures of Keats, Shelley, and Kant as they espouse the logic of the material sublime. In the latter works, poetic and technological making are not cures meant to surmount problems of unmaking, they are part and parcel of them, revealing the losses, and grappling with the costs of unbuilding and undoing that are yoked to acts of creation and creative invention alike.

Letters published in 1750 document a rare English earthquake that would prime Britain's interest in Lisbon's cataclysmic event and the scores of tremors arriving in its wake.[18] Various epistles recount England grappling with what were reported to be "great" shocks, but which amounted to little more than upended interiors and overturned household objects. A representative example relates how people "catched at the Walls, Tables, and such things as stood next them, expecting they should be thrown down: ... [with no] Damage being done by [the quake] more than some Chimnies thrown down, but nobody hurt by them."[19] Chimneys fared worst in even the most delicate tremors. They were often separate from main foundations and not built into a house's primary structure. Standing in relative isolation rendered them more likely to collapse. For instance, an entry penned in response to a later British tremblor in 1795

[18] Earthquakes aside, a long-standing trade relationship forged between England and Portugal also fueled British interest in Lisbon's fate. Richard Hamblyn provides a brief and helpful history of this partnership: "several thousand [Britons] were long-term residents of (Lisbon). The scale of the British presence was due to a series of binding trade agreements dating back to 1385, when England had agreed to protect the vulnerable Portugal 'as though she were England herself', in return for the right to export and sell unlimited quantities of valuable homespun textiles and, later, port wine; these agreements proved so favourable to British commercial interests that by the time Charles II married the Portuguese princess, Catherine of Braganza (whose legendary dowry included Bombay, Tangier and the Sri Lankan port of Galle), the bulk of Portugal's valuable import and export business was being handled by British merchants, whose offices and warehouses commandeered the length of the Lisbon waterfront." "Notes from Underground: The Lisbon Earthquake," *Romanticism* 14, no. 2 (2008): 113.

[19] Mr. Steward, "An Account of the Earthquake Which Happen'd about a Quarter before One O'Clock, on Sunday, September 30. 1750. By Mr. – Steward to the Earl of Cardigan," *Philosophical Transactions of the Royal Society of London* 46 (1750): 722–3. See also Henry Green, "Extract of a Letter from Mr. Henry Green to Mr. James Ayfchough, Optician, in Ludgate-Street, relating to the Earthquake felt Sept. 30. 1750," *Philosophical Transactions of the Royal Society of London* 46 (1750): 723–8.

The Seismograph and a Keatsian "Material Sublime"

first bespeaks the death of miners smothered by the earth and then goes on to recount how "several chimnies were thrown down, and several families left their habitations; indeed," the author continues, "such a general alarm was never known in this neighborhood."[20] Both accounts activate normative sublime tropes as they note sensations of shock and alarm coupled to uncertainty and confusion while nonetheless offering a degree of reassuring safety.

But here a keen eye can also detect the material sublime at work in the above examples, as they yoke together sublime nature (unexpected earthquakes) and technology (fallen chimneys, fleeing one's house), each carrying a sense of shared uncertainty and intimacy as neighborhoods, hearths, and homes once deemed safe and previously taken for granted now become something to fear, something thrown into question. As an aesthetic that indexes dangerous forces harbored first within the natural world and then consequently within what is invented and created out of the natural world, the material sublime necessarily applies to us, surrounds us, is close at hand, proximate and ubiquitous. This dimension of the material sublime undermines the fantasy of safety tendered in conventional sublime narratives that would place terror, repulsion, or horror at some safe remove.

Descriptions of physically riven earth or someone's toppled hearth so often recounted in contributions sent to the Royal Society speak to larger psychological gashes, as reports of damaged structures and downed chimneys chipped away at the idea of any perpetually secure earthly foundation. Regardless of being an ocean away, eighteenth-century New England publishers continuously reprinted accounts referencing that notorious November day in 1755. On both sides of the Atlantic presses ran hot with earthquake compendia describing recent frays between the planet and its human residents. This was the case even as many of such metaphoric bouts produced little more than minor structural damage or toppled furniture. As if to encourage readers to closely link smaller tremblors at home to larger ones felt elsewhere, London and Boston presses affixed narratives of their local, more minor tremors to at least ten retrospectively published compilations of earthquake accounts. This meant, for example, that these publications paired stories recounting the minor upheaval recently experienced in New England and Britain with such records as those documenting the utter ruination wrought upon Lima, Peru in 1746. Similarly, narratives of only slight upheaval in Boston and Britain were included in book-length earthquake compilations reaching back to Jamaica's deadly 1692 shock.[21]

---

[20] Edward Whitaker Gray, "Account of Earthquake Felt in Various Parts of England, November 18, 1795; With Some Observations Thereon. By Edward Whitaker Gray, M.D.F.R.S," *Philosophical Transactions of the Royal Society of London* 86 (1796): 353–81.

[21] Charles Edwin Clark, "Science, Reason, and an Angry God: The Literature of an Earthquake," *New England Quarterly* 38, no. 3 (1965): 342–6.

The Romantic Sublime and Representations of Technology

It is easy to suggest that Bostonians and Britons unsuitably cataloged their harried nerves and relatively small seismic activity alongside Lisbon's annals of utter collapse, not to mention other accounts of great catastrophes. However, these publications, as with the Royal Society's documents chronicling fallen chimneys touched off by milder tremors, did much to unite Britain's and New England's readers with those under greater geographical threat, linking anxieties born from shelters and homes made unsafe by unpredictable earthly shudders to larger fears and questions arising over nature's capacity to level humanity's built environments. For example, testimonies printed soon after the Lisbon quake placed a relatively banal review of rumblings felt in Derbyshire in 1750 adjacent to a horrific first-hand account of Lisbon's 1755 earthquake.[22] In the latter report, the author estimates Lisbon's loss to be on the order of 30,000 lives, recounting the "shocking sight of the dead bodies, together with the shrieks and cries of those, who were half buried in the ruins." Referencing a breached confidence in the concept of house-as-home, the author states that in Lisbon "twenty-two different shocks" ensured that "no body yet ventured[d] to lie in houses."[23] Legend would have it that Lisbon's own King refused to sleep under any roof ever again.[24] Other writers rushed to proclaim that "all the world [was] running out of their houses"; across the Atlantic Bostonians saw chimneys "dislocated" and roofs "leveled;" people in Spanish Madrid watched their churches, towers, and houses fall; shops were demolished in Tangier; "a great number of houses" crushed and killed "many people" in Morocco; and the "famous city" of Taffo "was wholly swallowed up; no remains left."[25]

Confirming the sublime status held by Lisbon and "55" throughout the Anglophone reading world, a settler colonist living in Sumatra remarks how "severe earthquakes, felt" even there prove that the Lisbon disaster "was certainly the most awful tremendous calamity, that has ever happened in the world." Painting the quake's vast reach in tones evocative of normative sublime

---

[22] William Bullock et al., "An Account of the Earthquake, Novem. 1, 1755, as Felt in the Lead Mines in Derbyshire; In a Letter from the Reverend Mr. Bullock to Lewis Crusius, D.D.F.R.S., *Philosophical Transactions of the Royal Society of London* 49 (1755–1756): 398–407.

[23] Richard Wolfall, "An Account of the Earthquake at Lisbon, Nov. I. 1755, in Two Letters from Mr. Wolfall, Surgeon, to James Parsons, M.D.F.R.S.," *Philosophical Transactions of the Royal Society of London* 49 (1755–1756): 403, 405.

[24] Wolfall, "An Account of the Earthquake at Lisbon," 405; Hamblyn, "Notes from Underground," 112.

[25] John Hyde, "An Account of the Earthquake felt at Boston in New-England, Novem. 18, 1755. Communicated by John Hyde, Esq. F.R.S.," *Philosophical Transactions of the Royal Society of London* 49 (1755–1756): 441; Don Antonio d'Ulloa, "An Account of the Earthquake at Cadiz, in a Letter to the Spanish Ambassador at the Hague, from Don Antonio d'Ulloa, F.R.S.," *Philosophical Transactions of the Royal Society of London* 49 (1755–1756): 422, 423–6, 429, 431, 432.

The Seismograph and a Keatsian "Material Sublime"

discourse, he writes: "its effects are extremely wonderful and amazing; and it seems, ... to have been felt in all parts of the globe."[26] The sublime logic and tropes marshaled here fuel the account's sensationalizing rhetoric. Full expressions of sublime nature articulate the sublime's signature ambivalence, its telltale mixture of wonder and stunned amazement as a response to calamity on a grand scale. While such rhetoric at play in aesthetic discourse is often put on trial when it depends upon relative positions of safety enjoyed by the remote viewer or reader, in this case the relativity of any safe distance warrants serious consideration. As Alexander Regier notes, the "Lisbon earthquake, rather than being limited in its location and consequences to one place, immediately becomes a European catastrophe felt throughout the western world."[27] Regier likewise identifies the literary outpouring inspired by the Lisbon disaster as belonging to the category of the sublime, observing that "the insistence on the mental quality of the experience immediately tempts [one] to figure the catastrophe and its representations in terms of the sublime, thereby following a number of authors who use earthquakes as an illustration of the sublime."[28] The sheer magnitude of Lisbon's devastation made even the smallest homegrown shock a source of deep concern and a well of shared sublime drama: how could one know that these small quakes might not presage equal ruin in England?

Accounts conjecturing causes of earthly "convulsions," as they were then called, connected a constellation of thinkers residing across the globe, especially those closest to active volcanoes or what we now know to be the planet's fault lines and subduction zones. What Tresch traces in his detailed account of Romantic-era Paris was also occurring earlier and elsewhere. Relative to Paris of the 1830s and 1840s, he notes how "new instruments and machines were theorized as extensions of human senses and intentionality, as fluid mediators between mind and world, and as the ligaments of society; they appeared as transformative, even sublime devices."[29] The longer arc of this history includes sublime accounts of awe and alarm arriving hand in hand with scientific thinking and experimentation occurring not just in Britain and New England but also in other sites. These locations were determined less by shared language and culture or one city, as in the case of Tresch's study of Paris. Instead, these thinkers, writers, and inventors were linked by way

---

[26] Mr. Perry and William Stukeley, "An Account of the Earthquake Felt in the Island of Sumatra, in the East-Indies, in November and December 1756. In a Letter from Mr. Perry to the Rev. Dr. Stukeley, Dated at Fort Marlborough, in the Island of Sumatra, Feb 20. 1757. Communicated by the Rev. Wm. Stukeley, M.D.F.R.S.," *Philosophical Transactions of the Royal Society of London* 50 (1757–1758): 491.

[27] Alexander Regier, *Fracture and Fragmentation in British Romanticism* (Cambridge: Cambridge University Press, 2010), 78.

[28] Regier, *Fracture and Fragmentation in British Romanticism*, 81.

[29] Tresch, *The Romantic Machine*, 5.

The Romantic Sublime and Representations of Technology

of being subject to particular agencies and forces home to the environments within which they lived; forces which in turn the inhabitants of these places felt, and their communities and buildings had to absorb.

Within this network of thinkers and tinkerers, some theorized that earthquakes were preceded by eerily calm weather. Then, overturing this view, John Winthrop charted weather conditions and barometric pressures associated with an earlier 1727 New England tremor, comparing it with data on the 1755 activity, proving that, at least for "smaller shocks," calm, serene "earthquake weather" is not in fact directly tied to any subterranean shudders.[30] Following the far-reaching 1755 earthquake, John Michell's 1769 report from Britain would connect Lisbon's fate to volcanic forces. He jettisoned a standing hypothesis that such ruptures came from the skies—either due to "compressed air" or some lightningesque airborne force (230).[31] Michell suggested in turn that the source must be underground, and he noted that the majority of these "extraordinary motions" happen not at random, but repeatedly in the same areas: Italy, Iceland, Peru, and Chile. These sites exist near "burning mountains" and so might be subject to more of the earth's sudden "subterraneous fires."[32] As for the intimidating rumbling that witnesses heard coming and going with each shock, these sounds signaled to him a wave-like tremulous nature felt in the movement of shifting ground. He correctly took the simultaneous passage of sound waves that many likened to raucous coaches or thunderous carriages to be akin to the "wave-like motion of the earth."[33] Scientific responses to these phenomena proliferated almost on a par with the efflorescence of popular earthquake literature, as if to match the rising level of anxiety with reassuring theories of causation.

The massive outpouring of earthquake literature at this time enjoyed a large and far-flung audience in part because of the undeniable charge of its

---

[30] John Winthrop, "An Account of the Earthquake Felt in New England, and the Neighbouring Parts of America, on the 18th of November 1755. In a Letter to Tho. Birch, D.D. Secret. R.S. by Mr. Professor Winthrop, of Cambridge in New England," *Philosophical Transactions of the Royal Society of London* 50 (1757–1758): 16–18.

[31] John Michell, *Conjectures concerning the cause, and observations upon the Phaenomena, of earthquakes; Particularly of That great Earthquake of the first of November 1755, which proved so fatal to the City of Lisbon, and whose Effects were felt as far as Africa, and more or less throughout almost all Europe. By the Reverend John Michell, M. A. Fellow of Queen's-College, Cambridge* (London, 1760), 230. For more information on the compressed air hypothesis, see John Andrew Peyssonel, "Observations upon a Slight Earthquake, Tho' Very Particular, Which May Lead to the Knowledge of the Cause of Great and Violent Ones, That Ravage Whole Countries, and Overturn Cities. By John Andrew Peyssonel, M.D.F.R.S. Translated from the French," *Philosophical Transactions of the Royal Society of London* 50 (1755–1756): 645–8.

[32] Michell, *Conjectures*, 232, 230.

[33] Michell, *Conjectures*, 233.

The Seismograph and a Keatsian "Material Sublime"

sublime ambivalence. If Kant is right that a defining feature of the sublime is the attraction–repulsion response it engenders in a safe observer, here we encounter a different formulation of sublime experience. Thus, one finds the sensational appeal of sublime, sudden, spectacular disaster happening *over there*, coupled to an encroaching sense that these shocks seem to compromise the solid ground beneath one's feet *right here*—throwing into question the idea of assumedly secure earthly homes and stalwart built environments. Residing within the space between a safe and distant and thus ultimately comfortable, resolvable sublime and one without the promise of safety, we find the aesthetic terrain and narrative frame of the material sublime.

In consuming a literature more in line with strands of sublime discourse that ameliorate or resolve the threat of danger, either by tempering associated horrors or by offering more vanilla varieties of wonder—or both—in addition to becoming privy to observations and hypotheses about the nature of these tremors, readers soon learned of inventions fashioned to detect the causes of these ruptures and even bring about possible "cures" for them.[34] This development surfaces a stripe of technological salvationism on a par with what we encounter in today's literature addressing how to engineer our way out of climate peril. In the wake of Michell's conjectures gleaned from the Lisbon cataclysm, the next major leap forward in seismology came with the 1783 Calabrian earthquakes.[35] That year areas near Mount Vesuvius endured six great tremblors in the months of February and March alone. Continuing a now well-established trend of funneling news of "planetary seizures" back to Britain, Sir William Hamilton, living near Naples at the time, famously reported on the devastation of the nearby kingdoms.[36] Hamilton's observations include how "at Cedraro, [he] found the first symptoms of the earthquake, some of the principal inhabitants of that city having quitted their houses,

---

[34] For more sources on instruments developed and used in this period that were also catalogued in this journal's letters, see "An Account of an Earthquake Felt at Lisbon, December 26, 1764: In a Letter to the Rev. Samuel Chandler, D.D.F.R.S.," *Philosophical Transactions of the Royal Society of London* 55 (1765–): 43–4; William Hirst, "An Account of an Earthquake in the East Indies, of Two Eclipses of the Sun and Moon, Observed at Calcutta: In a Letter to the Reverend Thomas Birch, D.D. Secret. R.S. from the Reverend William Hirst, M.A.F.R.S.," *Philosophical Transactions of the Royal Society of London* 53 (1763): 258–61.

[35] Erhard Oeser, "Historical Earthquake Theories from Aristotle to Kant," in *Historical Earthquakes in Central Europe*, eds. Rudolf Geutdeutsch, Gottfried Grunthal, and Roger Musson (Vienna: Geologische Bundesanstalt, 1992), 11.

[36] Sir William Hamilton, *An Account of the Earthquakes in Calabria, Sicily, etc. As communicated to the Royal Society* (Colchester: J. Fenno, 1783). For another source that both cites Hamilton and confirms the fame and familiarity of his earthquake chronicles, see William Guthrie, "A New Geographical, Historical, and Commercial Grammar; and present state of several kingdoms of the world," vol. 2, *History and Geography* (London, 1790).

The Romantic Sublime and Representations of Technology

and living in new erected barracks."[37] These very same months helped to usher in the seismograph, a device styled in various publications as a pivotal counterweight to the splintering earth presented as sublime foe in accounts like Hamilton's. Clockmaker D. Domemico Salsano from Naples put a pendulum to new work, paring it with ink and brush to map the seismic waves of the earth's interior. This mechanism produced a continuous record of ground motion, and onlookers stood by to witness what would be later known as tectonic shifts. Records show that his *geo-sismometro* might have detected "earthquakes [as far as] 300 km away and was equipped with a bell, which would ring when the motions were large." Then in 1796 Duca della Torre "added a hair to the pendulum" making a rudimentary *sismographo* that was hooked up to a clock.[38] The resulting amalgamation joined parts animal and metal to allow for the earth's oscillations and undulations to be recorded relative to standardized time. Ever more delicate, sensitive machines revealed and recorded the earth's most fearsome and forceful movements.

Here Joceyln's Holland and Susanne Strätling's "sublime tools" and "writing tools" converge. For Holland and Strätling, sublime tools function as an intermediary between the pragmatic and artistic by extending human limits of knowledge and agency, often spurring great cultural transformations, while writing tools are designated more broadly as tools participating in scenes of creativity that "cannot be extricated from the processes of artistic creation."[39] Marrying sublime tools with writing tools, Italian inventors effectively transformed the event of an volcanic eruption into one of earthly performance for an audience of surveyors—hailed to come and see by the ring of bell. Onlookers were treated to a view of the planet writing and self-recording its otherwise mysterious and previously unscripted activities. If we could watch the earthquake perform or read the earth's movements, perhaps they would be less troubling; this is the quintessential formula found in normative sublime accounts that ultimately sublimate natural horrors.

Other memorable seismic events prompted additional scientific advances, all reinforcing pervasive sublime narratives that the likes of Nye and Theodor Adorno would find so troubling precisely because they reductively and imprudently set nature against culture or simply domesticate the natural world.[40] In the boot-heel of what is the state of Missouri today, along a sizable length of the Mississippi River Valley and throughout the months of December 1811 through February 1812, the Midwest absorbed a rare, seemingly unprecedented

---

[37] Hamilton, *An Account of the Earthquakes in Calabria*, 6.
[38] Trifunac, "75th Anniversary of Strong Motion Observation," 592.
[39] Holland and Strätling, "Introduction: Aesthetics of the Tool," 203, 205.
[40] See Nye, *American Technological Sublime* and Horkheimer and Adorno, *Dialectic of Enlightenment*.

The Seismograph and a Keatsian "Material Sublime"

middle-American quake, which was "followed by a relentless aftershock sequence."[41] As land suddenly transformed into liquid, for some, the idea of Missouri's secure earthly foundation was quickly eroded, triggering sheer terror. For others, the New Madrid quakes presented a unique opportunity and thus also prompted delight and wonder. As if bringing to fruition anxieties fostered by falling chimneys and shuddering lands—of a planet bereft of any sure stability, even in places without a history of tremors—"loose soils in the Mississippi River Valley were shaken until they lost their internal cohesion and behaved like liquids rather than solids. Sand erupted from the ground via the phenomenon known as liquefaction ... over a swath many tens of kilometers long."[42] Complicating a model purporting a special relationship between quaking earth and volcanic activity, the fertile Mississippi valley lies far from any burning mountain. Drawing from the work of Italy's Giovanni Maria Cavalleri, who "used six pendulums with different periods and recorded their motion in fine powder" to "study the frequency content of earthquake waves" and thus "'embrace every undulation occasioned by any earthquake,'" a man from Louisville, Kentucky used pendulums of varied lengths to track the undulations of the New Madrid quakes—resulting in the first recorded use of multiple pendulums to estimate the period and amplitude of shockwaves.[43] While this technological development helped scientists to better understand earthquakes, which made them less frightening for some, the liquefaction process that ate away at the Mississippi River Valley's banks also advanced a troubling hypothesis: perhaps no ground offers the guarantee of remaining solid; reports on this quake suggested to readers that much of the earth is more dynamic than static, that land can be forced apart by its volcanic mountains and elsewhere can seemingly melt, dissolve, and slip away.

This instance of an unexpected change from one state of matter to another evokes meanings and feelings linked to the verb form of the word *sublime*, which retains the more arresting dimensions of the material sublime, pertaining alike to nature and technology, including forms of sublime nature and technology on display in earthquake literature and reports on seismological inventions. The material sublime speaks to astounding, often sudden transformations, with examples including the fallout from earthquakes, the leveling of a long-established structure, or the Mississippi Valley's once solid landscape turned liquid. A commonly cited example of the material process of sublimation, which is associated with the verb *to sublime*, is that of ice subliming off into the air without first becoming water. Strictly speaking, *to sublime* a substance

---

[41] Susan Elizabeth Hough and Roger G. Bilham, *After the Earth Quakes: Elastic Rebound on an Urban Planet* (New York: Oxford University Press, 2006), 64.

[42] Hough and Bilham, *After the Earth Quakes*, 62.

[43] Trifunac, "75th Anniversary of Strong Motion Observation," 593.

The Romantic Sublime and Representations of Technology

means to heat it such that it transforms directly from solid to vapor, flouting the more typical transformation sequence between states of matter that would run from solid, to liquid, then gas. When a substance sublimes it appears to be out of order even though it is not. In this case, what fuels the shock of surprise is being accustomed to a different sequence of things, to a different order—in this case a three-fold process shrinks to a two-fold one and thus renders the transformation more rapid and sudden, if not extraordinary to the uninitiated observer. Prompting such awe and alarm, the material sublime reminds us that the order we become used to or that we come to take for granted does not necessarily align with overriding orders of matter and processes of the natural world.

To better cope with examples of perceived disorder experienced during earthquakes and documented in their accounts, time and again inventors and inventions from this period were presented as scientific saviors. By the mid-nineteenth century the formula of combining sublime man and machine to counter sublime nature had become well worn, with Robert Mallet and the seismoscope appearing as the next set of coordinated figures of sublime culture battling the material sublimity home to earthquakes.

Upping the ante, the seismometer and the seismoscope would prove sublime for making the earth move at humanity's behest for a change, adding a sense of control where none existed previously. Questions of control, agency, or the lack thereof have long driven sublime narratives and the degree to which the sublime indexes human vulnerability relative to overpowering, sudden, or stunning godlike forces of nature cannot be overstated. Accounts of sublime nature described in eye-witness testimonies or scientific documents addressing the transformative process of sublimation historically turned upon not only a sense of surprise but also a powerful sense of human disempowerment. Rather than falling prey to powers of the material sublime, with grounds and structures seeming to defy so-called natural law, as in the case of solid earth suddenly becoming fluid or longstanding houses and hearths rattling to the ground in seconds, experimenters sought to empower themselves by creating ever more sensitive tools and then doubling down by initiating smaller earthquakes on demand. Next in the long line of Italian contributions to seismology, in 1856 Luigi Palmieri assembled the *seismographo-electro-magnetico*, crafted to survey the "direction, intensity, and duration of an earthquake."[44] At the same time in Britain, Mallet began to test and study these types of measurements to learn about the dynamism of the earth. Mallet documented his elaborate use of explosions and seismoscopes in North Wales, sending word of his methodology and results to that great storehouse of eighteenth- and nineteenth-century scientific study, *Philosophical Transactions for the Royal Society of London*.

---

[44] Trifunac, "75th Anniversary of Strong Motion Observation," 593.

The Seismograph and a Keatsian "Material Sublime"

Reporting from 1851 through 1861, Mallet played no waiting game with the planet, but rather "experimentally determined" the transit-velocities of the "waves of impulse produced by the explosion of charges of gunpowder," which he engineered along the east coast of Ireland. Mallet's manufactured concussions were not simply the stuff of science for science's sake. His first operation, "dislodging vast masses of rock by means" of explosion, coincided opportunely with a project run by the government of Holyhead for the "formation of Asylum Harbour."[45] Mallet routinely folded his projects into the major infrastructure and transportation ventures undertaken in his area. Working with entities like the City of Dublin Steam Packet Company, the Electric Telegraph Company, and the Chester and Holyhead Railway Company, he would make much of the brief openings provided by each company's regular lunch hours. Operating from noon to one to avoid hindering the progress of any commercial endeavor or injuring any workers, Mallet and his team probed and investigated the quaking ground by pairing seismoscopes, telescopes, and chronographs with explosive blasting materials.[46] Reflecting on the outcome produced across

---

[45] Robert Mallet, "Account of Experiments Made at Holyhead (North Wales) to Ascertain the Transit-Velocity of Waves, Analogous to Earthquake Waves, through the Local Rock Formations," *Philosophical Transactions of the Royal Society of London* 151 (1861): 655.

[46] Mallet, "Experiments," 656–7. Mallet's description of the inner workings of the seismoscope and chronograph provides more detailed information about the devices themselves: "Briefly, the seismoscope (fig. 3*, Plate XXIII.) consists of a cast-iron base-plate, on the centre of the surface of which is placed an accurately formed trough (*b*), 12 inches long, 4 inches wide, and 2 inches deep, containing an inch in depth of pure mercury, with its surface free from oxide or dust, so as to reflect properly. The longer axis of this trough is placed in the direction of the wave-path, the base of the instrument being level. At the opposite end of the trough are placed standards with suitable adjustments; that at the end next the centre of impulse carries a tube (*c*) provided with an achromatic object-glass at its lower end, and a pair of cross wires (horizontal and vertical); its optic axis is adjusted to 45° incidence with the reflecting-surface of mercury in the trough. At the other end of the trough an achromatic telescope (*a*) with a single wire is similarly adjusted, so that when the moveable blackened cover (*ee*) is placed over the trough, &c., no light can reach the surface of the mercury except through the tube *c*. The image of the cross wires in the latter is therefore seen through the telescope *a*, clearly reflected and defined in the surface of the mercury, so long as the fluid metal remains absolutely at rest; but the moment the slightest vibration or disturbance is by any means communicated to the instrument, the surface of the fluid mirror is disturbed and the image is distorted, or generally disappears totally. … In the present case … the impulse transmitted from these powerful explosions produced in all cases the most complete obliteration of the image, and in those of the most powerful mines experimented on caused a movement in the mercury of the trough that would have been visible to the naked eye. Indeed in that of the 24th of November 1860, the amplitude of the wave that reached the seismoscope was so great as to cause the mercury to sway forwards and backwards in the trough to a *depth* that might have been measured.

"After the earth-wave has reached this instrument, a certain interval of time is necessary

a decade, whether knowingly or not, Mallet made explicit the sublime stakes of this project. He first claims that "more interesting conditions could thus scarcely be found for experimental determination of the transit-rate of earth-waves, or more desirable for future comparison with that of earthquake-waves themselves," suggesting an equivalence between a creation of sublime nature, an earthquake, and a creation of his own invention, blasting the earth to then track its movements with his seismoscope.[47] Next heralding the wonder and wider appeal of his achievement as a coordinated event, as a kind of carefully orchestrated aesthetic display, Mallet writes, "I had thus presented visibly before me the 'tremors' that nearly invariably are described as proceeding and following the main shock and destructive surface movement in every great earthquake."[48] The sublime charge of "every great earthquake" is diminished and redirected, channeled instead into Mallet's framing of himself as a force powerful enough to make the earth quake at his command. Mallet, then, offers an early example of what Heidegger chalks up to "monstrousness," as modern technology such as the Rhine's hydroelectric plant renders the powerful river as no more than "a water-power supplier" and so "even the Rhine itself appears to be something at our command."[49]

In an ironic turn, Mallet's findings point to "*three* elements upon which the wave-transmissive power of a rock formation mainly depends, viz. the modulus of elasticity of its material, the absolute range of its compression by a given impulse or impact, and the degree of heterogeneity and discontinuity of its parts."[50] From all of his pummeling of Holyhead (Isle of Anglesey, North Wales), Mallet's conclusions suggest that it is not solid rock we should trust

for the production of the wave in the mercury, and for its transit from the end of the trough next *c*, where it is produced, to the mid-length where it is observed. ...

"The chronograph (originally devised by Wheatstone) is shown in fig. 1* Plate XXIII. It consists, in fact, of a small and finely made clock, deprived of its pendulum, but provided with a suitable detent, shown more at large in fig. 4*, by which the action of the weight upon it is kept always arrested, but can immediately be permitted to take place in giving it motion, upon pressing the hand quickly upon the lever *g*.

"The running down of the weight causes the anchor and pallets of the escapement (*k*) rapidly to pass the teeth of the escapement-wheel (*a*), so that the clock "runs down" by a succession of minute descents, and thus the motion is practically a uniform one. It follows that as more weight is added this velocity becomes greater, and by such addition the instrument may be made to measure more and more minute fractions of time.

"... The value in actual mean time, due to the movement of the instrument as thus recorded, requires to be ascertained by reference to a clock beating seconds, so that the number of revolutions of the index *b*, and parts of revolutions of that *a*, during an interval of, say, thirty seconds, may be determined by the mean of several experiments" ("Experiments," 665–6).

[47] Mallet, "Experiments," 662.
[48] Mallet, "Experiments," 676.
[49] Heidegger, "The Question Concerning Technology," 321.
[50] Mallet, "Experiments," 676.

The Seismograph and a Keatsian "Material Sublime"

as our so-called *terra firma*—for it is that which shatters first, while diverse, fragmented composites of rock unite to stand strongest under earthen push and pulse. In a dynamic environment made up of waves, earthly or oceanic, Mallet's projects, his mechanized, explosive, visually sensational events, all point to a world compromised when its "elasticity [becomes] permanently impaired."[51] Here we can see how even in more normative renditions of sublime technologies pitted against sublime nature, we yet find traces of a material sublime counternarrative. This counternarrative tells the story of an aggregate, not-necessarily combative material world in flux, a natural world never fully controlled nor conquered, which instead creates and ensures shared uncertainties for humanity, nature, and technology.

The broad concept of a sweeping, planet-wide sublime agency resonates across literary and cultural studies. There is, of course, the literary response itself, from Shelley's "Mont Blanc," where seismic activity is part of an amoral creative and destructive nature that cannot form the basis of human value, and Anna Laetitia Barbauld's comparison of war to "Ruin, as with an earthquake shock," to Mary Alcock's desire that "Should fire, or water, spread destruction drear, / Or earthquake shake this sublunary sphere, / In Air Balloon to distant realms I fly, / And leave the creeping world to sink and die."[52] And Mary Wollstonecraft rounds out her account of a shaken mind with a nod to how recent earthquakes had transformed the idea of solid ground into a terrifying question: "a mental convulsion, which, like the devastation of an earthquake, throws all the elements of thought and imagination into confusion, makes contemplation giddy, and we fearfully ask on what ground we stand."[53] Thus, the literature of the period reflects the uncertainty and anxiety that arose as the earth challenged the presumed dominance of built environs. The most obvious response to this anxiety may have been the scientific advances cataloged here, but there are other important cultural responses as well. While some might think of the British empire as moving knowledge and technology from the metropole outward, the response to seismic activity shows local, regional, and remote responses shaping thought and work back in London, and we hear non-British voices prominently in the conversation. These various reporters, scientists, and inventors worked heterogeneously to catalog and to respond to global and natural crises—and of course, such a network did not need to be

---

[51] Mallet, "Appendix to the Account of the Earthquake-Wave Experiments made at Holyhead," *Philosophical Transactions of the Royal Society of London* 152 (1862): 669.

[52] Anna Letitia Aikin Barbauld, "Eighteen Hundred and Eleven, A Poem" (London: J. Johnson 1812), line 49, https://quod.lib.umich.edu/b/bwrp/barbaeight; Mary Alcock, "The Air Balloon," in *Poems, &c. &c. by the Late Mrs. Mary Alcock* (London: Printed for C. Dilly, Poultry, 1799), 107–11, lines 69–72.

[53] Mary Wollstonecraft, *The Wrongs of Woman; or Maria*, in *The Works of Mary Wollstonecraft*, vol. 1, eds. Janet Todd and Marilyn Butler (London: William Pickering, 1989), 92.

The Romantic Sublime and Representations of Technology

under the auspices of colonial command; indeed many were not.[54] People like those reporting to the Royal Society or from New England's presses proved flexible enough to submit the germinal empirical data that channeled into the inventions inventoried here, along with many others. For better or worse, even the most misguided responses to the era's great quakes tended to occur in concert, in aggregate, communally.

As we have seen, Mallet's work identifies "perfectly unshattered" rock to be the most dangerous. He also acknowledges that "we cannot but be struck with this beneficent result (amongst others) arising from the shattered and broken-up condition of all the rocky masses forming the habitable surface of our globe."[55] If Hannah Arendt is correct when she gnomically states that "the earth is the very quintessence of the human condition," then perhaps we ought to mind Mallet's lesson (however ill-begotten): it just might be the case that as earthlings our strength too lies in our heterogeneity and elasticity, our ability to embrace the disparate and the fractured.[56] Contrarily, Kant opens his treatment of the Lisbon quake with reference to the shock such disasters hand us, in effect agreeing with Voltaire's idea that Lisbon's catastrophe signaled an unavoidable reign of evil. But, later in the same work, Kant offers a very different reflection on sublime worldbuilding and unbuilding relative to both humanity and the planet:

> As men, who were born to die, why cannot we bear that a few should die by an earthquake, and as such, who are strangers here below and possess no property, why are we inconsolable, when goods, which had shortly been abandoned by the universal way of nature, are lost? It may be easily divined that, when men build upon a ground, which is filled with inflammable substances, sooner or later the whole magnificence of their building may be destroyed by concussions. … Were it not better to judge thus: It was necessary, that earthquakes should happen upon the earth; but it was not necessary for us to build upon its gorgeous habitations.[57]

---

[54] For further direct evidence on how *Philosophical Transactions* united readers in far off places and enabled its audience to become "more acquainted with the countries and places where [the great natural events of the world] happen," see W. W. Weymarn, "An Account of an Earthquake in Siberia: In a Letter from Mons. Weymarn to Dr. Mounsey, Principal Physician of the Emperor of Russia, F.R.S. Translated from the French. Communicated by Mr. Henry Baker," *Philosophical Transactions of the Royal Society of London* 53 (1763): 201–10, 203.

[55] Mallet, "Experiments," 673.

[56] Hannah Arendt, *The Human Condition* (Chicago, IL: University of Chicago Press, 1958), 2.

[57] Kant, "History and Physiography," 133–4.

The Seismograph and a Keatsian "Material Sublime"

Kant's words might make us wonder how we became so inflexible and rigid so as to make necessary the sublime inventions devised by Cavalleri, Palmieri, and Mallet, leaving us to gaze at blasted rock, pendulum, scope, map, and clock—for with all of this technology, trained experts still did not know when the next quake would hit, with only animals knowing enough to run to safe ground just before a truly great tremor.[58] But, we do know now that it is indeed what we build upon the earth—especially where, how, and with what materials—which can and will most certainly bring destruction from earthly "concussions." We are still very much pulled to the idea and spectacle of earthly devastation beyond repair—reading it in narrative and watching it or even orchestrating it with advanced technologies—and, for a good portion of the Anglophone world, we are still largely watching the planet's intermixed processes of worldbuilding and unbuilding from a fraught seat of safety, albeit an increasingly shaky one.

The "Abuse of All Invention" and "the Inequality of Mankind"

If in "Mont Blanc" (1817) Shelley explored the earthquake daemon as one of many potential creators of the famous Alpine mountain, in *A Defence of Poetry* (1821) he considers larger, more sweeping frameworks of creation, including broader forces of human invention and destruction. Steven E. Jones notes that Shelley would compose *A Defence of Poetry* shortly after becoming a fervent supporter and financial backer of the development of a steamship.[59] The poet mentions the steamer and its engine in prose letters and the verse epistle, *Letter to Maria Gisborne*, works I treat in full in the next chapter. Here it serves to note that Shelley pens the *Defence* only months after not just investing in engineer Henry Reveley's projected steamship, but also on the heels of living in his home and writing in his workshop in Livorno, Italy, then called Leghorn. There Shelley worked and wrote while being surrounded by nuts and bolts, tools and gadgets, drafting plans and mathematical books. Jones suggests that "if the poet intended to engage the material world of politics and society, as Shelley

---

[58] Alexander Caldcleugh, "An Account of the Great Earthquake Experience in Chile on the 20th of February, 1835; With a Map. By Alexander Caldcleugh, Esq. F.R.S. F.G.S. &c.," *Philosophical Transactions of the Royal Society of London* 126 (1836): 22. This text documents dogs, rats, and birds who, according to the author, were able to sense the major Chilean tremors and relocate to safer locations. See also Robert Whytt, "An Account of the Earthquake Felt at Glasgow and Dumbarton; Also of a Shower of Dust Falling on a Ship between Shetland and Iceland; in a Letter from Dr. Robert Whytt, Professor of Medicine in the University of Edinburgh, to John Pringle, M.D.F.R.S.," *Philosophical Transactions of the Royal Society of London* 49 (1755–1756): 510.

[59] Steven E. Jones, "Shelley's 'Letter to Maria Gisborne' as Workshop Poetry," *The European Legacy* 24, Issue 3–4 (2019): 382.

did, the materials of the civil engineer might have seemed more immediately tantalizing in their potential" compared to the "materials of poetry": "language and culture."[60] For Jones, "at a time when romantic claims for poetry as the purest form of invention had to be reasserted against common sense, in the face of a general enthusiasm for scientific invention and inventors ... the whole purpose of *A Defence of Poetry* is to assert such claims."[61]

Jones rightly connects inventions both mechanical and poetical due to the great transformative potential they bear for Shelley, but what Jones does not discuss is how the discourse of the sublime reinforces this link and complicates it. Only after writing of sublime steam engines and steamships and seeing mechanical parts and instruments of all sorts in an engineer's workshop, not to mention writing there, does Shelley pen his *Defence* and therein puzzle over how human practices of poiesis might be tethered to other systems and instruments of creation and destruction. In his *Defence*, Shelley repurposes sublime aesthetics to talk a good deal about invention, and not simply artistic or poetic invention.[62] Enlarging his range of inquiry, Shelley's famed poetic manifesto resists theorizing sublime technē in a vacuum. While the ancient Greek term technē places arts, crafts, and various technologies together under one umbrella, if Shelley had adopted the term, it would have likely encompassed much more, expanding to include vast machines and cultural systems.

For Shelley, tools, devices large and small, and greater technological systems, as well as inventions of word and thought, are considered adjacently and contingently—in a continuum spanning histories and particularities of making, genesis, and creation, all occurring across a natural world inclusive of culture. It is not simply that in Shelley's work, technē, or technology more broadly conceived, qualifies as sublime because it operates ambivalently, always both extending and threatening human agency and security. This point has been well established. As Holland's work reminds us, the "untimely modernity of Romantic thinking," already alerts us to the fact that "what was at stake in the technics of the modern world was the capacity for a loss that could extend beyond the body to include the very being of mankind."[63] Beyond this, Shelleyan artistic inventions, both physical and ideological, are not at risk of being abstracted from their respective cultures and environments. As Cian Duffy observes, "the standard critical approach to the 'Shelleyan sublime' is not only premised upon mistaken notions about the 'romantic sublime.' Rather, it is also intimately bound up with a misreading of Shelley's own

[60] Jones, "Shelley's 'Letter to Maria Gisborne,'" 391.
[61] Jones, "Shelley's 'Letter to Maria Gisborne,'" 391.
[62] See Cian Duffy, *Shelley and the Revolutionary Sublime* (Cambridge: Cambridge University Press, 2009), 6.
[63] Jocelyn Holland, "From Romantic Tools to Technics: Heideggerian Questions in Novalis's Anthropology," *Configurations* 18, no. 3 (Fall 2010): 291.

political thought: namely the claim that he 'moves progressively' from a radical empiricism to an increasingly apolitical idealism." That is, instead of accepting standard approaches suggesting Shelley's sublime becomes increasingly Kantian for espousing disinterested idealism, Duffy, for example, reads "Mont Blanc" "in relation to complex, early nineteenth-century discourse on the alpine sublime."[64] The important point to bear in mind is that in "Mont Blanc" and elsewhere, Shelley's sublime is attuned to a politics of earthly place, to environmental affordances that make aesthetics possible, that make cultural politics possible.

In the *Defence*, Shelley's well-known figuration of humanity's creative process and potential—"the mind in creation is as a fading coal … when composition begins, inspiration is already on the decline"—closely follows a discussion of the mechanical arts, invention, and what Shelley calls "the grosser sciences": "moral, political, historical, … scientific and œconomical knowledge."[65] Shelley's formulation for the creative faculty conceives of invention and inspiration in limited terms. The conditions upon which they depend are anchored by the transformative energies of sublime nature. The inspired, inventive mind relies upon a concentrated source of fuel steadily approaching exhaustion, working at a quickening yet ever ebbing pace. Creation and invention, even at their start, already belong to processes of decline and transformation. Inspiration is touched off by a possibility and potential that is ever on the wane and that only arrives after being indebted to histories and systems much larger than itself. Coming not only from the work and tools of miners but first from a process spanning millions of years, coal forms out of energy stored in decayed plant matter long compressed and heated by layers of earth. Shelley, an early proponent of consuming a plant-based diet, here likens "the mind in creation" to recently unearthed ancient plant matter set alight and thus on the verge of assuming yet another new form. And by alluding to the at once generative and deleterious work of fire, Shelley's simile evokes ancient Greek mythology, where fire was first handed down to humanity from Prometheus, the Titanic god of forethought. As discussed in the opening chapter of this book, since the Prometheus myth often positions sublime technology as a defense against sublime nature, the myth serves as a widely recognizable example of how the sublime stories we tell about technology come to redefine humanity's relationship with the natural world. If we take the poet's reference to coal as mere simile or no more than a convenient historical example, we risk emptying out the technological and ecological implications at play in Shelley's aesthetic and lexical choices. The mind in creation, Shelley's fading coal, is a child of the material sublime.

[64] Duffy, *Shelley and the Revolutionary Sublime*, 6.
[65] Percy Shelley, *A Defence of Poetry*, in *Shelley's Poetry and Prose*, eds. Neil Fraistat and Donald H. Reiman, 2nd ed. (New York and London: W. W. Norton & Company, 2002), 531, 530.

The Romantic Sublime and Representations of Technology

In step with his representation of the inspired creative mind running akin to smoldering coal, Shelleyan invention, creation, and making are always both ideological and material, born of nature and mind, culture and history—all always in tangled nexus. Invention for Shelley, as with his usage of poetry and poets, is a term that functions capaciously: at once applying to immaterial and material invention. To fully fathom Shelleyan technological aesthetics inclusive of poetry as technē, it helps to recall the profound sublimity and ambivalent agency Shelley ascribes to poetry: "Poetry cannot be made subservient. Poetry is a sword of lightning, ever unsheathed, which consumes the scabbard that would contain it."[66] Following suit, borne out both in the poet's grammatical usage of the term *invention* (discussed below) and its implied meanings, Shelley tethers his understanding of poetic invention to other modes of knowledge production in the immaterial realm, as well as to physical, invented objects or systems encountered in the material world. Ideas and words are invented in a fashion comparable to that of social systems or durable artifacts. These are connected intrinsically, such that when creative, inventive powers of mind are abused so too the earth and anything living or working on it are likewise mistreated, undervalued, wronged. Thus, as Alan Bewell rightly observes, Shelley sees the abuse of any and all poetry, imagination, and invention as being linked to abuses of nature and people, ultimately underwriting systems of inequity and injustice running throughout the interwoven material and immaterial worlds we inhabit.[67] Humanity may have limited control of material sublimity and its ambivalent creations and inventions but humanity nonetheless remains obligated to do right in the face of sublime uncertainty and unknowing.

Just one short paragraph separates Shelley's lengthy consideration of the "abuse of all invention" and his fading ember rendering of the imaginative mind whose inventions cannot be controlled, "contained," or "made subservient." The well-known paragraph referencing invention warrants full consideration as it documents the poet's ethical understanding of the mechanical arts as they relate to "those sciences which have enlarged the limits of the empire of man over the external world":

> We have more moral, political and historical wisdom, than we know how to reduce into practice; we have more scientific and œconomical knowledge than can be accommodated to the just distribution of the produce which it multiplies. The poetry, in these systems of thought, is concealed by the accumulation of facts and calculating processes. There

[66] Shelley, *A Defence of Poetry*, 520.
[67] See Alan Bewell, "Percy Bysshe Shelley and Revolutionary Climatology," in *Romanticism and Colonial Disease* (Baltimore, MD: Johns Hopkins University Press, 2000), 205–41.

The Seismograph and a Keatsian "Material Sublime"

is no want of knowledge respecting what is wisest and best in morals, government, and political œconomy, or at least, what is wiser and better than what men now practise and endure. But we let "*I dare not* wait upon *I would*, like the poor cat in the adage." [*Macbeth*, I.vii.44–5, emphasis Shelley's.] We want the creative faculty to imagine that which we know; we want the generous impulse to act that which we imagine; we want the poetry of life: our calculations have outrun conception; we have eaten more than we can digest. The cultivation of those sciences which have enlarged the limits of the empire of man over the external world, has, for want of the poetical faculty, proportionally circumscribed those of the internal world; and man, having enslaved the elements, remains himself a slave. To what but a cultivation of the mechanical arts in a degree disproportioned to the presence of the creative faculty, which is the basis of all knowledge, is to be attributed the abuse of all invention for abridging and combining labour, to the exasperation of the inequality of mankind? From what other cause has it arisen that the discoveries which should have lightened, have added a weight to the curse imposed on Adam? Poetry, and the principle of Self, of which money is the visible, incarnation, are the God and Mammon of the world.[68]

Here the mechanical arts operate akin to sublime poetry by proffering control while eating away at it, by pointing to a moral high ground we never really had, not least because of a lack of collective, unselfish will to work toward equitable and ethically guided approaches to "cultivat[ing] the mechanical arts." By these lights, Shelley resists a technological sublime of the determinist or salvationist sort, embracing instead a technological sublime premised upon a material sublime world where worldbuilding and unbuilding go hand in hand and thus restraint and constraint are required whether or not we recognize either as an ethical obligation, goal, or intrinsic good. The mechanical arts, poetry, and other classes of human technē here bear the sublime's commonplace if not signature moral ambiguity. Like Kant, for Shelley such inventions highlight moral tensions rather than resolve them because the onus is on us to confront and address those tensions. From failing to think with the sublimities of both nature and culture, in the pursuit to expand the limits of humanity's control over itself and the natural world, Shelley finds little more than "the exasperation of the inequality of mankind." Due to this failure, much if not all of mankind has been mishandled and the elements have been enslaved.

When Shelley points out what we *want* in his paragraph on the abuse of invention, tellingly, he intimates not what we might gain or desire but what we routinely lack. He highlights our collective inability to think with what he calls

---

[68] Shelley, *A Defence of Poetry*, 530–1.

The Romantic Sublime and Representations of Technology

the "poetical faculty," but which may as well double for sublime worldbuilding, *qua* the material sublime—where sublime worldbuilding is always ambivalent, uncontrollable, collaborative, and dependent on, but not necessarily as unjust as, the world Shelley laments. After all, in Shelley's definition, "poets, in the most universal sense of the world ... express the influence of society or nature upon their own minds ... [and their language] marks the before unapprehend relations of things."[69] As Regier reminds us in his study of the Lisbon quake, the "Burkean sublime relies on [a] breaking force because it structurally and logically precedes the process of reconstruction within the framework of the aesthetic. Burkean distance ultimately relies on a shattering of relations."[70] In stark contrast, the aesthetic of the material sublime foregrounds the inescapable relation of things, suggesting expansive political and ethical obligations not limited to humanity, and raising sweeping questions pertaining to human responsibility and indebtedness.

Key in this case is embracing the material sublimity of the world and so throwing off the mantle of the selfishness and solipsism that drive practices of abused invention, which emerge in part from misaestheticized mechanical arts being packaged as either more distant and thus less pressing on our lives than they really are, or as easy answers "which should have lightened, [but in reality] have added a weight to the curse imposed on Adam." Shelley's evocation of Mammon in this context is telling. He worries over the ethics propelling any given human invention, creation, or act of poiesis, especially since in his mind we are foolhardy to fancy that we could contain whatever we might create—a problem addressed in his material sublime representation of poetry as "a sword of lightning" that "cannot be made subservient." To be sublime is to exist beyond our grasp, where to grasp means to hold or control both physically and mentally. The way to proceed then is to leave off from inventing things or ideas that are born out of a self-serving, narrow place and instead adopt a Shelleyan formula of recognition coupled with love, yielding freedom through "a going out of our own nature," which would mean, in this setting, to tarry with the fraught nature of nature to best confront our dependency upon it, debts to it, and our abiding affective relationship with it.[71] Shelleyan inventors, worldbuilders, and creators worthy of such names resemble "The Provençal Trouveurs, or inventors, ... whose verses are as spells, which unseal the inmost enchanted fountains of delight which is in the grief of Love. It is impossible to feel them without becoming a portion of that beauty which we contemplate: it were superfluous to explain how the gentleness and the elevation of mind connected with these sacred emotions can render men

---

[69] Shelley, *Defence of Poetry*, 512.
[70] Regier, *Fracture and Fragmentation in British Romanticism*, 87.
[71] Shelley, *Defence of Poetry*, 517.

The Seismograph and a Keatsian "Material Sublime"

more amiable, more generous, and wise, and lift them out of the dull vapours of the little world of self."[72]

Shelley does more than invite us to take a bath in the aesthetic pleasure of sublime, lofty, uplifting verse. His logic here instructively applies to human engagement with the natural world and inventions of sorts other than poetry. Tellingly casting poets as "inventors" and yoking "verses" to "enchanted fountains" that afford us capacities for deep feeling and connection, Shelley prescribes transformative aesthetic experience as a remedy for a dulled life tantamount to no more than "the little world of self." The ethical–aesthetic rubric instantiated in these lines presses humanity to refrain from reducing the poetic, the mechanistic, the technological to any Mammon-esque extension of self, and instead to envision them as belonging to much larger aesthetics of invention that allow us to commune with transcendent beauty.[73] For Shelley we will only be able to recognize pervasive immaterial and material sublimities and therefore the consequent beauties of the world (fraught as they are as in the "grief of Love") when we at last rise above "the dull vapours" of the self and so finally cease crafting ever more woefully misguided cages for the elements and ever more cultures of enslavement.

"Something of Material Sublime": "Things Cannot to the Will / Be Settled"

If Kant and Shelley expose dark questions only proffering solutions without providing a clear path to resolve them, within Keats's work exists a response, a way forward, a hypothesis to test: what if we re-see the entire world as sublime?[74] Keats's "Epistle to Reynolds" aligns with sentiments expressed in

---

[72] Shelley, *Defence of Poetry*, 525.

[73] Here Holland's work is again salient. See Holland, "From Romantic Tools to Technics," 291, 306.

[74] In relation to noted Keatsian scholarship on the material sublime, my reading departs most from Jack Stillinger's and perhaps agrees most with that of Louise Z. Smith. Smith notes that because Stillinger's account "ignor[es] [the] 'material' altogether, he misreads the passage and hence the poem. The sublime is not 'uplifted from the world' and 'unearthly'; it is firmly grounded in material phenomena, e.g. the sunset. Stillinger's reading makes no sense in terms of the earlier lines [of the poem]; why would Keats wish to return to the 'fantastic dreams' when he has already wished to be among the 'few are there who escape these visitings' (13)? Stillinger's conclusion, that 'sublime dreamings are preferable to the mental repetition of daytime world jostling,' (p. 596) is correct, but he defines 'sublime dreamings' incorrectly. Definition must cope with the 'material sublime.' 'Sublime' means either grandeur, magnitude, and power or the elevated emotions of awe, fear, and rapture occasioned by perception of these phenomena. If the words mean 'material which is sublime,' Keats probably refers to the mountains and sunset." Smith, "The Material Sublime: Keats and 'Isabella,'" *Studies in Romanticism* 13, no. 4 (Fall 1974): 302. Jack

The Romantic Sublime and Representations of Technology

his famous letter on what he calls "Negative Capability." Across both texts Keats's words cut against hyperbolic accounts of humanity's creative agency that still permeate narratives of technological invention, innovation, even salvation. Keats reveals a world built upon stories of relational agency and collective potential. Crucial to both ecological thought and Romanticism, these stories stress the limits of making as well as the limits of repair. They dethrone the Romantic figure of the lone, godlike, genius creator. They tear down easy techno-utopic fantasies suggesting that we can build anything, repair whatever we break, our earthly world included. Intriguingly, Keats grounds our necessary uncertainty not only in an overwhelming nature—"the core / Of an eternal fierce destruction," as he will call it—but also in a shifting and shaking built environment: while the buildings in Keats's epistle may not be shaken by earthquakes, interlinked forces of building and unbuilding in the poem emphasize the fragility of our earthly and built structures every bit as powerfully.[75]

Writing an ekphrastic poem to an ailing friend, Keats offers as salve the agential sublime aesthetic he locates in Claude Lorrain's landscape painting known as the "Enchanted Castle." For Keats, Lorrain brings to life a natural and built environment that "elsewhere [is] but half animate" (37). These part nature-created, part human-created environs betoken a charged agential force, forming anything but a static background, dull landscape, or unshifting, unreceptive world: "Here ... they look alive to love and hate ... they seem a lifted mound ... pulsing underground" (38, 39, 40). Lorrain's image moves Keats because of the astonishing movement and activity it implies. The built and natural worlds comprising the painting's landscape suggest manifold kinetic energies—even responsive affective agencies—not simply appearing to "pulse" but also endowed with the potential to harbor "love and hate." Echoing how the epistle's built environs work with and not against the natural landscape, throughout the poem Keats appears to be working out a variation on the theme of sublime forces operating in aggregate, a theme articulated by way of a series of unexpected combinations and protean forms.

Antecedent to Keats's ever-animated surrounds and buildings is a parade of incongruent human bodies (6–12), what Grant F. Scott calls a "bizarre gallimaufry of historical figures that appears in the beginning of the poem."[76]

Stillinger, "Keats and Romance," *Studies in English Literature, 1500–1900* 8, no. 4, Nineteenth Century (Autumn 1968): 593–605.

[75] John Keats, "[Dear Reynolds, as last night I lay in bed]," lines 96–7. Hereafter citations are noted in-text by line number.

[76] Grant F. Scott, "Words into Pictures: Ekphrasis in 'Fragment of Castle-builder,' 'Epistle to John Hamilton Reynolds,' and 'The Eve of St. Agnes'" in *The Sculpted Word: Keats, Ekphrasis, and the Visual Arts* (Hanover and London: University Press of New England, 1994), 73.

The Seismograph and a Keatsian "Material Sublime"

For Scott, "Keats' dream violates historical, natural, and physical boundaries. It is prone to uncanny combinations and has a disturbingly anarchic quality that is manifest in the humorous, if inappropriate, transposing of the various figures' wardrobes: thus, Alexander should have military gear; Voltaire, the nightcap; Brutus, the cravat, and so on. A natural order is disrupted."[77] That is, the poem activates the aesthetic of the material sublime well before Keats deploys that phrase, with the poet's "uncanny combinations" evoking disorder and challenging perceived notions of natural order. In such fashion, the poem opens with a dream vision of wonderous material mutability: "There came before my eyes that wonted thread / Of shapes, and shadows, and remembrances, / That every other minute vex and please: / Things all disjointed come from north and south" (2–5). As Stuart Sperry notes, nothing seems fitting or normal—very little seems to fit here at all. "The poem as a whole seems strangely disjointed and even, at times, incoherent, especially when compared with the poet's more polished work," observes Sperry.[78] Later I'll address Sperry's comment about polish, but for now I would like to stress that the disjointed and incoherent aesthetic Sperry detects is none other than that of the material sublime, the aesthetic category built of what simultaneously vexes and pleases, where conjunction meets disruption and disjunction, where ambivalence and paradox reign across the material world, where profound wonder arises much more than any certain or safe answer. Think of the material sublime's lightning-riven skies, molten earth, tremulous foundations, collapsed hearths, and seismographic machines manifesting largely unusable legers.

Also prior to penning the phrase "material sublime," Keats writes of self-opening doors and Merlin-esque castle walls (49, 34). Working in this spirit, Keats notes the dim approach and consequent sudden vanishing of a "golden galley" with lightning oars (55–60). As alluded to in the previous section, lightning has long been the calling card for sublime nature as well as sublime culture thanks to the Prometheus myth, where the Titan steals Zeus's lightning to endow humanity with the technics of fire. The poet likewise calls attention to the sudden materialization and dematerialization of the vessel. In so doing, he threads together two standard tropes of sublime nature's offshoot, the material sublime (with lightning and worldbuilding yoked to unbuilding), where the stuff of the material world announces its overriding agency by manifesting rapidly constructed worlds and just as quickly tearing them down, reducing them to nothingness, making them disappear in a moment, forever. This built environment moves, seemingly of its own accord or apart from human agency. He writes: "The doors all look as if they oped themselves, / The windows as

---

[77] Scott, *The Sculpted Word*, 74–5.
[78] Stuart Sperry, "The Epistle to John Hamilton Reynolds," in *Keats's Poetry and Prose*, 583.

The Romantic Sublime and Representations of Technology

if latched by fays and elves" (49–50). Keats imagines what might otherwise appear to be solid, static, stalwart built structures in more empowered terms (as being more agential, more forcefully motile—in a phrase, more materially sublime), all thanks to a painting he sees, a painting fixed upon a wall and seemingly bereft of any movement. The work of art in this case enables Keats to envision his world differently, which in turn prompts him to reconsider the work of art, its genesis and production, and ultimately its relationality and debt to the natural world. Keats's understanding of the natural world here turns upon his understanding of art, creative faculties, human inventing. And so, his work expresses the powerful role our technē and technics play in influencing the degrees of agency we grant to the natural world—or better, to worlds that reach beyond the human and the cultural, but upon which humanity's culture grows with, grows from, and cannot grow beyond.

As Sperry reminds us, Keats's "hasty and impromptu verses" from "The Epistle to Reynolds" are penned at just that point when the poet had become increasingly interested in the sublime.[79] Sperry notes how

> Keats's method in the lines to Reynolds is progression by way of contrasts and oppositions. ... The imaginative scene he has created ... has slowly crystalized the major preoccupation of his poem: the degree of idealization—both in a good and bad sense—that art can achieve in its transcendence of actuality. The theme, of course, is one intimately connected with his growing interest in the sublime, both as a general and long-established ideal of art and in its relation to his own more particular sense of the process of aesthetic sublimation by which the materials of art are purged of 'disagreeables,' fused in the imagination, and 'put into etherial existence for the relish of one's fellows.'[80]

It is right to suggest that by this time Keats is deeply concerned with questions surrounding the sublimity of the work of art—both in terms of a distinct type of art that can be produced to move audiences in unique and powerful ways and in terms of how sublime aesthetics engages with the disagreeable. But rather than transcending actuality with the aim of purging "disagreeables" or cleansing the materials of art by taking recourse to the ethereal over the material, Keats puts life's painful realities on full, visceral display in his poem. He does so not for anyone to relish them naïvely but to recognize them honestly, inviting readers to contemplate the role of the work of art in aiding us to exist with the material world's ambivalence and uncertainty rather than to run from it. It is important to recall that it was only three months earlier

[79] Sperry, "The Epistle to John Hamilton Reynolds," 584.
[80] Sperry, "The Epistle to John Hamilton Reynolds," 586.

The Seismograph and a Keatsian "Material Sublime"

that Keats came to his famed formulation of "Negative Capability" after being inspired and moved by a different work of artistic worldbuilding, Shakespeare's *Richard III*, performed by celebrated actor Edmund Kean. There Keats famously praised Shakespeare for "possess[ing] so enormously ... *Negative Capability*, that is when man is capable of being in uncertainties, Mysteries, doubts, without any irritable reaching after fact & reason."[81]

By these lights, it is challenging to read Keats's catalog of the disjunctive and disjointed as signifying nothing in the manner that Sperry does; Sperry suggests, "It is not merely that the images themselves are ludicrously inconsistent with each other; but they neither suggest nor lead to anything more."[82] At the same time, Sperry aptly notes how Keats's verse demonstrates that "once again there is the device Keats had used so often in the past of working into the poem by elaborating a chain of images and associations that he hoped might lead on to a major theme."[83] Instead of Keats's chain of incongruent images being tantamount to a failure of his art or a failure of Keats's polish rendering the images "totally inconsistent with [Keats's] ideal [creative or artistic] process," these images do succeed in allowing Keats to develop a major theme. Keats presents human life as a jostling, disjointed affair reflected by the unsettled world within which we reside and from which we invent and create. Rather than working against such earthly fears and uncomfortable realities, truly sublime art and technics challenge us to come to terms with our ineluctable relationship with a world of unsettled, unwilled, unconquerable aggregates in flux.

A prime example of one of the poem's sublime aggregates arrives in the collection of builders who take part in helping to form the castle. Rather than springing from one lone, unknowable, perfect godhead, the part physical, part metaphysical origin story Keats weaves for the built structure is of a multiplicitous nature, weaving together disparate religious and ritualized examples of sacred, storied creation. Instead of a pure, absolute deity, readers encounter a morally ambiguous conglomeration of religious figures from diverse traditions and competing stories of the sacred and the magical, all arising from various parts of the globe. Together they co-build Keats's sublime castle, and not by instant fiat as in narratives that prop up lone godlike creators and inventors but in an account of the material sublime that runs across great swaths of time: "Part of the building was ... Built by a banished santon of Chaldee; / The other part, two thousand years from him, / Was built by Cuthbert de Saint Aldebrim; / Then there's a little wing ... Built by a Lampland Witch

---

[81] John Keats, "Letter to George and Tom Keats, 21, 27? December 1817," in *Keats's Poetry and Prose*, 107–9.

[82] Sperry, "The Epistle to John Hamilton Reynolds," 584.

[83] Sperry, "The Epistle to John Hamilton Reynolds," 584.

95

The Romantic Sublime and Representations of Technology

turned maudlin nun— / And many other juts of aged stone / Founded with many a mason-devil's groan" (41–8). Keats writes against the single-author model of one original sublime cause. Here we find no monotheistic tale of sublime worldbuilding where an omnipotent, humanoid god manifests the world in seconds with just his invented words. Keats composes a different script to attempt to account for the mystery, the ambivalence, and overall sublime nature of worldbuilding wherein reside wide varieties of immaterial and material agencies. Intersecting and divergent cultural ideologies of faith, folklore, and legend, which represent orders of the immaterial, here join "juts of aged stone" changed by numerous material bodies and historical contingencies, akin to Shelley's fading coal.

It is telling that Keats's poem pertaining to art and architecture—to the sublime making of our interlocked immaterial–material worlds—would have to encourage readers to be mindful of the materials with which they build, dream, imagine, create, and construct. On the heels of poetic lines recounting an unheeded story of a herdsman who visited the "enchanted spot" and felt its eerie ambivalence, its sublime uncanny core, its telltale mixture of "sweet music" (delight) and "fear" (62, 63), Keats hopes his reader might finally heel, heal, and take heed. Keats entreats his sick friend, Reynolds, to imbibe a formula for collective repair. That is, Keats invites Reynolds to take in his apostrophe to a sublime of the everyday, to an abiding and overriding material aesthetic foregrounding humanity's inescapable relationality, interdependence, and uncertainty:

> O, that our dreamings all of sleep or wake
> Would all their colours from the sunset take:
> From something of material sublime,
> Rather than shadow our own soul's day-time
> In the dark void of night. For in the world
> We jostle,—but my flag is not unfurl'd
> On the Admiral-staff,—and to philosophize
> I dare not yet!—Oh never will I prize,
> High reason, and the lore of good and ill,
> Be my reward. Things cannot to the will
> Be settled, but they tease us out of thought; (67–77)

Instead of taking comfort in high inventions of philosophical reason and morality (lines 63–6), and without recourse to any reassuring certainties, Keats embraces a material world wherein "We jostle" and "Things cannot to the will / Be settled." Here, humanity, along with all that it would dream, envision, and create, ultimately does not get to decide, choose, or determine. There is no room for the shallow utopias of techno-determinism or techo-salvation here.

The Seismograph and a Keatsian "Material Sublime"

The unsettled world Keats paints does not bend to human will. When we assume that we can will what we want into existence, we engineer for ourselves a world that can only "shadow our soul's day-time." This Keatsian complement to Plato's cave holds even less light and delusionary promise than the original, given that in Keats's next line these shadows are quickly extinguished "In the dark void of night." Like Shelley, for Keats, when we make, invent, and manifest worlds in accord with our own solipsistic visions, in accord with naught but our own image or selfish desires, then we ourselves and what we create are necessarily benighted and bankrupt.

Leading up to these lines, in a canny move, the poet wishes for what he knows he cannot will into existence: sweeping cultures, practices, and patterns of creative invention not in thrall to myths of individual sublime creators, but inspired instead by a sublime of the everyday permeating every place. Keats expresses this desire through an ironic use of poetic apostrophe when he writes: "O, that our dreamings all of sleep or wake / Would all their colours from the sunset take: / From something of material sublime, / Rather than shadow our own soul's day-time / In the dark void of night." Readers familiar with poetic tradition will recognize that Keats works strategically within the apostrophic mode in this instance to both activate and critique the creative force of words, poets, and poetry. This mode is known for exposing a poet's most passionately hoped for desires which fly in the face of the reality confronted by the poet or poetic speaker. Here Keats's wish is less for himself than for the collective community. What would Keats will into being with his words, as if by sublime, godlike fiat? A world that better accepts our jostling, unsettled, unexpected fates, rather than clinging to individualized desires and whatever consensus has calcified to human-centered day-time norms, to kinds of guiding light that lead to no more than darkness and void. Notably the sentence bearing Keats's apostrophe concludes not with the excessive emotive charge and heightened tension of an exclamation mark—as with many examples of apostrophe—but instead with the measured finality of a period. Keats's apostrophe reads less as an embarrassed confession or the self-centered, impassioned plea of one individual, and assumes instead the feel of a sound declarative judgment assessing the actual state of things. It betrays ardent hopes tempered by a prudent admission that we have yet to take in the chief lesson of the colorful sunset—Keats's grounding image for the "material sublime," which the poet hopes could act as a guiding light for what we dream and go on to invent. Keats's proposed alternative world bears out dreams and desires both conscious and unconscious ("our dreamings all of sleep or wake") that would begin not with us, the self, the subject, and by extension, humanity, but instead find their prime origin and inspiration from a wider material sublimity betokened by the uncontrollable, un-willable, unknowable aesthetics of interplay and emblematized by the perennially shifting colors of the everyday sunset. An omnipresent material sublime, a somewhere always setting sun, ever receding but nonetheless ubiquitous, which we may not always behold but nonetheless persists, serves as the ethical–aesthetic basis for Keats's prescription for better, less selfish dreams, putting into play more realistic and more responsible created things, cultures, and worlds.

Keats's poem concentrates on the production of sublime technē which Shelley sees as foundational for any and all ethically bound cultural inventions, practices, and ideologies. When we do not bear in mind this "material sublimity," our artifacts, activities, and habitual thinking tends to fall back on cycles of cold, base predation or unjust consumption. Shelley's discussion of cultural corruption in the *Defence* turns upon two key metaphors of overconsumption leading the world to the brink of illness, first with a body politic eating more than it could possibly digest, and then again in an image of an excessively accumulating body grown "too unwieldy for that which animates it."[84] In parallel, because of the disturbing patterns of invention and consumption he finds all around him, Keats himself ends up feeling ill at the end of his verse letter to his sick friend. Like Shelley, the sickness Keats points out is metaphorical and sublime, mysterious and pervasive, more vexing than pleasing, and checks even a poet's verbal prowess. That is, Keats's verse epistle goes on to align with stock sublime narratives containing the trope of sublime experiences that transcend the limits of language, expression, and communication. Keats is made sick by a sublime world darkly bent upon eating away at itself. This world is all but evacuated of any buoying sources of wonder. It is nearly emptied out of any promise or any spark of sublime beauty typically held in tension with the darker side of the material sublime:

> Dear Reynolds! I have a mysterious tale
> And cannot speak it. ...
> I was at home
> And should have been most happy,—but I saw
> Too far into the sea, where every maw
> The greater on the less feeds evermore,—
> But I saw too distinct into the core
> Of an eternal fierce destruction,
> And so from happiness was far gone.
> Still am I sick of it: and tho' to-day
> I've gathered young spring-leaves, and flowers gay
> Of periwinkle and wild strawberry,
> Still do I that most fierce destruction see,—
> The Shark at savage prey,—the hawk at pounce,—

---

[84] Shelley, *A Defence of Poetry*, 530, 531.

The Seismograph and a Keatsian "Material Sublime"

> The gentle Robin, like a pard or ounce,
> Ravening a worm,—Away, ye horrid moods,
> Moods of one's mind! You know I hate them well,
> You know I'd sooner be a clapping bell
> To some Kamschatkan missionary church,
> Than with these horrid moods be left in lurch—
> Do get your health—and Tom the same—I'll dance,
> And from detested moods in new romance
> Take refuge.—Of bad lines a centaine dose
> Is sure enough—and so 'here follows prose.'— (86–113)

This is not the sublime beheld from some remote, reassuring distance. Keats is feeling it. Keats is in it. He feels sick because of it. "Rather than moving away from the painting, then, as most critics believe, [Keats] moves into it. Adopting the perspective of the pensive figure, who is gazing out at the ocean," as Scott puts it.[85] Echoing Kant's piece that opened this chapter, Keats's growing sentences build pressure and a sense of encroaching proximity, with image after image crowding together within the shared world of each sentence. He is not disinterested, disaffected, or suggesting that he stands apart from these sublime figures and his syntax reinforces the idea of a sublime that is all too close for comfort. They are with him, in him, whether he likes it or not. This sublime permeates Keats's world, resides there during would-be quiet moments at home, and is impossible to escape, even through communing with the beauty of flowers or writing romantic verse. The poem's dalliance with sublime realities that continue to press Keats into his "horrid moods" all but evacuates the promise of refuge Keats hopes to find in the arms of a "new romance."

Shelley echoes Keats on key points, chief among these being an overriding generative and destructive sublimity inherent in the external material–immaterial world that is not ours to possess, control, or fully know. How these poets (and Kant) view creation, invention, and creative capacities, in the end leads to them framing human contingency and our curtailed agency differently, but nonetheless, in each of their sublime accounts it is we who are responsible and held accountable, not technē or technics, not art or nature. More precisely whatever agency humanity does possess (creative, inventive, or otherwise) arises only in aggregate, only in tandem with forces and processes of making and unmaking distributed throughout our built and natural worlds. Under the rubric of the material sublime nothing is given or granted but is instead aggregately built, ambivalently born. In the best case scenario, we arrive at an uneven field—playing together unexpectedly at times, uncertainly most of the time, and always running both out of our dreams and against

---

[85] Scott, "Words into Pictures," 81.

The Romantic Sublime and Representations of Technology

our dreams. Attending carefully to the Janus-headed nature of technology and invention begs important questions about what exists beyond any tool or tool user, about context, contingency, and agency. What comes of linking sublime technology together with its larger earthly, material, immaterial, and cultural contexts is that technology's, and by extension humanity's, interdependence and fundamental relationality becomes starkly clear, pervasive, and impossible to write off.

Like the natural world that bears a future changed by the ideas and inventions we make, so too humanity is remade and unmade by what it creates. This is a prime lesson of Romantic-era material sublimity. We are not only reshaped through the work of worldbuilding we inact through and in narrative and nature, but just as a poet cannot predict the cultural or environmental impact of their words and (pace Paul de Man)[86] each word inevitably disfigures the next, so goes our relationship with the technological: to write is to unwrite, to build is to unbuild, with each case being made possible only by virtue of a changeling natural world that, like all sublime things, we can never fully grasp.

Thus, worldbuilding goes hand in hand with unmaking and unbuilding. When we recognize this often-frightening reality, as Kant, Shelley, and Keats do, questions arise pertaining to earthly and human worldbuilding: how they relate to one another, how they diverge, how best to proceed in light of apparent differences. Questions about worldbuilding, unbuilding, and ethics persist today in current debates about the very idea of repair. Jack Halberstam, in a recent interview, reaffirms his anarchist leanings, again calling for "'fewer strategies of repair'" given the type of world capitalism has built.[87] "[I]n an era of environmental decline, financial corruption, right-wing populism," for Halberstam the most pivotal question now becomes "how do we unbuild the world? Queer theory in the mode of Eve K. Sedgwick and even José Muñoz espoused was very committed to world making. I honor that lineage and queer genealogy, but I also want to turn for a while toward world unmaking. Another world is possible, but only when this one ends."[88] While it stands to argue that new worlds and old worlds might indeed coexist, Halberstam's point is well taken: we ought to consider seriously questions pertaining not only to worldbuilding but also unbuilding. In the same vein, although not directly pertaining to Halberstam's modes of anarchist or abolitionist thought, Steven J. Jackson's work on media and information technology in

---

[86] Paul de Man, "Shelley Disfigured," in Harold Bloom et al., *Deconstruction and Criticism* (New York: Continuum, 1979).

[87] Jack Halberstam, "Public Thinker: Jack Halberstam On Wildness, Anarchy, and Growing Up Punk," interview by Damon Ross Young, *Public Books*, 26 March 2009, https://www.publicbooks.org/public-thinker-jack-halberstam-on-wildness-anarchy-and-growing-up-punk.

[88] Halberstam, "Public Thinker."

The Seismograph and a Keatsian "Material Sublime"

the twenty-first century sounds a similar call. Jackson calls for rethinking repair as an "exercise in broken world thinking."[89] He wonders "what happens when we take erosion, breakdown, and decay, rather than novelty, growth, and progress, as our starting points in thinking through the nature, use, and effects of information technology and new media."[90] Whereas Halberstam urges readers to consider unbuilding the inequitable, precarious world that capital built, Jackson aims to counterpoise "broken world thinking" with ideas central to nineteenth-century frontier thinking: novelty, development with no end, and the dream-myth of progress.

To wit, across the eighteenth and nineteenth centuries, during a time of unparalleled British and continental industrialization and imperialism, and throughout the so-called age of improvement, there already existed a line of thought on par with Jackson's twenty-first century "broken world thinking." The material sublime, as an iteration of the Romantic sublime, arrives by way of one of Romanticism's most prestigious and promiscuous aesthetic categories. This offshoot of the Romantic sublime advances nuanced notions of repair that do not necessarily propagate myths of progress nor simply reaffirm conventional wisdom. As Keats suggests, an opportunity confronts us in the routine example of the sunset, "from something of material sublime." From it we might daily take inspiration, not to enact linear progress, with flag "unfurld" assuming the posture of a conqueror, but as a dreamer alive in a tremulous, jostling world within which we all collectively reside, and where there is also a light, a potential, and an abiding responsibility in never being "settled."

[89] Steven J. Jackson, "Rethinking Repair," in *Media Technologies: Essays on Communication, Materiality, and Society*, eds. Tarleton Gillespie, Pablo J. Boczkowski, and Kirsten A. Foot (Oxford: Oxford University Press, 2014), 221.
[90] Jackson, "Rethinking Repair," 221.

CHAPTER THREE

Lyres, Levers, Boats, and Steam

Shelleyan Technologies of Sublime Correspondence

Nature's vast frame, the web of human things,
Birth and the grave, that are not as they were.

—Shelley, *Alastor; or, The Spirit of Solitude*, lines 719–29

Like a child from the womb, like a ghost from the tomb,
I arise, and unbuild it again.

—Shelley, "The Cloud," lines 83–4

Percy Shelley correlates birth and death with models of technological making
and undoing in the above lines from *Alastor* and "The Cloud." Yet at the
same time, and as readers might expect from a Romantic poet, here he also
yokes birth and death to models of natural growth and decline. The lines
from *Alastor* doubly circumscribe humanity: first within "Nature's vast frame,"
and then again within an organically styled technics spanning the "web of
human things." Vast spaces of nature exist in league with sprawling networks
of fabricated objects, each underpinning the boundaries of human life ("Birth
and the grave") and change (rendering nothing "as they were"). Humanity is
not simply subject to overwhelming forces of nature but also to unpredictable
dynamics of human culture, to myriad "human things" inclusive of our fabricated objects and artistic creations.

Operating in similar spirit, the second set of lines from "The Cloud"
naturalizes humankind's simultaneous technological and natural entanglements: the cloud as would-be child of nature and the cloud as would-be ghost

103

The Romantic Sublime and Representations of Technology

of culture together become the cloud as future unbuilder. While each poem gestures toward the genesis, terminus, and continuance of human life, these cycles are haunted by irrevocable change and loss attributed to humanity's technological contingency, with Shelley's "ghost from the tomb" resonant with "human things ... that are not as they were." For Shelley, cultural artifacts like the tomb exist within a wide arena of made objects, where even the most powerful invention commemorates our limitedness and limitations (our undoings).[1] Shelleyan technologies, then, connote rousing creative agencies as well as dispiriting, delimiting, or even dangerous ones. In essence, the poet's figurations of technology echo sublime aestheticizations of the natural world, where thrilling yet daunting accounts of Nature challenge the autonomy of human agency. Of note is how Shelley recalibrates the notoriously fraught aesthetic category of the sublime. Channeling the ambivalent logic long home to sublime ecological aesthetics, Shelleyan renditions of technological agency position poetry within a continuum of auspicious inventions all shaded by uncertain change and unintended consequences.[2]

The vexed discourse of the sublime becomes a resource for Shelley, allowing him to showcase the transformative promise and peril he attributes to machinery and poetry alike. Moreover, sublime ecology and technology intermingle in Shelley, each heralding what we may never fully understand but what indeed demarcates the conditions of everyday life and verbal art, and perhaps most significantly for Shelley, what might enable or render impossible degrees of human communication, communion, and control. By putting into

---

[1] This ambivalent account of technology marks a departure from more techno-utopian renderings exhibited in early works such as *Queen Mab*. Discussing Shelley's youthful optimism toward, quite literally, engineering change, Alan Bewell notes that while "An anti-imperialist on one level, Shelley nevertheless shares with the promoters of empire the 'techno-utopian' belief that European science should contribute to the transformation of global environments" (213). Bewell also detects what I argue comprise the seeds of a poetics of ecological and technological entanglement, anticipating contemporary thought suggesting a fundamental link between social and ecological justice: "Shelley shared with many nineteenth-century imperialists the idea that the world's geographies were epiphenomena that could be radically transformed through education, technology, and political change. Unlike them, however, he also recognized that such changes would be ineffectual if they increased, rather than decreased, social inequalities" (241). See Bewell, "Percy Bysshe Shelley and Revolutionary Climatology," in *Romanticism and Colonial Disease*, 205–41.

[2] As we saw in the Introduction to this book, Sianne Ngai likewise acknowledges how "the sublime is still western philosophy's most prestigious example of an aesthetic category that derives its specificity from mixed or conflicting feelings." Distinct from performative acts of judgement built into the aesthetic of the *merely interesting*, as Ngai calls it, where "[j]udging something interesting is often a first step in *actually making it so*," the "reverse" is true "for [the] material sublime." In the case of the material sublime "we don't make it sublime via judgement but the judgement reflects sublime being." Jasper and Ngai, "Our Aesthetic Categories: An Interview with Sianne Ngai."

Lyres, Levers, Boats, and Steam

dialogue Shelley's oft-remarked lyres from *The Defence of Poetry* (1821) and *Ode to the West Wind* (1819) with various technologies chronicled in his letters and verse epistle *Letter to Maria Gisborne* (1820), it becomes clear that Shelley ascribes sublimity to inventions deemed especially generative, destructive, or inescapably ubiquitous. Poetry, dread engines, even teacups become sublime. Shelley's sublime figurations of musical instruments, marvelous machinery, and domestic objects at once foreground great transformative potential as well as acutely diminished agency.[3] Shelley ascribes sublimity to a range of cultural artifacts as if to negotiate unavoidable ecological and technological circum-scriptions. Technological contingency, like a necessary ecological contingency, both extends and curtails human agency, a point that Shelley's writing often grants if not laments. It follows that Shelley places poetry and technology within a dynamic and complex social ecology, pointing the way not to naïve utopia but to sublime paradox, to an ironically fragile yet powerfully intimate socioecological field of sublime technological entanglement.[4]

We find evidence of such inexorable entanglements in the fifth and final stanza of *Ode to the West Wind*, particularly where Shelley likens the poet to a lyre—to a responsive instrument made vocal by environmental force and ecological contingency. Lines of pleading verse beg autumnal blasts to "Drive [the poet's] dead thoughts over the universe / Like withered leaves to quicken a new birth ... Be through [the poet's] lips to unawakened Earth / the trumpet of a prophecy!"[5] While Shelley is renowned for evoking the

---

[3] My analysis diverges from Timothy Morton's largely damning assessment of Shelley's intertwined ecological and technological aesthetics, particularly insofar as Morton suggests that "Shelley is forever thinking of planetary and solar disaster. He favors the global over the local in a way that would scandalize the typical Romantic ecocritic. For this very reason his writing seems apt for an era of global warming. The poetry performs aesthetically what ecological damage and global positioning technology perform in the real, swallowing horizons and worlds" (para. 12). Alternatively, my reading of Shelley's technological aesthetics charts how Shelley marshals the discourse of the sublime to figure technologies as emblematic of our larger, celestial, even cosmic aims, while simultaneously also evoking proximate loss and the inevitable costs bound up with local and contingent being. See Morton, "Romantic Disaster Ecology: Blake, Shelley, Wordsworth," *Romantic Circles Praxis Volume: Romanticism and Disaster*, eds. Jacques Khalip and David Collings (2012), paras. 1–32, https://romantic-circles.org/praxis/disaster/HTML/praxis.2012.morton.html.

[4] Here I refer to Karen Barad's account of entanglement, where she contends that "To be entangled is not simply to be intertwined with another, as in the joining of separate entities, but to lack an independent, self-contained existence. Existence is not an individual affair ... individuals emerge through and as part of their entangled intra-relating" (ix). See Barad, *Meeting the Universe Halfway: Quantum Physics and the Entanglement of Matter and Meaning* (Durham, NC: Duke University Press, 2007).

[5] Percy Bysshe Shelley, *Ode to the West Wind*, in *The Poems of Shelley, Volume 3: 1819–1820*, eds. Jack Donovan, Cian Duffy, Kelvin Everest, and Michael Rossington (London: Longman, 2011), 211–12, lines 63–4, 68–9.

The Romantic Sublime and Representations of Technology

lyre "in various contexts as a figure for his persuasion that inspiration originates in a power independent of the mind," critics have yet to acknowledge the assortment of sublime inventions and devices he enlists to represent poiesis.[6] Shelley's mobilizing tools, mechanical objects, and built environments accrue great tropological power as creations that could become creators. In this capacity, Shelley's sublime technologies mirror the sublime poetry of the ancient Longinian tradition, wherein literary works were celebrated and deemed sublime for their inspirational charge and the degree to which they were deemed capable of moving contemporary readers or future audiences.[7] In like fashion, Shelley's more aspirational writing showcases engines of sublime genesis figured analogously to a sublime poetry capable of stunning if not lasting change. This is especially true for instruments and technological systems seemingly capable of generating renewed community or alternate models of sociality.[8] Resonating with the English radical tradition of the 1790s wherein the likes of Thomas Paine transformed the lever into a galvanizing symbol of political potential, and the British abolition movement that dubbed antislavery crusader Thomas Clarkson the "moral steam-engine," Shelleyan lyres, levers, and larger technologies of conveyance such as sailboats and steamships become agents of change in their own right. Pregnant with rejuvenating energies not unlike the wind, they too might quicken Shelley's thoughts to "new birth." Machines as well as nature can move the poet. Yet just as crucially, sublime machines and sublime nature betray the limits of human license, poetic liberty, and technological agency such that they become topoi wherein

---

[6] Headnote to *Ode to the West Wind*, in *The Poems of Shelley, Volume 3: 1819–1820*, 211.

[7] See Longinus, *On the Sublime*, in *The Loeb Classical Library*, 2nd ed. (Cambridge, MA and London: Harvard University Press, 1995), 159–307. See also Morton's recent assessment of the long history of sublime objects and artifacts, where he reminds us how, at its core, the "Longinian sublime is about the physical intrusion of an alien presence … it's a matter of contact with an alien presence" (220–1). In this sense the Longinian sublime is profoundly ecological in its thinking because it assumes an essential spatial relationality and contingency between humanity and nonhuman others and because it foregrounds human encounters with various agentive alterities that humanity can neither master nor assimilate. Morton, "Sublime Objects," *Speculations II* (2011): 207–27.

[8] It is important to bear in mind that, as Barbara T. Allen points out, "romantic responses to industrialization were by no means universally hostile. William Godwin, for example, always suspicious of the uneducated masses, looked to machine labor to free the working classes from the drudgery which prevented their reading and meditation. In *Enquiry Concerning Political Justice* he wrote that the inventions of mills, weaving machines, and steam engines may 'alarm the laboring part of the community' and produce 'temporary distress,' but such inventions will ultimately benefit 'the most important interests of the multitude' … Robert Owen, renowned for his creation of model industrial communities, also believed that if properly managed, machines could facilitate the emergence of a utopian society'" (53). See Allen, "Poetry and Machinery in Shelley's 'Letter to Maria Gisborne,'" *Nineteenth Century Studies* 2 (1988): 53–61.

Lyres, Levers, Boats, and Steam

Shelley confronts his own fragility. For Shelley, regenerative technological and ecological forces pivot around the politics of loss.

Plagued as he was by the loss of children and a lack of readers, it should come as no surprise that Shelley would champion reanimating impulses or entertain fantasies of a people or a poetry reborn. "Hope" the poet writes, "is a solemn duty which we owe alike to ourselves & to the world—a worship to the spirit of good within, which requires before it sends that inspiration forth, which impresses its likeness upon all that it creates, devoted & disinterested homage."[9] Daring to hope in the aftermath of the 1819 Peterloo massacre that mowed down his fellow Englishmen assembled in peaceful protest, and after the death of his daughter Clara (September 1818) and son William (June 1819), Shelley writes in exile in Pisa and other Italian locales, often casting technologies as sublime and otherworldly arbiters of poetic life and death. Such is the case for the acclaimed *Ode to the West Wind*, which enlists the bittersweet promise of an externally activated lyre, where a lone instrument responds to autumn's somber yet cyclical winds mirroring an isolated poet driven by death-in-life, animated by the many faces of death that Shelley attempts to work through—that of his children, distant countrymen, and unread verse.[10] As we shall see, a painful mixture of loss, failure, and estrangement presses Shelley to imagine community beyond human terms.

The *Ode*'s lyre *qua* poet prefigures another Shelleyan wind harp-turned-human, one described in greater detail within the pages of his poetic manifesto, *A Defence of Poetry*. Shelley's authoritative discussion of poetics aestheticizes human beings in not-quite-mechanistic terms but nearly so, coloring humanity and perhaps other sentient beings with shades of necessity tempered with spirituality.[11] Attuned to external and internal impressions, each of us—as the equivalent of some incarnate instrument—cannot help but produce polyphonic

---

[9] Shelley to Maria Gisborne, 13 or 14 October 1819, in *The Letters of Percy Bysshe Shelley, Volume II: Shelley in Italy*, ed. Frederick L. Jones (Oxford: Oxford University Press, 1964), 125.

[10] In a letter to Thomas Love Peacock written 12 July 1820, Shelley addresses his scant readership and negative reviews: "I am told that the magazines, etc., blaspheme me at a great rate. I wonder why I write verses, for nobody reads them. It is a kind of disorder, for which the regular practitioners prescribe what is called a torrent of abuse" (213). Shelley to Thomas Love Peacock, 12 July 1820, in *The Letters of Percy Bysshe Shelley, Volume II: Shelley in Italy*, 213.

[11] Morton goes so far as to suggest that the "harp image evokes the idea that human beings in some sense *are* their environment," and notes how Shelley's lyre "revises a strong and varied tradition of imagining people as fleshly instruments both in Pythagorean and Neoplatonic philosophy and in Christian liturgy and poetry, which accounts for the image's spiritual resonance" (187, 186). Morton, "Nature and Culture," in *The Cambridge Companion to Shelley*, ed. Timothy Morton (Cambridge: Cambridge University Press, 2006), 185–207.

The Romantic Sublime and Representations of Technology

sound. In the following lines, our inherent making eclipses that of melody, necessarily moving into sublime harmony:

> Man is an instrument over which a series of external and internal impressions are driven, like the alternations of an ever-changing wind over an Æolian lyre, which move it by their motion to ever-changing melody. But there is a principle within the human being, and perhaps within all sentient beings, which acts otherwise than in the lyre, and produces not melody alone, but harmony, by an internal adjustment of the sounds or motions thus excited to the impressions which excite them.[12]

While one might safely assume that Shelley would wed poetic expression to the creation of sound, these words in fact mount a much larger claim. By this logic, to make is to sound. For Shelley, all human making necessarily entails multiplicitous sounding. In this broad account of sound's integral place within our movements and our makings, it is not simply sound or even one lone song that the many soundings of our makings produce. Here sounds and songs seem continuously to breed companions and are thus never actually alone or in exile from one another. Shelleyan sounds move and mark off together as if to resemble the collaboration of a chorus as sounding community. In the *Defence*, Shelley's emblem for the poet as maker (*homo faber*) is first instrumental, mechanical, and monophonically melodic. Then Shelley begins to pick and choose what elements belong more exclusively to the organic sentient being which "produces not melody alone." Shelley builds collectivity into the sentient being by way of song and sound. As harbingers of numerous "sounds or motions," we adjust internally, respond excitedly, and in kind, multiply, harmoniously together. Even singly, in Shelley's view, it seems impossible to sing a melody alone. And perhaps surprisingly, Shelley's prose next produces a child: "*as the lyre trembles and sounds after the wind has died away, so the child seeks, by prolonging in its voice and motions the duration of the effect*, to prolong also a consciousness of the cause. In relation to the objects which delight a child, these expressions are, what Poetry is to higher objects" (emphasis added).[13] The inspiring wind trembles the lyre into attenuating sound as the child prolongs its voice, its motions, hoping to stay the company of expression that engendered delight for as long as humanly possible. Shelley's child, like the lyre, is ostensibly alone, but ever-poised to produce a heavenly, nearly godlike harmony that announces our higher, potential condition: that of being in sublime accompaniment—with others and the external world. Sublime being, for Shelley, entails not being alone, but being necessarily together, necessarily

---

[12] Shelley, *A Defence of Poetry*, 511.
[13] Shelley, *A Defence of Poetry*, 511.

Lyres, Levers, Boats, and Steam

entangled. Notably, Shelley's model of sublime entanglement cuts against overblown, grandiose narratives of sublime individuation famously marked by Keats as the "egotistical sublime" wherein a poet seemingly "stands alone."[14]

While the Aeolian harp's receptive and responsive posture emphasizes a more or less ubiquitous collaboration and contingency, Archimedes's lever assumes the sublime charge of transformative lightning. Jocelyn Holland's recent study of the lever's centrality to eighteenth- and nineteenth-century thought, marks an "historical tendency to understand certain aspects of being human, such as making judgments, thinking, or organizing concepts, in terms of the activity of the lever."[15] Shelley, for one, appended the ancient Greek mathematician's aphoristic saying, "Give me a place to stand, and I will move the earth," to some of his most notorious works. Serving as paratext for *Queen Mab; A Philosophical Poem; With Notes* (1813) and *Laon and Cythna; or, The Revolution of the Golden City* (1817), the epigraph first foregrounds the long poem that helped to establish Shelley's infamy and utopic leanings, and then frames an even longer poem that would cement the poet's scandalous reputation and signature radical optimism. The emboldened wager at the heart of "Give me somewhere to stand, and I will move the earth" has everything to do with the transformative potential of the lever, but gives no mention of that tool, grants no explicit credit to the sublime power of the lever itself. The latent presence of Archimedes's lever in Shelley tacitly confirms conventional wisdom surrounding Romantic-era renderings—or better, erasures—of the requisite technological artifact: human subjectivity and the natural world loom large; the pivotal instrument recedes. In this sense, Archimedes's syntax models a structuring logic and wider cultural grammar—the word *lever* never appears, yet this unvoiced mechanism is just as crucial as earth or humanity in effecting even a modicum of change. The absent presence of the lever recalls the lyre that is left behind as Shelley turns to the figure of the child to discuss poets and poetics and whatever external impressions might drive the child to delight. The lever, like the lyre, becomes the shadow figure that makes possible Archimedes's resulting figurations of human being and earthly movement, of revolution and change. *With* lyre and lever, so goes the fate of humanity.

Paradoxically, to ignore the presence of the lyre or lever is to distance humanity from the environment. We lose a fundamental bridge that binds external world to sentient subject. This is the function of the Romantic instrument and Romantic machine: it ushers forth aesthetic communion which in turn makes room for making sound and sense for the making of poetry. Admittedly, the very phrase "Romantic machine" might ring oxymoronic if not blasphemous. This reaction

---

[14] John Keats, "Letter to Richard Woodhouse, 27 October 1818," in *Keats's Poetry and Prose*, 295.

[15] Holland, *The Lever as Instrument of Reason*, 14.

The Romantic Sublime and Representations of Technology

stems in part from the primacy placed on Romanticism's pre-Marxist critiques of industry and commerce that understand technology more or less monolithically—as an alienating force estranging humankind from the natural world. The phrase is also haunted by the pervading idea that Romantic organicism (often betokened by a fungible, mutable, and sensitive plant) replaced Enlightenment models of a mechanistically determinist, teleologically bound universe (epitomized by Newton's world machine or the clockwork cosmos). As a result, strict Marxist or organicist readings of Romantic literature risk overlooking key roles played by devices in the very narratives they seek to embrace and disseminate. Case in point, by adopting Archimedes's words early on Shelley already harnesses the storied scientist's "enthusiasm for the power of the lever, a trope frequently used by radicals ... to link mechanical forces with revolutionary actions."[16] As Shelley's twice-deployed epigraph suggests, Romantic technologies underwrite related revolutionary potencies of earthly and human being.

Operating in similar spirit to the technē that is poetry, whether here receding to the background or elsewhere appearing at the fore, machines and everyday technologies underpin Shelleyan notions of collective, co-determining action, even radical change. Technological indebtedness exists at the core of anthropogenic making. As James Chandler notes, Shelley "invokes the sense of instrumentality implicit in the Romantic topos of the Aeollan harp ... [to manifest a] representation of mutual making."[17] Furthermore, for Shelley the radical potential of such mutual making comes at a cost, a cost that accrues regardless of whether or not we lionize the lyre or disavow the lever upon which our making depends. Shelley renders this cost legible by aestheticizing technological and poetical agency within an especially intimate rendition of sublime discourse, one that pushes back against "the way in which sublime Nature, objectified as wilderness, is set up to loom around, beyond and behind human activity like a distant mountain range."[18] As Timothy Morton suggests, traditionally "reified sublimity passes too quickly over the distressing intimacy ... of human and nonhuman interaction;" in contrast, Shelley foregrounds humanity's close interaction with, and at times, resemblance to the technological milieu, countervailing clichéd and reductive iterations of sublime, objectified nature that risk divorcing humanity from technology.[19] Poets become wind-driven lyres that morph into singing children. Sublime revolutions entail earth and levers—not humanity alone.

---

[16] Radical enlightenment thinkers such as Thomas Paine popularized rhetorical links between the work of mechanical forces and the work of revolutionary politics. See Fraistat and Reiman, *Shelley's Poetry and Prose*, 16, n. 3.

[17] James Chandler, *England in 1819: The Politics of Literary Culture and the Case of Romantic Historicism* (Chicago and London: University of Chicago Press, 1998), 544–5.

[18] Morton, "Romantic Disaster Ecology," para. 26.

[19] Morton, "Romantic Disaster Ecology," para. 26.

Lyres, Levers, Boats, and Steam

Shelley's longstanding penchant for making boats out of leaves of paper emblematizes how the poet links sublime figurations of tools, machines, and built environments to poetic process. As close acquaintances knew, Shelley made a habit of building paper boats, alighting them upon whatever body of water was close at hand. Shelley records this very tick in the teasing verse epistle *Letter to Maria Gisborne*. "[F]or," the poet explains, "I / Yield to the impulse of an infancy / Outlasting manhood—I have made to float / A rude idealism of a paper boat: / A hollow screw with cogs—Henry will know / The thing I mean and laugh at me—if so / He fears not I should do more mischief."[20] The poem's layered metaphoricity conjoins motile metal parts with the symbolic potency of sublime poetry borne aloft *by* and *as* sea craft. Folds of paper metonymically manifest turns of verse in the same spirit as the turn of the screw, cog, or wheel might. Here and elsewhere, Shelley's boats double for poetic mechanisms of conveyance, cradling thought and propelling it onward, outward, and aloft on currents of air or cresting waves.[21] Strikingly in this case, the boat's visionary agency playfully encompasses the more ordinary promise of a hollow screw and cogs. Humble mechanical parts and impromptu paper boats join poetic lines in being vehicles of sublime imagination.

While Shelley's preoccupation with boats and sailing is much remarked, his fervor for the modern steamboat is less so, and to date has rarely been studied in relation to Shelleyan poetics or aesthetics. Yet during the latter part of what Stuart Curran taught us to understand as Shelley's *annus mirabilis* of 1819 and throughout much of 1820 (the year that would yield his celebrated *Prometheus Unbound* volume), the steamboat appears again and again in Shelley's writings.[22] The steamer, combined with the process of its making, becomes a controlling metaphor for Shelley. The ambivalent figure of the ship accrues a representational value capacious enough to account for any

---

[20] Shelley, *Letter to Maria Gisborne*, in *The Poems of Shelley, Volume 3: 1819–1820*, 425–61, lines 72, 72–8. Hereafter citations are noted in-text by line number.

[21] D. J. Hughes notes that in Shelley, the "boat is the vehicle or container of the individual mind or consciousness," with the "boat [being] imitative of thought ... and the boat [working] as a technical device to stir the poem to movement, [which can] combine to inaugurate ... great visions." Hughes, "Potentiality in Prometheus Unbound," in *Shelley's Poetry and Prose*, eds. Neil Fraistat and Donald H. Reiman, 1st ed. (New York: W. W. Norton & Co., 1977), 607. More recently, Michael Demson traces how in Shelley, the "boat ... becomes a 'bearer of knowledge' ... 'a vehicle for conveyance of the disembodied spirit' ... [as well as] 'a vehicle of Shelleyan love.'" See Demson, "Percy Shelley's Radical Agrarian Politics," *Romanticism* 16, no. 3 (2010): 82. See also, Neville Rogers, *Shelley at Work: A Critical Inquiry* (Oxford: Clarendon Press, 1956), 91–105; Mandy Swann, "Shelley's Utopian Seascapes," *Studies in Romanticism* 52, no. 3 (Fall 2013): 389–414.

[22] Stuart Curran, *Shelley's Annus Mirabilis: The Maturing of An Epic Vision* (Pasadena, CA: Huntington Library Press, 1975).

111

The Romantic Sublime and Representations of Technology

recuperative or disruptive impulses alike that might inform the making of life and poetry, home and community, dialogue and descant. In 1819 Shelley financially backed the production of a steamboat to the tune of £250–£350.[23] The ship was to be built by Henry Reveley, an aspiring nautical engineer and son of Maria Gisborne, one of Shelley's dear friends. The poet met Maria Gisborne and her second husband, John, the previous year, with Shelley becoming especially fond of Maria Gisborne, partly because of her links to Mary Shelley's past and partly out of admiration for her special cast of mind.[24] Indicative of such bonhomie, in exchange for Shelley contributing funds to Henry's project, Maria Gisborne offered him Spanish lessons, and in letters between the two Shelley compares the task of reading and thinking in Spanish without her to undertaking perilous and lonesome seafaring expeditions:

> Madonna
>   I have been lately voyaging in a sea without my pilot, & although my sail has often been torn, my boat become leaky, & the log lost, I have yet sailed in a kind of way from island to island, some of craggy & mountainous magnificence, some clothed with moss & flowers … some barren deserts.—*I have been reading Calderon without you.*[25]

In Shelley skiff and pinnace typically mark the intellectual spirit of poetry, the imaginative power of language, and visionary thought, in addition to representing the poet himself. But here the Shelleyan sailboat is acutely alone, pilotless, "torn," "leaky," "lost"—and yet the poet asserts that he nonetheless "sailed in a kind of way," suggesting that he and his imagination rudder on, albeit wrongly, dispiritedly, without the guiding hand of close intellectual support or any pervading sense of sublime accompaniment.[26] Indeed, it is precisely this sense of sublime accompaniment that the steamer promises.

Reveley's incipient steamboat brought much-needed levity and artistic inspiration to an anxious and alienated Shelley. The modern vessel features

---

[23] Headnote to *Letter to Maria Gisborne*, in *The Poems of Shelley*, 430.

[24] Maria Gisborne cared for Mary Shelley when her birthmother, Mary Wollstonecraft Godwin, died in childbirth. Mary Shelley's father, William Godwin, once Percy Shelley's prime political inspiration, proposed to Maria Gisborne but she demurred, wedding instead John Gisborne, an English merchant.

[25] Shelley to Maria Gisborne, 16 November 1819, in *The Letters of Percy Bysshe Shelley, Volume II: Shelley in Italy*, 154 (original emphasis).

[26] On the trope of poets being piloted by likewise able minds, see Michael O'Neill's discussion of *Adonais* which recalls Dante being "piloted first by Virgil (in the *Inferno* and the *Purgatorio*) and then by Beatrice, reversing roles and serving as the fit reader's guide." See O'Neill, "'The Mind Which Feeds This Verse': Shelley," in *Romanticism and the Self-Conscious Poem* (Oxford: Oxford University Press, 1997), 129.

Lyres, Levers, Boats, and Steam

in Shelley's pages as a figure for poiesis understood broadly, with metalwork and castings by turns representing the materialization of the earth and the inception of sentient beings, in addition to mercurial outpourings of the written word. Serving as a technological counterpart to the Romantic lyric's multivalent nightingale, Shelley's steamer at times represents poetry, the poet, or the modern invention itself, separately or all at once. For example, in one of Shelley's epistolary exchanges with Reveley, the ship is first the product of a sublime, godlike process of poiesis, only later to become an ethereal voyager or ersatz poet traversing high seas resembling sublime heavens. First Reveley informs Shelley of the casting process that molded two key parts of the ship: steam cylinder and air pump. Knowingly or not, the engineer's letter leans heavily upon the genre conventions of the celestial and sublime creation story. A momentous occasion—a harnessing of swift Promethean fires coupled with "the perfection of the furnace" bring metal "into its proper form":

> The event is now past—both the steam cylinder and air-pump were cast at three this afternoon. ... The fire was lighted in the furnace at nine, and in three hours the metal was fused. At three o'clock it was ready to cast, the fusion being remarkably rapid, owing to the perfection of the furnace. The metal was also heated to an extreme degree, boiling with fury, and seeming to dance with the pleasure of running into its proper form. The plug was struck, and a massy stream of a bluish dazzling whiteness filled the moulds in the twinkling of a shooting star. ... I expect them to be perfect.[27]

Stringing together a sequence of events occurring in passive voice (fire was lighted, metal was fused, the plug was struck), the letter all but writes out the role of the engineer as human laborer. Either the casting process assumes an air of quasi-divine predestination, or it is as if metal itself desired to bend to Reveley's will, acting somehow as an agent in its own right. Only after chronicling a creation event now past, does Reveley include the self-referential pronoun "I," recalling divine fiat. The engineer's late use of the subjective pronoun suggests divinely inspired powers of utterance and underwrites the quasi-divine judgement of Reveley's works and words, which here redundantly pronounce perfection upon a sublime creation formed by a faultless creator. Far from narrating a fragile or intimate story of technological entanglement and sublime contingency, Reveley instead fashions himself as a solitary and sublime creator, and so reactivates the individuating logic of the egotistical sublime.

---

[27] Henry Reveley to Shelley, 17 November 1819, in *The Letters of Percy Bysshe Shelley, Volume II: Shelley in Italy*, 157–8, n. 3.

The Romantic Sublime and Representations of Technology

Shelley takes the engineer's creationist rhetoric and runs with it, styling him a divine maker bringing the world swiftly into being as if by fiat. The poet's prose transforms Reveley into a smiling creator god, pleased and made proud by the works he's forged. Shelley writes:

> Your volcanic description of the birth of the Cylinder is very character-istic of you & of it. One might imagine God when he made the earth, & saw the granite mountains & flinty promontories flow into their craggy forms, & the splendor of their fusion filling millions of miles of the void space, like the tail of a comet, so looking, & so delighting in his work. God sees his machine spinning round the sun & delights in its success, ... Your boat will be to the Ocean of Water what the earth is to the Ocean of Æther—a prosperous & swift voyager.—
>
> When shall we see you all? *You* not I suppose until your boat is ready to sail, & then, if not before I must of course come to Livorno.—Our plans for the winter are yet scarcely defined—they tend towards our spending February & March at Pisa where our communication will not be so distant, or so epistolary—Charles [Clairmont] left us a week ago, not without many lamentations as all true lovers pay on such occasions. He is to write me an account of the Trieste Steam Boat which I will transmit to you— ...
>
> Most affectionately yours
P B S[28]

Each letter's rendering of man and metal exposes a tension at play within the genres of monotheistic and classical creation stories. Such genesis narra-tives turn upon a central dyad consisting of a divine maker and the divinely made, leaving Reveley and Shelley little room for the figure of the common inventor understood as mortal being and necessary collaborator. Equivo-cating between collapsing humankind into a creator god or swapping the future of humanity for the trajectory of a ship, the epistle either suggests that the engineer assumes the seat of a godhead or the human hand disap-pears altogether. Playfully drawing on familiar religious tropes and classical associations, Shelley conjures images of a lone creator God newly delighting in the company of his spinning machine, with its retinue of freshly molded earth and stars. In this sense, Reveley recalls the lyre that would become a child, both of whom respond to a delightful accompaniment they find in an external material world that is otherwise unpeopled. But instead of making sonic harmonies on earth, Shelley envisages something all the more sublime

---

[28] Shelley to Henry Reveley, 17 November 1819, in *The Letters of Percy Bysshe Shelley, Volume II: Shelley in Italy*, 157–8, n. 3.

Lyres, Levers, Boats, and Steam

for Reveley: the godly engineer fashions Earth itself, populates vast celestial spaces with the harmonious spheres of the cosmos.[29] The yet-unformed steamboat assumes the place of humankind, or better, displaces humanity given that it is the boat, not any sailor or thinker, which will take shape as "a prosperous & swift voyager." If Archimedes's old adage only ever implies a lever, in these letters Shelley's technological aesthetics pitch humankind offstage—out of reach; only after Shelley concludes his fanciful response to Reveley's description of the "birth of the Cylinder" does the poet return to the pressing absence of distant friends. The overblown dualisms of Promethean Romanticism and reductive dyads of egotistical sublime aesthetics can disavow but cannot dissolve the larger and more fragile communities of interlocked actors from which they emerge.

Reveley's status as sublime creator is echoed first in the steamship's personified role as sole voyager and then again in Shelley's account of himself as an isolated poet desperate for comradery.[30] Henry as lone creator, steamship as sole voyager, Shelley as sequestered thinker: each figure differs in type but not kind, amounting to a variation on the theme of solitary being and the extent to which invented words or things exacerbate or ameliorate loneliness. On the heels of a singular engineer comes an isolated planet, next a secluded boat—all vessels seem afloat in an abyss, orbiting and transiting alone, metonymically standing in for a poet estranged and writing in exile. And so, the letter shifts from envisioning a "boat [that] will be to the Ocean of Water what the earth is to the Ocean of Æther" to a poignant disclosure of the poet's pronounced aching for community. Plying between subjects old and new, Shelley's dispatch propels headlong from the topic of remote seafaring to that of shared longing and back again. Amounting to a call-and-response-dialogue-turned monologue, each pang of lonesomeness is answered by a pivot to the ship, to a swift voyager able to collapse agonizing distance: "When shall we see you all? *You* not I suppose until your boat is ready to sail, & then, if not before I must of course come to Livorno.—Our plans for the winter are yet scarcely defined." Shelley desires to be proximate, accessible, to be where "communication will not be so distant, or so epistolary."

---

[29] As Yasmin Solomonescu suggests, for Shelley harmonies and acoustic rhythms "'echo ... the eternal music,' [where t]he latter phrase alludes to the half-mystical, half-mathematical cosmology of the pre-Socratic philosopher Pythagoras, who held that the heavenly bodies moved according to the same mathematical ratios that created musical concordances and in so moving produced a heavenly music, or what his followers called *harmonia mundi*, the universal harmony." Solomonescu, "Percy Shelley's Revolutionary Periods," *ELH* 83, no. 4 (2016): 1107.

[30] For an influential assessment of how dominant renditions of the Romantic sublime informed thinking about the concept of the individual or disparate unit, see Ferguson, *Solitude and the Sublime.*

The Romantic Sublime and Representations of Technology

And after noting the elegiac lament "all true lovers pay" upon parting, the epistle returns again to the question concerning technology, bookending an appeal to the fleeting togetherness of kindred beings by swerving back to the figure of the steamer that by this point serves as more than a source of common interest shared between friends, now bearing as it does the promise of more intimate community and proximate communication.[31] Shelley's letter deploys intersecting models of sublime technological aesthetics, oscillating between narratives of spectacularly individuated agency and astonishingly vulnerable contingency. The requisite ambivalence of Shelleyan technology tethers fantasies of sublime solitude to daunting realities of lived material and social relations.

Poetry and machinery might embolden and empower but cannot erase what are in essence the more sublime limits of language and life. Whereas Shelley's steamboat brings with it new communities of life—foregrounding conversations, reunions, and places to come, it nonetheless cannot be divorced from loss and privation. On the one hand, Shelley's optimistic view of the steamer anticipates Victorian-era enthusiasm for the steamship, wherein "[s]team … facilitat[ed] a vision of how the future might differ from the disappointing present."[32] Later Romantic-era treatments of the steamboat document the emergence of this trend, which can be traced back not just to Shelley but also to poems by the likes of William Wordsworth and Joanna Baillie. "Steamboats, Viaducts, and Railways" (c. 1833) fittingly assumes the Italianate sonnet form traditionally associated with Petrarchan love poetry as Wordsworth ascribes a hopeful, cheerful aesthetic to the steamer and related symbols of modern transport.[33] In this work Wordsworth—a poet commonly cited as proof of a Romantic resistance to the technological given his early opposition of the rail system—here devotes the closing sestet of his love sonnet to a technological sublime wherein Nature embraces the steamer:

> In spite of all that beauty may disown
> In your harsh features, Nature doth embrace
> Her lawful offspring in Man's art; and Time,
> Pleased with your triumphs o'er his brother Space,

---

[31] Students of the British abolition movement would find progressive or utopian figurations of the steamship unsurprising. As previously alluded to, Thomas Clarkson was famously named the "Moral Steam-Engine" after publishing *An essay on the impolicy of the African slave trade* in 1788. See May, "Coleridge's Slave Trade Lecture," 425–9.

[32] J. P. Parry, "Steam Power and British Influence in Baghdad, 1820–1860," *The Historical Journal* 56, no. 1 (2013): 172.

[33] William Wordsworth, "Steamboats, Viaducts, and Railways," in *The Poetical Works of William Wordsworth*, vol. 7, ed. William Knight (London and New York: Macmillan, 1896), 389–90. References cited in-text by line number.

Lyres, Levers, Boats, and Steam

Accepts from your bold hands a proffered crown
Of hope, and smiles on you with cheer sublime. (lines 9–14)

Even more, Joanna Baillie's "Address to a Steam Vessel" (1840) resembles Shelley's account of steamship sublimity as, like Shelley, Baillie in this poem also considers technological agency relative to agencies of humanity and nature.[34] Baillie's steamer appears to be an independent actor, a "Rover at will on river, lake, and sea" (line 92). Yet at the same time, it is celebrated as the "Offspring of Watt, that philosophic sage ... whose fame / Shall still be linked with Davy's splendid name!" (lines 94, 97–8). Intriguingly, for Baillie, the ship numbers as one among many willed agents to whom humanity is indebted: she marks not just "whate'er we owe to thee [the steamer]" but also to Watt and Davy, described here as "those to whom men owe high meed of thanks / For genius usefully employed" (lines 91, 96–7). And yet, a Shelleyan sublime tension sounds across Baillie's closing lines, as she strives to account for the conflicted feelings prompted by the steam vessel. Baillie first evokes the "fleeting shadows of a feverish dream," then underscores a "gaze" made "fitful," "with adverse humours teased" out by the presence of the ship, leaving the poet "Half sad, half proud, half angry, and half pleased" (lines 130–2).

Mary Godwin Shelley confirms that her husband linked Henry's project to visions of a better tomorrow, noting his "fervent interest in the undertaking, for its own sake" distinct from any motive of economic reward.[35] In this spirit Shelley evokes the steamboat in "vital[ly] metaphorical" ways, grafting it to generative agencies of word and myth—to language and narratives that might likewise bring new futures to life.[36] As Steven E. Jones rightly suggests, "what the steamboat represented and what Shelley was seeking in analogous form for his poetry—was a source of power, a way to move through the world and to move the world."[37] Then, complicating this analogy, the ship reappears in another letter to the Gisbornes, and just as before, the mythopoetic steamboat arrives in the wake of a "disappointing present" and a discussion of distant intimates, reinforcing not simply that "Shelley's longing for community suffuses many of his letters," but also how Shelley yokes technology to cycles of loss and communion.[38] Directing his missive back home to London (where the Gisbornes had traveled to sell their English holdings before returning to

---

[34] Joanna Baillie, "Address to a Steam Vessel," in *Fugitive Verses* (London: Edward Moxon, Dover Street, 1840), 248–54. References cited in-text by line number.

[35] *The Poems of Shelley, Volume 3: 1819–1820*, 429.

[36] Shelley, *A Defence of Poetry*, 278.

[37] Jones, "Shelley's 'Letter to Maria Gisborne' as Workshop Poetry," 393.

[38] Madeleine Callaghan, "'Any thing human or earthly': Shelley's Letters and Poetry," in *Letter Writing Among Poets: From William Wordsworth to Elizabeth Bishop*, ed. Jonathan Ellis (Edinburgh: Edinburgh University Press, 2015), 119.

The Romantic Sublime and Representations of Technology

their residence in Livorno), Shelley composes a *de facto* letter of introduction meant to connect old and new friends—friends whose proximity the poet himself cannot enjoy—and here, by way of playful association, Reveley's still incipient steamer becomes yet another prized but all too remote character:

> We go to Bagni [di San Giuliano] next month—but still direct to Pisa as safest ... I am undergoing a course of the Pisa baths, on which I lay no singular stress,—but {they} soothe. I ought to have peace of mind— leisure tranquility; this I expect soon—Our anxiety about Godwin is very great, & any information that you can give a day or two earlier than he might, respecting any decisive event in his lawsuit would be a great relief. Your impressions about Godwin (I speak especially to Madonna mia, [Maria Gisborne] who had known him before) will especially interest me—You know, that although I believe he is the only sincere enemy I have in the world, that added years only add to my admiration of his intellectual powers, & even the moral resources of his character.—Of my other friends I say nothing—To see Hunt, is to like him—and there is one other recommendation which he has to you, he is my friend—. To know Hogg, (if anyone can know him) is to know something very unlike & inexpressibly superior {to} the great mass of men.—
>
> Will Henry write me an adamantine letter, flowing not like the words of Sophocles with honey, but molten brass & iron, & bristling with wheels & teeth? I saw his steamboat asleep under the walls. I was afraid to waken it & ask it whether it was dreaming of him for the same reason that I w^d. have refrained from waking Ariadne after Theseus had left her—unless I had been Bacchus.—
>
> Affectionately & anxiously yours,
P.B.S.[39]

Here is Shelley's dream of a correspondent machine. Leave it to the author of *The Sensitive-Plant* to envision a sensitive machine, which likewise blurs boundaries of common or easy classification.[40] It would seem that if Shelley could not be with his kindred few, he may as well enlist the alchemy of language to invent some for him—but even Shelley's modern machine is at risk of being left behind, compared as it is here to an abandoned Ariadne. Although Shelley distances Reveley's would-be "adamantine letter" from naturalized modes of aesthetic creation (belonging to the ephemeral bee and the mortal, honey-tongued

---

[39] Shelley to John and Maria Gisborne, 26 May 1820, in *The Letters of Percy Bysshe Shelley, Volume II: Shelley in Italy*, 202–3.

[40] Shelley, *The Sensitive-Plant*, in *The Poems of Shelley, Volume 3: 1819–1820*, 287–316.

Lyres, Levers, Boats, and Steam

tragedian, Sophocles), these lines nonetheless style page and pen as elements of an organic machine.[41] After likening the origin of written words to a once mercurial state of "molten" metal, words and thoughts coalesce into durable form, embodied mechanomorphically "with wheels" and zoomorphically with "teeth." Pivoting slightly from this almost alchemical representation of language and print as ambivalent organic machines, the poet flirts with a representation of the steamboat that nearly humanizes it (or animalizes it) as a sleeping being, as a fellow sentient companion. Dreaming organisms metaphorize into dormant machines. Then the next sentence places Shelley's dreaming steamboat squarely within the anthropomorphic provenance of the divine, within a mythological albeit humanoid pantheon that would make gods of both Reveley and his invention. New words are born of brass and iron; steamships take on the dream-life, mental theater, and amorous politics of ancient gods. This account of poetic invention intermingles tropes of anthropomorphism, mechanomorphism, and zoomorphism, suggesting interpenetrating levels of dependence and inter-involvement, not least because each metaphorical reference builds and turns upon the other. This is not simply a fanciful story of manifesting the written word. In this case meaning itself is made possible because of a rebounding interplay between images animal, mechanical, and human.

The less-noted steamships of Shelley's letters reposition his more familiar Aeolian lyre, the child it becomes, and the entangled harmonies and cacophonies they make. If, as M. H. Abrams suggests in his classic study of Romantic poetry, *The Correspondent Breeze*, the "wind is not only a property of the landscape, but also a vehicle for radical changes in the poet's mind ... [often associated] with a complex subjective process: the return to a sense of community after isolation, the renewal of life ... after apathy and a deathlike torpor, and an outburst of creative power following a period of imaginative sterility," the same could be said of Shelley's instruments and machines.[42] Abrams's analysis of the trope of the wind in Romantic poetry similarly applies to Shelley's figurations of Romantic technologies, and not simply those featured in his prose letters. An example that establishes a link between the Aeolian lyre of Romantic lyric poetry and the steamships of Shelley's everyday letters arrives in the verse epistle *Letter to Maria Gisborne*. Shelley's epistolary poem echoes his everyday prose letters: here again readers encounter a correspondent machine that becomes a figure for subjective process and a notably qualified

---

[41] John Tresch recognizes how during the Romantic era, "there was a shift in the image of the machine from an idea of balanced, inhuman clockwork to a 'romantic machine' exemplified by the steam engine and other technologies of conversion and transmutation. Concepts of mechanism and organicism merged in several ways." Tresch, *The Romantic Machine*, 5.

[42] M. H. Abrams, "The Correspondent Breeze: A Romantic Metaphor," in *The Correspondent Breeze: Essays on English Romanticism* (New York: Norton & Co., 1981), 26.

The Romantic Sublime and Representations of Technology

collective creative promise. While a close poetic precedent exists in Erasmus Darwin's *Botanic Garden* (1791), with its mythologized inventors, marvelous inventions, and cantos made of couplets, Shelley's poem assumes a different tone and form—trading Darwin's ambitious didacticism and philosophical notes for dark humor and epistolary intimacy.[43] Aimed at like-minds, Shelley's letter in verse correlates rousing elements of nature and sublime technologies, both being capable of generating communion and loss—or, more accurately, an entanglement of the two.[44]

One of only two verse letters known to be composed by Shelley, this work marks a rare foray into the genre of the house poem, with its signature rhyming couplets, conversational style, and place-based genre conventions.[45] The house poem or estate poem, a mainstay of seventeenth- and eighteenth-century literature, traditionally studies poiesis and wider processes of making by way of depicting landscape, labor, and leisure as they occur in the everyday space of the home.[46] Any portrait of those personal, private spaces of the house, its

---

[43] Ann Thompson's careful consideration of the *Letter*'s most immediate audience accounts for the fact that "Maria Gisborne was an intimate friend from whom Shelley did not usually attempt to conceal his problems, either domestic ones or those relating to his literary career. The very fact of this intimacy allows Shelley to be brief and even playful when alluding to serious matters." Thompson, "Shelley's 'Letter to Maria Gisborne': Tact and Clutter," in *Essays on Shelley*, ed. Miriam Allott (Liverpool: Liverpool University Press, 1982), 149.

[44] See Jeffrey N. Cox, *Poetry and Politics in the Cockney School: Keats, Shelley, Hunt and Their Circle* (Cambridge: Cambridge University Press, 1998); William Keach, *Shelley's Style* (New York: Methuen, 1984). Although full-length examinations of the poem remain rare, *Letter to Maria Gisborne* has long been acknowledged as an important coterie poem. Cox cites the poem as one that self-consciously "celebrated the bonds of friendship that gave rise to [it]" (80). Keach remarks how Shelley's comedic play in *Letter to Maria Gisborne* was in part cultivated by the "congenial stimulus of what would become his 'Pisan Circle'" (185). Frequently writing for dear friends during the summer of 1820 and the year following, certain strands of Shelleyan poetry became "broadly and conspicuously open to possibilities of wit and humor" (185). Composing his missive from the Gisborne home in Pisa and directing it to their temporary residence in London, Shelley adopted a posture of frank comedic openness. The honesty so often resident within comedy is here emboldened by the intimate security offered by coterie poetry, revealing key insights into the ways that technology and proximity inform late Shelleyan sublimity.

[45] The Longman edition of *The Poems of Shelley* (*Volume 3: 1819–1820*) offers a helpful consideration of *Letter to Maria Gisborne*'s generic influences, noting that "[a]part from the epistolary doggerel of S[helley]'s 1811 letters in verse to Edward Fergus Graham ... this is S[helley]'s only verse-letter" (432).

[46] See David Hill Radcliffe, "Genre and Social Order in Country House Poems of the Eighteenth Century: Four Views of Percy Lodge," *Studies in English Literature, 1500–1900, Restoration and Eighteenth Century* 30, no. 3 (Summer 1990): 445–65, 461. For a broader consideration of eighteenth-century house poetry, see Robert Arnold Aubin, *Topographical Poetry in XVIII-Century England* (New York: Modern Language Association of America, 1936).

Lyres, Levers, Boats, and Steam

interiors and attendant human labors always doubles as a self-reflexive examination of poetic verse and its scribbler. These dual levels of signification are reinforced by its verse form. The couplet form accentuates the genre's ability to intertwine spaces poetic and domestic such that each is intimately, inextricably fused to the other and such that poetry's most sublime imaginings ultimately remain anchored to domestic ecologies.

Knitting together spatial technologies of place and page, particularly as they relate to subjective experience, practices of inscription, and the production of art, Shelley opens with a lighthearted study of contrasting modes of habitation lived out by the lonely spider and the lowly silkworm. Shelley presents two technological imaginaries attributed to silkworm and arachnid realms, which bring with them seemingly opposing ways of knowing and being in and with the world—and yet each seems to live alone in Shelley's lines and each leads a life circumscribed jointly by technology and ecology. Weaving and winding organisms afford Shelley a whimsical opportunity to examine inextricable technologies and fundamental practices of making as they might exist in the natural world, wherein building and dwelling are inevitably bound to making, writing, and thinking:

> The spider spreads her webs, whether she be
> In poet's tower, cellar or barn, or tree;
> The silkworm in the dark green mulberry leaves
> His winding sheet and cradle ever weaves;
> So I, a thing whom moralists call worm,
> Sit spinning still round this decaying form,
> From the fine threads of verse and subtle thought—
> No net of words in garish colours wrought
> To catch the idle buzzers of the day—
> But a soft cell, where when that fades away,
> Memory may clothe in wings my living name
> And feed it with the asphodels of fame,
> Which in those hearts which most remember me
> Grow, making love an immortality. (lines 1–14)

The spider's ubiquitous webbing and the silkworm's perpetual weaving find their counterparts in Shelley's unending technological contingency. Thanks to the poem's amphibious syntax, Shelley is both continuously "spinning" his words and portrayed as being always affixed to them, being fixed in place and being still even while "spinning." Like the spider and the silkworm, all that he produces surrounds him, suggesting not fantasies of forward progress through poiesis, but rather a delicate feedback loop of writerly practice and existence. A circling of "threads of verse and subtle thought" enswathe his undeniably

121

The Romantic Sublime and Representations of Technology

"decaying form." In casting himself as maker, Shelley eschews biblical or classical genesis narratives that would transform him into an all-powerful god manifesting his spinning machine out of the void. He is instead a vulnerable being spinning alongside fellow makers, all earthly inhabitants at best able to author a gossamer web or a "soft cell," transitory homes and impermanent connections. Significantly, wherever Shelley's weaving arachnid and cocooned larvae alter the given naturescape they bind themselves to it. But their parallel lives end there. Resembling the harsh literary critic or cloying writer, the spider's technics of predation and opportunism seem all too prevalent, adaptable, and ubiquitous. In contrast, the silkworm, with whom Shelley explicitly identifies, seems too rare—grafting itself sparingly to trees, only as necessary for a pivotal conversion into something more, something undeniably intimate yet sublimely alien—into something not merely self-sustaining but other-creating.[47]

While spiders and worms commonly figure the vanity of writerly wishes in satiric works by Jonathan Swift and Alexander Pope, other key Shelleyan influences such as Erasmus Darwin championed such seemingly lowly beings as Shelley does here—as kindred agents of sublime transformation and technological change. Darwin writes of humankind's "kindred forms, / Thy brother Emmets, and thy sister Worms," suggesting that the "excellence of the sense of touch in many insects seems to have given them wonderful ingenuity so as to equal or even excel mankind in some of their arts and discoveries; many of which may have been acquired in situations previous to their present ones, as the great globe itself, and all that it inhabit, appear to be in a perpetual state of mutation and improvement."[48] This understanding of an especially Darwinian writerly worm recalls Shelley's Platonic inheritances, particularly from the *Phaedrus* where Plato's transformed soul finally becomes "perfect and fully winged."[49] If the poet is the worm, then the winged insect it becomes is not unlike the Keatsian "viewless wings of Poesy," which for Shelley makes "immortal all that is best and most beautiful in the world; [Poetry] arrests the vanishing apparitions which haunt the interlunations of life, and veiling them or in language or in form sends them forth among mankind, bearing sweet news of kindred joy to those with whom their sisters abide—abide, because there is no portal of expression from the caverns of the spirit which they inhabit

---

[47] O'Neill recalls how the "spider is an emblem used by Swift in *The Battle of the Books* for the modern writer who arrogantly 'spins and spits wholly from himself, and scorns to own any obligation or assistance from without' ... [but b]oth insects serve as emblems of the poet." O'Neill, "'The Mind Which Feeds This Verse': Shelley," 137.

[48] Darwin, *The Temple of Nature*, Canto III, lines 433–4, n. 35. During the Romantic period, the term "insects" was often used broadly to refer to what we today distinguish to be arachnids, invertebrate animals, etc.

[49] See Plato, *Phaedrus*, in *Five Dialogues: Euthyphro, Apology, Crito, Meno, Phaedo*, trans. G. M. A. Grube, 2nd ed. (Cambridge: Hackett Publishing, 2002), 246c.

122

Lyres, Levers, Boats, and Steam

into the universe of things."[50] Shelley, in his call for a "living name," then, seems torn. On the one hand, he toys with a vain, self-centered transformation aimed at winging toward fame; on the other, he marks a continuous process of reaching out for those "kindred joy[s]" that were previously sought by the poet-turned-lyre-turned-child. Either way, when the worm uses its threads to shape its cocoon, it is preparing not for stasis but change: a preparing that does not allow it to be what it once was. Paradoxically, the most temporary yet endless work belongs not to the spider and her predatory, tortuous "net" but to the worm's transformative process of becoming. His is not a cycle of endless worldly consumption but an ongoing sublime program of intimate estrangement and uncertain outcomes.

Shelley's house poem continues in this vein, questioning spatial relations in order to question thinking and writing as well as the technologically and ecologically bounded nature of being. Here "Shelley becomes, in a possibly therapeutic poem, for once a poet of common things," namely those particular things surrounding him in Livorno rather than his friends.[51] His verse next moves to the study where he writes, a room not of his own and wherein the poet is encircled by unfamiliar tools and devices. Shelley's house poem strives to be at home with creating poetry out of a place of intimate estrangement and a sense of uncertain futurity. This endeavor becomes especially legible when Shelley notes how apt *and* absurd it is that he writes from the workshop of Maria Gisborne's son Henry Reveley, the nautical engineer who was elsewhere contriving a steamboat as Shelley was crafting his poetic lines:

> Whoever should behold me now, I wist,
> Would think I were a mighty mechanist,
> Bent with sublime Archimedean art
> To breathe a soul into the iron heart
> Of some machine portentous, or strange gin,
> Which, by the force of figured spells might win
> Its way over the sea, and sport therein;
> For round the walls are hung dread engines, such
> As Vulcan never wrought for Jove to clutch
> Ixion or the Titans: (lines 15–24)

The trope of poet as sublime alchemist gains renewed charge here as Shelley reveals that he works in a room populated by strange mechanical inventions. And between couplets figuring an Archimedean Shelley and those

---

[50] Shelley, *A Defence of Poetry*, 532.
[51] James H. Hall, "The Spider and the Silkworm: Shelley's 'Letter to Maria Gisborne,'" *Keats-Shelley Memorial Bulletin* 20 (1969): 3.

The Romantic Sublime and Representations of Technology

writing him as being walled in by "dread engines," exists the dream of a steamer incarnate. Formal variance arrives in tow with the alien invention or "strange gin." Shelley forgoes his requisite couplets, installing instead an excess of three rhymed lines all working to house the pervasive, expansive, and potentially untamable nature of Shelley's Romantic machine. Paralleling Shelley's account of poetry in the *Defence* where "Poetry is a sword of lightning ever unsheathed, which consumes the scabbard that would contain it," this "machine portentous" is not easily contained by its erstwhile handlers; its creative energies are sublime.[52] But then again, like always-mediated forms of poetry, it is of course limited by degree, requiring the surface tension of the sublime seas for support and for its necessary field of play, for its animation, for its sport.

On one level, the poet's thinking anticipates ideas held by science-minded Whigs living in early nineteenth-century Britain.[53] A "steam intellect" mentality of 1830s British liberalism imagined steam power as emblematic of progress, in turn promoting widespread "optimism about the transformative material and moral power of steamships."[54] What was once water, now is suddenly steam. Bringing together forces mechanical and elemental, steam engines emblematized the godlike, sublime transformative power of Promethean fire and fomented renewed interest in a mysterious alchemy of the machine. At home in England and elsewhere, ideological investments in profound and seemingly unknowable powers of technological change grounded sublime portraits of steam engines and other modern technologies heralded for their transformative promise. Across the channel in France, "[d]uring the early nineteenth century ... images of self-moving machines were newly associated with the physics of ethers, conversions, steam and electricity, as well as animal magnetism; they also frequently had magical and religious associations."[55]

But at the same time, Shelley's empowering engines of transformation do not shore up inevitable degrees of disempowerment, limitation, or interdependence. Shelley's poem makes possible a simultaneous contemplation of the fraught spaces of poetry and modern technology through allusions to a technics of entrapment, first seen in the writerly webs, nets, and soft cells of the natural-technological world. For Shelley these beings seemingly *write* themselves as they *house* themselves; built environments double as preconditioning literary devices and vice versa. Of the few scholars who have worked with this poem in detail, most suggest that Shelley contrasts "mechanical

---

[52] Shelley, *A Defence of Poetry*, 520.
[53] Parry, "Steam Power and British Influence in Baghdad, 1820–1860," 160.
[54] Parry, "Steam Power and British Influence in Baghdad, 1820–1860," 145.
[55] John Tresch. "The Machine Awakens: The Science and Politics of the Fantastic Automaton," *French Historical Studies* 34, no. 1 (Winter 2011): 87.

Lyres, Levers, Boats, and Steam

and scientific knowledge with the magical powers of the imagination."[56] Steven Jones's recent consideration of the verse epistle loosely follows this trend as his reading of the poem turns upon Shelley envying the "hands-on work done" in Reveley's workshop.[57] Jones suggests that "at the very least ... the exchanges about the steamboat [between Henry Reveley and Shelley] often sound awkwardly competitive, even (or perhaps especially) in Shelley's displays of wit."[58] In this sense and well beyond it, Shelley's poem considers intellectual and embodied mechanisms of poetry in tandem with marvels of modern technology like the steamship.[59] Indeed, the poet scripts a sublime tragicomedy of the home, wryly comparing poetry to the various technologies modern subjects find almost impossible to escape, avoid, and live without. In keeping with this logic, Shelley's *Letter to Maria Gisborne* establishes an aesthetic rubric of sublime entanglement and adjacency, foregrounding a counternarrative of material sublimity not based upon comfortable aesthetic distance but discomfiting aesthetic proximity.[60] Shelley's opening images of encircling webs, nets, inventions, and lines of verse are reprised early on with troubling depictions of modern technology: self-fashioned technics of entrapment arrive via "sublime Archimedean" magic fostering a portentous machine or "strange gin" (*gin* being a Shakespearean term for "traps and snares").[61] The Shakespearean reference rekindles longstanding associations between invention and entrapment, devices and entanglement. Further emphasizing celebrated poetic accounts of sublime genesis and making that bespeak such technological ensnarement, Shelley next recalls the chains and ties that Hephaestus forged to "clutch" Prometheus and which bound Ixion to an ever-turning wheel in Hades.

Complicating simple accounts of humanity's relationship to technology, Shelley characteristically employs a poetics of negation, which ultimately

[56] Fraistat and Reiman, *Shelley's Poetry and Prose*, 329. For important exceptions to this rule see the aforementioned work of Barbara T. Allen as well as Timothy Webb, "Scratching at the Door of Absence: Writing and Reading 'Letter to Maria Gisborne,'" in *The Unfamiliar Shelley*, eds. Alan M. Weinberg and Timothy Webb (Surrey, England: Ashgate, 2009), 119–36, esp. 134.

[57] Jones, "Shelley's 'Letter to Maria Gisborne' as Workshop Poetry," 381.

[58] Jones, "Shelley's 'Letter to Maria Gisborne' as Workshop Poetry," 382.

[59] Webb observes that "the mechanist (who will soon represent the unimaginative and routinely calculating tendency in contemporary society in 'A Defence of Poetry') is here identified with the poet himself and given a favorable shading by Shelley's use of Spenser's preferred adjective 'mighty'" (134).

[60] Edmund Burke's *A Philosophical Enquiry into the Origin of our Ideas of the Sublime and Beautiful* (1757) famously establishes aesthetic distance as a defining feature of sublime experience, which Immanuel Kant's *Critique* later confirms. See section VII, "Of the Sublime."

[61] Fraistat and Reiman, *Shelley's Poetry and Prose*, 329, n. 6.

The Romantic Sublime and Representations of Technology

undermines the logic of the kind of technological sublime at play in his letters, which mythopoetically displaces the work of human hands and whereby Reveley becomes a god and his steamer seems to voyage with no one at the helm. In contrast, in Shelley's verse epistle, Reveley's "dread engines" are "such / As Vulcan *never* wrought" (line 23, emphasis added). As Shelley continues an inventory of the engineer's workshop, he remarks upon various stupefying technologies *that the gods never made.* "[O]ther strange and dread / Magical forms" spread about the room that even "Proteus transformed to metal *did not make.*" (lines 43–4, 45, emphasis added). "[S]hapes of unintelligible brass," "tin or iron not to be understood" and "forms of unimaginable wood" could "puzzle" even "Tubal Cain and all his brood" (lines 47, 49, 50, 51). Given Tubal Cain was the first metalsmith to appear in the biblical myth of Genesis (4:22), by this point the poem has roundly rejected reductionist understandings of technology that might leverage Judeo-Christian or Greek mythological systems to cede humanity's technological responsibility. Shelley questions narratives that fabricate divine origins for technology, repeating— that for good or ill—these technologies the gods *did not make.* Shelley reminds us, that like the lines of poetry he writes, if we use technologies to trap and torture on any extraordinary or more domesticated basis, it is an undivine hand that forges its own prison and frames its own hell.

Shelley's verse epistle insists upon coeval humanity and technology, stressing that we must live with the technology we create and cannot forget the degree to which technologies in turn recreate us. This technological imaginary suggests technology is neither divine nor godly and therefore can neither save nor destroy us as techno-utopic or techno-apocalyptic narratives might have it. Instead, we salvage or dismantle *with* the earth and technology, *in* the earth and technology. Indeed, Shelley's lines take full advantage of the metaphoricity and malleability of narrative space as well as the couplet form's ideological implications to provide a scaled down study of humanity's simultaneous coupling with the earth and technology. While, as Dipesh Chakrabarty famously contends in "The Climate of History: Four Theses," history may be at an impasse when reckoning with the complex realities of climate change—because we cannot experience *species being* (that is, as Chakrabarty puts it, "We humans never experience ourselves as a species") and nor can we experience climate change's macrocosmic, large-scale global effects—literature, ironically perhaps, provides a mechanism for imagining such daunting realities and complexities of scale.[62] After zooming in, as it were, documenting the room's various "screws and cones, and wheels and grooved blocks," its "knacks and quips," Shelley turns to "[a] pretty bowl of wood" that later doubles for the cradle of the globe (lines

---

[62] Dipesh Chakrabarty, "The Climate of History: Four Theses," *Critical Inquiry* 35, no. 2 (2009): 197–222, 220.

Lyres, Levers, Boats, and Steam

52, 55, 57). By transposing geological space onto domestic space, the poem allows the reader to conceive a more intimate relationship with land and sea, with both surface and depths of terraqueous earth. Shelley inventively recounts how Henry's "pretty bowl of wood" is "not full of wine, / But quicksilver, that dew which the gnomes drink / When at their subterranean toil they swink, ... call[ing] out to the cities o'er their head— / Roofs, towers, and shrines, the dying and the dead, / [all] Crash through the chinks of earth" (lines 57–9; 62–4). Shelley does not sugarcoat the cost of modernity's intermingling with earthly and technological being. Nor does he fantastically imagine away the reality that every space of human life and death depends upon the earth. The poet continues, next framing the mercurial waters beside him as the sea in miniature, by extension making the rest of the room into a technologically populated *terra firma*. Deploying "a distinctive feature of [late Shelleyan] style," the poet "holds in balance opposing perspectives on the grand scale," this time juxtaposing domestic microcosm with earthly macrocosm to gesture toward what it might mean to be at home with being with technology— not domesticating technology nor any of its sublime strangeness, but rather acknowledging the sublimely ubiquitous, intimate nature of our technological contingency.[63] Formally documenting myriad technological and ecological inter-involvements that defy separation, frustrate compartmentalization, and effectively refuse consideration in isolation, line after poetic line binds together sprawling associative sentences. And when these sentences finally syntactically "conclude," Shelley draws his readers to the next adjacent object or contingent idea by frequently deploying dashes and opening with terms such as "And," "Then," "next," or "Near" that indicate conjunction, sequence, and proximity. The poet writes:

> And in this bowl of quicksilver—for I
> Yield to the impulse of an infancy
> Outlasting manhood—I have made to float
> A rude idealism of a paper boat:
> A hollow screw with cogs—Henry will know
> The thing I mean and laugh at me,—if so
> He fears not I should do more mischief—next
> Lie bills and calculations much perplexed,
> With steamboats, frigates and machinery quaint
> Traced over them in blue and yellow paint.
> Then comes a range of mathematical
> Instruments, for plans nautical and statical;

---

[63] Alan Weinberg, "Freedom from the Stranglehold of Time: Shelley's Visionary Conception in *Queen Mab*," *Romanticism* 22, no. 1 (2016): 92.

127

The Romantic Sublime and Representations of Technology

> A heap of rosin, a queer broken glass
> With ink in it, a china cup that was
> What it will never be again, I think,
> A thing from which sweet lips were wont to drink
> The liquor doctors rail at—and which I
> Will quaff in spite of them—and when we die
> We'll toss up who died first of drinking tea,
> And cry out heads or tails, where'er we be.
> Near that a dusty paint box, some odd hooks,
> A half-burnt match, an ivory block, three books
> Where conic sections, spherics, logarithms,
> To great Laplace, from Saunderson and Sims,
> Lie heaped in their harmonious disarray
> Of figures—disentangle them who may— (lines 72–97)

Shelley's miniaturized sea is destined to reside amidst a thoroughly relational world and an almost wholly technologized milieu. The poet here plays the part of engineer, with Shelley's longstanding emblem for the politics of aesthetics, the "paper boat," now appearing as a "hollow screw with cogs," and now approximated as a mechanical yet still magical set of conjoined parts floating upon not water, not even air, but a sea of liquid metal. The poem's couplets and content intersect to reinforce the link between questions of technicity and relationality, granting Shelley access to an additional formal register within which to suggest that humankind needs to come to terms with being materially entangled and technologically contingent. In these ways, the verse epistle tacitly theorizes the modern technological condition as one circumscribed by technological proximity, its suggestive nearness, and its simultaneously extensive and immersive natures. The poem's swimming inventory of intimate yet unknowable things, devices, inventions, papers, gadgets, and calculations underscore that we are awash in technology "where[v]er we be."

In the poem, ordinary life spills over into things technological, spanning not just the presence of the poetic line on the page but also the entwined existence of hooks and books, a steamboat and a china cup, a "half-burnt match," a paper boat, spaces of thought, readers and writers, even spaces of death. Shelley's coupling of lives poetic and technic anticipates the logic of Langdon Winner. Winner theorizes technologies as forms of life inhabiting earthly space right along with us. "As they become woven into the texture of everyday existence," Winner argues, "the devices, techniques, and systems we adopt shed their tool-like qualities to become part of our very humanity. In an important sense we become the beings who work on assembly lines, who talk on telephones, who do our figuring on pocket calculators, who eat

Lyres, Levers, Boats, and Steam

processed foods, who clean our homes with powerful chemicals."[64] Shelley's modern technological imaginary humbles us in light of our relationship with and in technology—almost as if it were a form of life as Winner suggests. And in this light, Shelley's laughing letter laughs at all of us: for forgetting the entangled nature of our humanity and technology; for fantasizing that either we're a godlike power, or sublime technology is.

What instead reigns supreme in Shelley's verse is situational adjacency and transformational community. Borne aloft by quicksilver, Shelley's impromptu boat sails next to preliminary sketches of steamships. His emergent poetic verse lies with bills and "plans nautical and statical." Visionary poetry transits alongside projected steamers. But in place of realizing utopian plans, Shelley's skiff and ship meet with a "heap" and a "queer broken glass:" physical reminders of the costs that come of transformation and change. Shelley both weaves together and leaves behind figures he routinely associates with collective progress and poetic engagement to consider a futurity that pivots upon a humble cup, a relic left behind, one emblematic of an especially intimate and fleeting communion and exchange made possible by the simple ceremony of drinking tea together. Regardless of the animating powers of poetry or modern machinery, it is the cup that finally ushers in the future tense, a future wherein it is "What it will never be again ... A thing from which sweet lips were wont to drink." The poem later makes light of the dangers of laudanum and even death itself as Shelley's technological imaginary becomes a steppingstone toward a future made full by imagined community and the creating that communal exchange enables. The prose letters formulate a pattern that remerges here: Shelley engages a technological object, aestheticizes it and mythologizes it, which then prompts longing and solitude, calls for communion, a drive to bridge the distance. Or the inverse occurs, where discussions of technology serve as a point of departure, offering an alternate outlet for possibilities of making and mythologizing, but also offering a point of shared communion. Importantly, as with the common cup, it is one thing to make the instrument, object, or machine but it is all the more crucial to make upon it. Shelley's Romantic machines allow for both—for different points of departure into mythology, literature, and poetry, while also providing a node of connection between and among people and across the earth and things.

The poem's following section links processes of artificial and natural creation through the power of sound and word, recalling the "insect" technics as well as poetics of organic machinery that figure questions of isolation and reunion in Shelley's poetry and letters. Again, an otherwise sequestered poet seeks comfort in accompaniment. "And here like some weird Archimage sit

---

[64] Langdon Winner, "Technologies as Forms of Life," in *Readings in the Philosophy of Technology*, ed. David M. Kaplan (Oxford: Rowman and Littlefield, 2004), 108.

I," the poet writes, "Plotting dark spells and devilish enginery, / [and here] The self-impelling steam-wheels of the mind" drive the poet's thoughts to new birth, "[w]hich pump up oaths from clergymen, and grind / The gentle spirit of our meek reviews / Into a powdery foam of salt abuse" (lines 106, 107–8, 109–11). While William Keach observes that in "*Letter to Maria Gisborne* Shelley anticipates having the Witch of Atlas's cave 'stored with scrolls of strange device, / The works of some Saturnian Archimage'" by composing "a self-portrait in which he puckishly casts himself as Spenser's arch-magician," Shelley's conjurer is notably limited in his powers and especially sensitive to sound.[65] Here the poetic subject bears a mind bidden by steam and a still sitting body respondent to external winds and internal pumps, manifesting words:

> Ruffling the ocean of their [the critics'] self-content—
> I sit, and smile or sigh as is my bent,
> But not for them—Libeccio rushes round
> With an inconstant and an idle sound,
> I heed him more than them ...
> The murmur of the awaking sea doth fill
> The empty pauses of the blast—
>   ... in sullen strain
> The interrupted thunder howls; above
> One chasm of heaven smiles, like the eye of Love
> O'er the unquiet world— (lines 112–16, 122–3, 125–8)

In dialogue with an "unquiet world," the poet joins an inconstant if not idle chorus of elegiac voices, "blast[s]," "howls," and "sullen strain[s]." Like Shelley's lyre or his child, the poet here hopes to stay the company of expression that engendered delight for as long as humanly possible. In these lines the poet seems at last to become the lyre thanks to a transformative figuration of steam, but this is not enough.

The heavenly "eye of Love" floats "above / One chasm" and appears just as Shelley will return to questions of friendship and directly address his coterie readers, readers necessarily hovering above the lines that carry Shelley's sullen strains and darkly comic couplets:

> The interrupted thunder howls; above
> One chasm of heaven smiles, like the eye of Love
> O'er the unquiet world—while such things are,
> How could one worth your friendship heed the war

---

[65] Keach, *Shelley's Style*, 113.

Lyres, Levers, Boats, and Steam

Of worms? the shriek of the world's carrion jays,
Their censure, or their wonder, or their praise?

You are not here ... the quaint witch Memory sees
In vacant chairs your absent images,
And points where you once you sat, and now should be
But are not—I demand if ever we
Shall meet as then we met—and she replies,
Veiling in awe her second-sighted eyes;
"I know the past alone—but summon home
My sister Hope,—she speaks of all to come."
But I, an old diviner, who know well
Every false verse of that sweet oracle,
Turned to the sad enchantress [Memory] once again,
And sought a respite from my gentle pain,
In citing every passage o'er and o'er
Of our communion— (lines 126–45)

Registering the harmonious disarray of Shelley's unquiet world, when Shelley's
couplets announce the reader's distance ("You are not here") and make Memory
read absence into a room of vacant chairs, the rhyme scheme is interrupted,
faltering intermittently as if to resemble disrupted communication and
communion. Taking recourse to the closing and brief, slight rhyme in "sees"
and "images," poetic lines repeatedly sound out the "jarring and inexplicable
frame / Of this wrong world" by at times resisting the perfect closure of quick
and simple rhyme, and at others foreclosing the easy auditory kinship proffered
by the couplet form. A sporadic intrusion of half and imperfect rhymes appears
at precisely that moment when Shelley demands a togetherness that he alone
cannot create. "[C]ome" follows "home." The bittersweetness of the "oracle"
Hope is a taste the poet knows too "well" to bind together "oracle" and "well"
in perfect rhyme *qua* perfect, chiming fulfillment. Although Shelley comes
strikingly close to a Wordsworthian investment in memory, memory is not
palliative enough for Shelley. A "sad enchantress," a "quaint witch," Memory—
the counterpart of "Hope"—brings only "a respite" from pain, leaving the poet
wistfully to collapse time and distance by "citing every passage o'er and o'er /
Of our communion," by reading already created words, making them live and
return again by recreating them in sound.

Less akin to Wordsworth, Shelley's words chime most with Plato's Socrates.
In the *Phaedrus*, Socrates casts human embodiment in terms of a relational
entombment or dynamic enshrinement. Like words and ships, bodies are
conveyed and carried; however, the self seems ensnared, trapped, confined—
somehow isolated within bodily form. Socrates states:

131

The Romantic Sublime and Representations of Technology

and then we beheld the beatific vision and were initiated into a mystery which may be truly called most blessed, celebrated by us in our state of innocence, before we had any experience of evils to come, when we were admitted to the sight of apparitions innocent and simple and calm and happy, which we beheld shining in pure light, pure ourselves and not yet enshrined in that living tomb which we carry about, now that we are imprisoned in the body, like an oyster in his shell. Let me linger over the memory of scenes which have passed away.[66]

Socrates, espousing a view of incarnate earthly experience negatively defined by boundedness and containment, grants himself permission to "linger over the memory of scenes which have passed away."

At once borrowing from Plato while also leaving him behind, Shelley does not consign himself to memory alone. In drawing out poetry's technological and natural affinities he locates not just wider communities of earthly sound evocative of the harmonious spheres of the cosmos. He also carves out a guardedly hopeful vision of meaningful human sociality carried out by the simple act of conversing together—all of which hinges on foundations both planetary and technological:

> If living winds the rapid clouds pursue,
> If hawks chase doves through the etherial way,
> Huntsmen the innocent deer, and beasts their prey,
> Why should not we rouse with the spirit's blast
> Out of the forest of the pathless past
> These recollected pleasures?
>
>   You are now
> In London, that great sea, whose ebb and flow
> *At once is deaf and loud*, and on the shore
> Vomits its wrecks, and *still howls on for more*.
> Yet in its depth what treasures! You will see
> That which was Godwin,
> …
> You will see Coleridge—
> …
> You will see Hunt—one of those happy souls
> Who are the salt of the earth, and without whom
> This world would smell like what it is—a tomb;
> …

[66] Plato, *Phaedrus*, 475–6.

Lyres, Levers, Boats, and Steam

> You will see Hogg—and I cannot express
> His virtues, though I know that they are great,
> Because he locks, then barricades the gate
> Within which they inhabit;—of his wit
> And wisdom, you'll cry out when you are bit.
> He is a pearl within an oyster shell,
> One of the richest of the deep.
>
> (lines 187–97, 202, 209–11, 226–32)

The unrhymed and thus unassimilable question of rousing "[t]hese recollected pleasures" literally hangs upon the page, above a break in Shelley's verse, calling attention to an unsuturable communal rupture that even the technology of poetry cannot bridge. While one may be entangled ecologically to technologies large and small, or bound to the earth both proximately and globally, these bonds cannot adequately stand in for those attributed to Shelley's lost community. Nor do they erase a loss of understanding, the limits of written language that cannot replicate spoken dialogue, or the ultimate unknowability of the things we make. After generating hundreds of lines of verse that document a sublime tragicomedy of everyday domestic life, a solitary poet sometimes weaves couplets into being, even as he acknowledges limitedness and all the while hearing harmony in the disarray that is. To close his verse epistle, Shelley rewrites the uncertain ending of *Ode to the West Wind*: "If Winter comes, can Spring be far behind?"[67] Asking Maria Gisborne and his other readers to read the stars with him—wherever they be—he then implores them to think of meeting again, soon, in the spring. Envisioning this possible future, Shelley imagines trading distant epistolary being for convivial repartee, suggesting that "To thaw the six weeks' winter in our blood ... we'll talk— what shall we talk about? / Oh! there are themes enough for many a bout / Of thought-entangled descant;—" (lines 307, 308–10).

Shelley's wind-driven and waterborne vessels scaffold a broader technics of poetic inception, an understanding of poetry that is as indebted to the poet's aesthetic treatments of a great range of artificial creations and human relations as it is to the animating forces of water, wind, and mind. Evoking lyric poetry's ancient lyres as well as modern inventions chronicled in commonplace letters and occasional verse, Shelley's broad account of poiesis uses technology as a metaphor for the ecological contingency of humanity. Shelley resists a simple opposition between nature and technological progress. His is a view of entangled natural, poetic, social, and technological process, which challenges narrowminded accounts of the environment just as it throws into question

---

[67] Shelley, *Ode to the West Wind*, line 70.

The Romantic Sublime and Representations of Technology

the quixotic figure of the solitary Romantic poet. Shelley's poetry and prose offer a model for thinking human finitude in conjunction with an account of ecological contingency that is complicated by technological contingency, where humankind is not of technology (as reductionist mythological or genesis narratives might suggest) but with technology (as contemporary environmental theory maintains in its models of social ecology). This is not to say that the poet is not seduced by sublimely mythopoetic visions of lone, godlike creators, or other imaginings which threaten to reinforce exceptional renditions of human autonomy—quite the contrary. It is only when the poet acknowledges how creation, invention, and transformation always arrive in lockstep with death, separation, and loss, that Shelley finally espouses an understanding of technological sublimity that would dispel the myth and misplaced glamour of being and creating alone.

CHAPTER FOUR

Suspension Bridges, Modern Canals, and the Infrastructural Sublime

Robert Southey, Thomas Telford, and the Traffic of Empire

We didn't build our bridges simply to avoid walking on water. Nothing so obvious.

—Jeanette Winterson, *The Passion* (1987)

I know of nothing sublime, which is not some modification of power.

—Edmund Burke, *A Philosophical Inquiry into the Origin of Our Ideas of the Sublime and Beautiful* (1757)

This chapter turns to Britain's imperial past to unravel a knotty link between celebrations of Britain's civil infrastructure and Romantic authors' accounts of poetic prowess. Tales of transformative agencies ascribed to engineers and architects drastically altering British landscapes come to sound an awful lot like stories of radical change and creative agency attributed to the poet, page, and pen—but why? A prime answer lurks in the sprawling logics and languages of the sublime. As Matthew Gandy's work on urban geography rightly suggests, "cognitive polarities between concrete and imaginary space can be explored with reference to the aesthetic categories of the sublime ... that have begun to permeate critical writings on ... industrial landscapes."[1] The sublime is the western aesthetic category most preoccupied with registering our ambivalence

[1] Matthew Gandy, "Cyborg Urbanization: Complexity and Monstrosity in the Contemporary City," *International Journal of Urban and Regional Research* 29, no. 1 (2005): 40.

The Romantic Sublime and Representations of Technology

toward what we can't make sense of and toward whatever might be grand, massive, or powerful enough to change us—whether we like it or not. In particular, sublime characterizations of the maker and the made link aestheticized accounts of poets and engineers and the overlapping worlds—imagined and lived—they create. Across the long arc of sublime aesthetics, the sublime consistently registers our discomfort with the powers of makers and creators, just as it indexes our anxieties about the made objects, artifacts, and spaces our most mighty makers create, even if all the while the aesthetic of the sublime also expresses our drive to quell such fears.

Indeed, it is well known that sublime aesthetics not only chronicled deep reservations about powers of creation but also held in abeyance abiding anxieties spurred by the idea of creative power on the grandest scales: belonging to godheads or natural forces as well as the forbidding things they might generate, be they eternal hellscapes or sudden earthquakes. Less known, however, is that writers take recourse to sublime aesthetics to speak of humanity at odds with itself, to voice our vexed relationship with powers of human invention and the formidable inventions we make—from wrought words to built worlds—and the abiding relationship between the two. This particular branch of sublime aesthetics is associated with what is today known as the technological sublime. The technological sublime lionizes craft, heralds the stuff of human fabrication. Long before it was called this, key Romantic-era writers such as Robert Southey and his friend, Thomas Telford (1757–1834), Britain's so-called father of civil engineering, already recognized how the technological sublime might just be the aesthetic register best suited to confront (honestly, in the best case) the unsettling agencies alive in all that we make and create. Romantic-era writers assign the sublime's telltale ambivalence (its signature attraction and repulsion, with its resulting charge of awe mingled with terror) to poetic verse and built structures alike. Sublime representations and figurations, then, make legible a kind of profound worry couched in guarded reverence. And in this case, the logic and language of the sublime remind us to be both wary and canny of the fearsome forces borne out by human worldbuilding, be they writ in water or preserved in infrastructure.

Although the relationship between poetics, landscape, and architecture remains a core concern within Romantic literary criticism, little work studies the widely celebrated innovations of this period's civil engineers.[2] Yet when

---

[2] For influential accounts of eighteenth-century and Romantic literature studying both interior and exterior architecture see Nicole Reynolds, *Building Romanticism: Literature and Architecture in Nineteenth-Century Britain* (Ann Arbor, MI: University of Michigan Press, 2010); Sophie Thomas, *Romanticism and Visuality: Fragments, History, Spectacle* (London and New York: Routledge, 2008); Tita Chico, *Designing Women: The Dressing Room in Eighteenth-Century Literature and Culture* (Lewisburg, PA: Bucknell University Press, 1999); and Simon Varey, *Space and the Eighteenth-Century English Novel* (Cambridge:

Suspension Bridges, Modern Canals, and the Infrastructural Sublime

we recognize how bridges, roadways, and canals from this era were rendered sublime both by influential poets such as Southey and Britain's popular presses we discover a troubling link between British infrastructural aesthetics, poetics, and empire. Studies on Romantic literature and architectural form tend to foreground ruins, and they typically theorize the decay of structures both actual and figurative. Here the figure of the ruin introduces questions concerning narratology and subjectivity, with issues related to narrative deformation, cultural memory, and fragmented consciousness leading the way.[3] Left virtually unconsidered in these accounts is the technology of the bridge, not to mention grand undertakings like Telford's work on the expansive London to Holyhead road project, its relation to colonial ideology, and to Southey, Telford's close acquaintance and Britain's Poet Laureate.[4] Yet to bring these massive and widely celebrated infrastructural developments into conversation with historical and literary inquiry compels us to reconsider key intersections between national politics, sublime aesthetics, and the architectural and poetic art born of the British Romantic movement.

At stake in discussions of sublime representations of celebrated works of civil infrastructure such as the modern suspension bridge and the British empire's sprawling roadways are two principal concerns: first, how liminal yet monumental infrastructural technologies mediate Romantic understandings of natural and built environments; and second, how these suspended and entrenched artifacts—these major arteries of transportation and communication—inform British national and colonial imaginaries as presented in British Romantic literature. Studying sublime figurations of the meeting points

Cambridge University Press, 1990). On landscape and Romantic literature and culture see Ann Bermingham, *Landscape and Ideology: The English Rustic Tradition 1740–1860* (London: Thames and Hudson, 1987) and Raymond Williams, *The Country and the City* (Oxford: Oxford University Press, 1973). For the exception that proves the rule regarding extant criticism on British canalworks, see Miranda Burgess, "Transport: Mobility, Anxiety, and the Romantic Poetics of Feeling," *Studies in Romanticism* 49, no. 2 (2010): 229–60, http://www.jstor.org/stable/41059287.

[3] See Katie Trumpener, *Bardic Nationalism: The Romantic Novel and the British Empire* (Princeton, NJ: Princeton University Press, 1997); M. H. Abrams, *Natural Supernaturalism: Tradition and Revolution in Romantic Literature* (New York and London: Norton, 1971); Jerome McGann, *The Romantic Ideology: A Critical Investigation* (Chicago, IL: University Chicago Press, 1983); and Thomas McFarland, *Romanticism and the Forms of Ruin: Wordsworth, Coleridge, and Modalities of Fragmentation* (Princeton, NJ: Princeton University Press, 1981).

[4] On Southey's relationship with Telford and the civil artifacts he designed, scholars note only that they were close friends, that they journeyed together with a group touring the Scottish Highlands, and that Southey was set to pen the famed engineer's biography but died before drafting it. See, for example, Lynda Pratt, "Introduction," and "Family Misfortunes? The posthumous editing of Robert Southey," in *Robert Southey and the Contexts of English Romanticism*, ed. Lynda Pratt (Aldershot: Ashgate, 2006), xvii–xxix, 219–38.

The Romantic Sublime and Representations of Technology

between natural and artificial landscapes (where the material sublime of Romantic nature meets the more technological sublime of British empire) reveal previously unnoticed aspects of Romantic life and Romantic imaginings underpinned by sublime discourses framing the external world through figures of material irony and temporal paradox.[5] While related architectural and economic aspects of British Romantic bridges and canals are of course at play, my primary concern in these pages is to demonstrate how Romantic representations of the material sublime in nature unfold in dialogue with a technological sublime, and in following to reveal how discourses of material and technological sublimity have been brought together both to challenge and advance the politics and aesthetics of empire. Ultimately, this chapter reveals how it is neither the technological nor the material sublime alone that would become a central aesthetic of imperial worldbuilding, but a marriage of the two extant in what I'm calling the infrastructural sublime.

Typifying this interplay between material and technological sublimity in celebratory British infrastructural discourse, a speech given on the opening day of Wearmouth Bridge at Sunderland (9 August 1796) highlighted the cultural and national significances of infrastructure by coloring it sublime. William Nesfield, the Provincial Grand Chaplain of Durham, repeatedly honored the Sunderland Bridge with nationally charged orations. First in 1792, he spoke after ceremoniously laying the "foundation" stone of a structure about to be, and later he would fête the bridge's fruition. Each occasion exalted engineered transformations of the British landscape with the language of the sublime. For both events, Nesfield would summon one of the sublime's signature temporal modes, signaling not any warlike sublime event of cataclysmic end times, but a charged instant of sudden creative force, a fiat-like sublime moment of transformative genesis.[6] To confer the bridge with infrastructural sublimity he paints the bridge as if conjured from thin air, and so compares the completed work before him to the bridge imagined at inception, before it had yet to exist

---

[5] My reading of supernatural landscapes both "natural" and "artificial" reads against the theoretical grain established by Max Horkheimer and Theodor W. Adorno in *Dialectic of Enlightenment* where they hold key thinkers such as Bacon and Leibniz responsible for a wholesale disenchantment of nature. See their "Concept of Enlightenment," for instance, in which they offer the following: "The 'happy match' between human understanding and the nature of things that [Bacon] envisaged is a patriarchal one: the mind, conquering superstition, is to rule over disenchanted nature. Knowledge, which is power, knows no limits, either in its enslavement of creation or in its deference to worldly masters. ... Technology is the essence of this knowledge. It aims to produce neither concepts nor images, nor the joy of understanding, but method, exploitation of the labor of others, capital. ... What human beings seek to learn from nature is how to use it to dominate wholly both it and human beings" (2).

[6] For a book-length study of the Romantic fiat see Eric Reid Lindstrom, *Romantic Fiat: Demystification and Enchantment in Lyric Poetry* (Basingstoke: Palgrave, 2011).

Suspension Bridges, Modern Canals, and the Infrastructural Sublime

and when seemingly only just conceived at that inaugural foundation-stone moment: "when I thought the undertaking but the fabric of a vision;--... [but] what must I now feel [he remarks], when all that I thought impossible stands realized before me, and when compliment and exhortation have given way to substance and effect?"[7] After extolling a vision made manifest, after musing over words and abstract signifiers (compliments, exhortations) transmuted into a physical reality (material substance), he underscores the sublime "wonder" and "astonishment" borne out by this "stupendous edifice" (12). Nesfield's bridge is a thing sublime:

> [W]here am I to find words to convey its adequate eulogium? or how
> am I to distinguish, in appropriate terms, its different and peculiar excel-
> lencies? Am I to describe the awful boldness of its height, the immensity
> of its span, the lightness of its texture, the simplicity of its design ...
> no ordinary ideas can well do justice to it; ... Examine it! View it from
> your shores with microscopic attention! You see *that* firm, substantial,
> and realized, which you thought had only existed on the fanciful canvas
> of the painter, or had been faintly conceived in the playful imagination
> of the poet. (6–7, original emphasis)

The bridge assumes sublime status via associations with whatever resists repre-sentation, with what both Kant and Lyotard would call the "unpresentable" and what Geoffrey Hartman theorizes as "sublime aphasia," or the phenomenon of being at a loss for words when encountering the unpresentable.[8] In addition, by heralding the bridge's paradoxical material aesthetic—its imposing "awful boldness" and "immensity" crossed with an ethereal "simplicity" and "lightness"—Nesfield enlists a Burkean sublime vernacular commonly attributed to natural and built landscapes unique in their perceived struc-tural antagonisms, material disjunctions, temporal anomalousness, or overall paradoxical form.[9] Baffling earthly manifestations or transformations previ-

---

[7] William Nesfield, *An oration, delivered at the opening of the iron bridge at Wearmouth, August 9, 1796. By William Nesfield, M. A. Provincial Grand Chaplain, Durham. And a sermon, preached in the chapel at Sunderland, on the same occasion, by John Brewster, M. A. Chaplain of the Lodge of Philanthropy, Stockton, No. 19. To which is added, an Appendix, Containing an Account of the Order of the Procession, Ceremonies, Used on that Occasion, &c.* (London: Christopher and Jennett, 1796), 4. Hereafter citations are noted in-text by page number.

[8] See especially Book One of Kant, *Critique of Judgment*; Jean-François Lyotard, "Presenting the Unpresentable: The Sublime," *Artforum* (April 1982), https://www.artforum.com/features/presenting-the-unpresentable-the-sublime-208373/; Geoffrey H. Hartman, "Blessing the Torrent: On Wordsworth's Later Style," *PMLA* 93, no. 2 (1978): 196–204.

[9] Arguing similarly, in *Reinventing Allegory* (Cambridge: Cambridge University Press, 1997), Theresa M. Kelley uncovers how certain representations of Devil's Bridge in

The Romantic Sublime and Representations of Technology

ously only associated with nature's prowess and the material sublime, now also belong to major civil engineering projects and come to commonly underpin accounts of sublime infrastructure. In turn, sublime infrastructural works metonymically guarantee the sublimity of the nation. Nesfield's account of the Sunderland Bridge is about much more than pragmatic issues entailed in finding new ways to avoid perilous straights while in transit on the ground; it is also about appropriating earthly agencies typically extolled in accounts of material sublimity to rebrand British culture as sublime by way of technological aesthetics and theater.

Regardless of the project's many challenges and setbacks, the Sunderland Bridge was understood as a work of infrastructure enabling the "conquest of natural obstacles and forces," and thus also accrued aesthetic value against a backdrop of the material sublime in nature.[10] In Nesfield's closing remarks, the chaplain entreats the audience to "call back to your minds the object of our assemblage here this day," that is, the built crossing, in order to pay proper tribute to this "ornament of our country at large; the pride and boast of this great country in particular" (12). The word "ornament" calls attention to the aesthetic valuation of this new addition to the British built environment, and as ever for the sublime as an aesthetic category—size matters. Although not explicitly referring to the vast magnitude of the bridge, Nesfield paradoxically miniaturizes the structure. It is a mere ornament decorating an even larger artificial creation: the at once physical and ideological "country at large" now boasting the comparatively diminutive and novel structure of the bridge. Deemed sublime both because and in spite of the iron arch's hazardous positioning, the Sunderland Bridge emblematizes how notions of nationalized geography are always engineered through delicate if not perilous feats of mental and material fabrication:

> Exposed, by its aerial situation, to the rude rock of the tempest, and the fury of contending winds, may it still rest firm on its foundations! unshaken [sic] by the conflict of the jarring elements, unimpaired by the ravage of devouring time! May it in our days stand a glorious monument of British taste, and of national grandeur! and [sic] may it in after ages maintain its proud eminence, permanent and durable as the work of the immortal Roman! (12–13)

St. Gothard Pass—with its "deep, Romantic chasm, … [and] where men and horses and munitions tumbled down or struggled across the Devil's Bridge"—qualify as "'sublime' by anyone's definition except Kant's" (191). Affirming my thesis on the sublime's mixed appeals to paradoxical temporalities and material conditions, Kelley highlights sublime treatments of Devil's Bridge, such as "Turners' view, [where] the bridge looks, to use phrases repeated in the nineteenth century guidebooks, 'thrown across' or 'cast' over the ravine," in contradistinction to traditional pastoral aesthetics (193).

[10] Nye, *American Technological Sublime*, 77.

140

Suspension Bridges, Modern Canals, and the Infrastructural Sublime

For Nesfield, the anticipated legacy of the structure's "national grandeur" is grounded upon an unflinching investment in repatterning imperial pasts. Nesfield links the civil artifact's symbolic value to Rome, to an empire that famously flourished by way of many well-wrought roads, all brought to fruition by many kinds of exploited labor. Furthermore, as to the relationships presented here between sublime discourse and figurations of the liminal space where infrastructure meets natural terrain—the threshold where natural and artificial landscape converge, intermingle, and unfold—Nesfield's account marks an early example of how an artificial colonial sublimity emerges in conversation with descriptions of numinous natural, material sublimity within national frontier narratives.

Romantic natural sublimity in effect called forth a titanic challenger: not just the reach of the imaginative mind understood through Kantian dynamic sublimity, but also its physical, manmade complement, a technological sublimity, a sublimity including massive infrastructural–colonial projects calling to mind a logic not of *deus ex machina* but *demos ex machina*: known more precisely as the infrastructural sublime. While the famed Latin phrase *deus ex machina*, roughly translating to "god from the machinery" connotes plot contrivance (forced if not facile narrative resolutions) my permutation of that phrase, *demos ex machina*, suggests a "polity from the machinery," connoting land manipulations contrived in part to betoken national adhesion and achievement, binding Britons together and installing national pride. This iteration of the technological sublime, the infrastructural sublime, reads unparalleled civil artifacts less as the work of earthen agencies or diverse hands and more as proud and wondrous products of one nation, one vision.

I: Robert Southey, the Wearmouth Bridge, and the Style of British Civil Engineering

In one of his bestselling epistolary achievements, the mock-travelogue *Letters from England* (1807), Southey describes a characteristically British type of bridgework.[11] Early on he addresses the aforementioned Wearmouth Bridge at Sunderland. Built in last decade of the eighteenth century, scholars of science and technology studies see it as a pioneering effort born from a particularly robust period in the history of British and Irish civil engineering:

---

[11] While Southey's first epistolary work, *Letters Written During a Short Residence in Spain and Portugal* saw a second edition, *Letters from England by Don Manuel Alvarez Espriella* went through three, with the last being a revised edition. See Lynda Pratt, Tim Fulford, and Ian Packer, "General Introduction: Southey as a Letter Writer," in *The Collected Letters of Robert Southey, A Romantic Circles Electronic Edition*, para. 4, https://romantic-circles.org/editions/southey_letters/letterEEd.26.genIntro.html; and Carol Bolton, ed., *Letters from England: By Don Manuel Alvarez Espriella* (New York: Routledge, 2016).

The Romantic Sublime and Representations of Technology

the decades of 1790–1830.[12] Planned and designed by the local Parliamentary Member Rowland Burdon and supervised by directing engineer Thomas Wilson, in 1796 the bridge featured the longest cast iron arch of its day, making it the first of its type to be built.[13] While the French had attempted unsuccessfully to create iron arch bridges since 1719, the first functional example of this kind was the Ironbridge over the Severn at Coalbrookdale in Shropshire (1779).[14] After Burdon secured a necessary Act of Parliament in 1792, the irons for Wearmouth Bridge at Sunderland were cast and sent from Rotherham. Meanwhile, Wilson began to devise its construction. Borrowing from a system Thomas Paine demonstrated at the French Académie in 1786, Wilson implemented an innovative method that contemporary engineering biographers continue to describe as vaguely ingenious and quasi-ethereal.[15] For instance, in reference to Wilson's plan to raise the basic framework, A. W. Skempton's recent account includes little about the whole process beyond noting how "[t]he ribs of the arch had been positioned by supporting them on scaffolding, [and then] floated into position."[16] For its storied method of construction, its unprecedented size, and signature "British" style, the Sunderland Bridge quickly—albeit inaccurately—assumed the status of a national triumph.

The important point to bear in mind is how sublime celebrations of innovative infrastructure risk occluding the long arc of the construction process. Often, when works of civil infrastructure are styled sublime, temporal emphases fall on staged foundation stones and inaugural ribbon cuttings. This pattern arises in Romantic literature of all sorts documenting infrastructural work partly because of existing parameters of sublime discourse. As many critics of Romantic-era aesthetics note, sublime discourse is organized around two prominent temporal registers: first, the instant or ephemeral, and second,

---

[12] A. W. Skempton, *A Biographical Dictionary of Civil Engineers in Great Britain and Ireland: 1500–1830* (London: ICE Publishing, 2002), xxix–xxx.

[13] With its 236-foot span, it was two and a half times longer than the Coalbrookdale Bridge in Shropshire, which opened in 1779. In his *Biographical Dictionary of Civil Engineers*, Skempton marks the "development of iron arch bridges" as a "characteristic feature of the period," with notable examples including the "pioneer Sunderland Bridge (Rowland Burdon and Thomas Wilson) to the mature bridges of Telford and William Hazeldine at Craigellachie and Tewkesbury and James Walker's Vauxhall Bridge in London, and the equally remarkable development of suspension bridges from the Union Bridge of Sir Samuel Brown to Telford's 580-ft. span Menai Bridge on the Holyhead Road" (xxx).

[14] Tom F. Peters, *Transitions in Engineering: Guillaume Henri Dufour and the Early 19th Century Cable Suspension Bridges* (Basel: Birkhäuser, 1987), 188.

[15] Thomas Paine's system, as borrowed by Wilson, was originally planned for Schuylkill in Philadelphia. See Peters, *Transitions in Engineering*, 189.

[16] Skempton, *Biographical Dictionary of Civil Engineers*, 788.

Suspension Bridges, Modern Canals, and the Infrastructural Sublime

the eternal or the long durée. Representations of noted British infrastructure bear similar temporal emphases. The figure of an enduring nation emerges from evanescent characterizations of a particularly British style of bridge, of a structure that transports astonished observers by making durable substance out of airy style.

Such formulas of sublime transport trade on figures of temporal paradox, which hazard collapsing time across human, biotic, and technological scales. Sublimity's telltale temporalities—barely conceivable deep time yoked to an immediate moment of reception—acknowledge process chiefly to aggrandize the final, beheld product. These hallmark temporalities of natural sublimity undergird the grounding structures of meaning for infrastructural sublimity. Under the rubric of the infrastructural sublime, those arduous human labors and gradual workings of time and materiality are overshadowed by the draw and allure of either the momentary fireworks of novel apprehension—of epiphanic time—or by the grand seductions of deep time, the pull of timespans far outpacing spaces of human life. These emphases on either extraordinary or nonhuman temporalities within sublime discourse tend to lend built structures the false promise of permanence, granting fantastic and impossible longevities, and suggesting civil artifacts without end. One's sense of being in the presence of a timeless built structure only intensifies the compressed and individuated instant of sublime apprehension, ultimately propping up fictions of national durability and exceptionality.

Emerging out of existing registers of traditional landscape aesthetics treating the natural or material sublime, the paradoxical language of infrastructural sublimity codes time and labor in terms that favor the epiphanic moment of the structure's reception, with much ado being made over the onset and conclusion of construction. As we have seen, Nesfield's speech repatterns conventional sublime discourse, lavishing the bulk of the attention upon the start and stop of work, not any gradual labor process. Most of all, Nesfield champions the bridge's completion, the charged moment of encountering the finished product, but as ever, such transport is charged by way of sublime temporal paradox, as he then emphasizes a limitless, unending, and thus, unknowable time attributed to the crossing, and by extension, to Britain. Here again sublime discourse turns upon temporal extremes—the awe-striking moment hinges upon imaginings of the infinite—conferring the bridge with both immediate import and the dress of immortality. Paradoxical sublime temporal registers afford Nesfield an easy link between an eternal iconography of the bridge and an horizonless British futurity.

Yet, in *Letters from England*, Southey both channels and challenges a sublime reception of the Sunderland structure that would read the bridge as unwavering and rightful national landmark. On the one hand the poet echoes Nesfield, professing a sense of undying national prowess made manifest in a

143

The Romantic Sublime and Representations of Technology

"glorious monument of British taste." Southey follows Nesfield most closely when he dwells upon a sublime, counterintuitive contrast amassed by the bridge's apparent ephemeral yet durable form. In particular, he lauds the "delicate" crossing's ability to bear its own weight in addition to that of its many travelers.[17] On the other hand, even with this emphasis on formal or material paradox, *Letters from England* does more to resist intertwined natural and technological sublime narratives that would read the artifact as an embodiment of some extreme, simultaneous dichotomy: either instant or eternal shrine or both. Southey likewise challenges the notion that it symbolizes the work of just one nation, as opposed to being a thing of joint labors, ordinary processes, and international crossings. Adopting the voice of a touring Spanish gentleman, the soon-to-be Poet Laureate published his *Letters* under a pseudonym: Don Manuel Alvarez Espriella.[18] While the entire travel narrative operates in the way of an anthropological study of British taste and manners viewed through the lens of an intimate outsider, one passage in particular foregrounds the nationalized significance ascribed to such infrastructural ventures. The same passage also recognizes key overlapping and gradual realities that the infrastructural sublime can obscure.

Southey's letter playfully showcases Espriella's contempt for the cast iron bridges of Britannia, all the while identifying hallmark features associated with these Romantic-era conduits, including the British bridge's refined ironwork that he and others read as an updated technological expression of the paradoxical if not ironic logic of the material sublime. Iron unexpectedly instantiates the bridge's light, airy, and insubstantial feel:

> [A]n adventurous iron bridge had been built at Sunderland, [with] one arch of monstrous span over a river with high rocky banks, so that large ships could sail under. ... I know not how these iron bridges may appear to an English eye, but to a Spaniard's they are utterly detestable. The colour, where it is not black, is rusty, and the hollow, open, spider work, which they so much praise for its lightness, has no appearance of solidity. Of all the works of man, there is not any one which unites so well with natural scenery, and so heightens its beauty, as a bridge, if any taste, or rather if no bad taste, be displayed in its structure. This is

---

[17] Bolton, ed., *Letters from England*, 102. Hereafter, citations are noted in the text by page number.

[18] In her scholarly edition of *Letters*, Carol Bolton notes how Southey "wanted to create the detached view of an outsider from which to critique his own society. His innocent ingénu comes from a sheltered, parochial background, and brings with him a strong, unquestioning, religious faith. This allows Southey to present naïve impressions that amuse and entertain (as Byron would do in Don Juan) but also to fulfil the role of 'truth-teller' for a sophisticated, elite audience" (15).

Suspension Bridges, Modern Canals, and the Infrastructural Sublime

exemplified in the rude as well as in the magnificent; by the stepping stones or crossing plank of a village brook, as well as by the immortal works of Trajan: but to look at these bridges which are bespoken at the foundries, you would actually suppose that the architect had studied at the confectioner's, and borrowed his ornaments from the sugar temples of a dessert. It is curious that this execrable improvement, as every novelty is called in England, should have been introduced by the notorious politician, Paine, who came over from America, upon this speculation, and exhibited one as a show upon dry ground in the metropolis. (102–3)

Southey's faux-foreign narrator teasingly describes the "adventurous" quality of the "monstrous" British arch. Although the letter mentions that the Sunderland crossing was modeled after that of an American colonial, Thomas Paine, to Southey's imagined Spanish eye it amounts to no more than a glaring shrine to repugnant British taste. Such pronouncements draw upon the conceptual currency of, and cultural exclusivity frequently granted to, the grand infrastructural artifact, which alike grounded Nesfield's speech; regardless of its genuine multinational origins such as those explicitly mentioned here with reference to Paine, Southey's sublime characterizations of the arch activate a political and professional mythology rendering bridges as depositories of national character and evolutionary histories. Suggesting a "distinctively British position in then-contemporary world culture" and moving toward the "revolution of manners" that James Chandler argues culminates in England in 1819, Southey's letter betrays the allegorical role of the bridge as infrastructural artifact betokening national efficacy and its role in developing a national aesthetic and structural taste.[19] Writ large, to be sublime means to be exceptional, uncommon, unassimilable, not communal. As Frances Ferguson would remind us, Romantic sublimity traditionally understood trades upon fictions of solitude and a politics of individuation. So too, in terms of technological aesthetics, sublime discourse swerves toward the particularizing example, *a* national achievement, one engineer's genius creation. Within the milieu of late eighteenth- and early nineteenth-century infrastructural customs and manners, blue blood courses throughout the delicate ribs of Sunderland's iron bridge.

Sublime discourse underwrites the style claimed for British structural engineering during the Romantic era, with authors as well as orators depicting an architecture of sweetness and light yet imbued with an unassailable resilience. The paradoxical logic of the sublime fit well with the paradoxical logic of British (infrastructural) imperialism: appear all sweetness and light, reside and remain with an iron grip. Troubling the logic of such nationalized infrastructural aesthetics, Southey makes a confectioner of the architect and takes

---

[19] Chandler, *England in 1819*, xiv.

The Romantic Sublime and Representations of Technology

the entire structure for a fragile, saccharine pastry. "[I]ts lightness" yields "no appearance of solidity," and Espriella sees scant cause for celebrating the weightless appearance of the "hollow, open, spider work, which [Britons] praise." These lines again attest to the ways in which "[t]echnological objects serve as ideal containers for nationalistic views. They allow feelings about nativeness and foreignness to assume a tangible form."[20] Moreover, historian of technology Gregory K. Dreicer observes how "infrastructure does seem to reflect the state of a nation by demonstrating a government's ability to maintain the networks that enable the nation to function," and Southey's words at once reinforce and undermine the national significance of the supposedly hearty if willowy Sunderland Bridge.[21] The passage suggests that the engineer, Wilson, must have "borrowed his ornaments from the sugar temples of a dessert" and with this image the writer begins to undercut the presumed durability of the pronounced arch. Rather than applauding the lightness of the structure, he invites an association between dissolving sugars of a dessert and corroding ruins of a desert. Southey does not stop there. Leveraging another routine trope of the infrastructural sublime, the Spanish narrator's metaphor makes light work of the prospect of raising other iron bridges, with the narrator blithely suggesting that Wilson might just "throw a similar but smaller bridge over the Thames" (102). To this loosely veiled critique of the going "English" mode of infrastructural design, Southey affixes a footnote; it reads: "The great Sunderland bridge has lately become liable to tremendous vibrations, and thereby established the unfitness of building any more such" (103, n. 15). Beyond any politics of style (the labyrinthine "spider work" of this structure) the ancient form of the sweeping arch recast here in metal failed to safely and consistently unite Britons from both sides of the River Wear, and thus failed to deliver on the strained promise of *demos ex machina*.[22] For Southey, the less overt iconography of the Sunderland Bridge entails its historical failures, its untenable fragilities, and thus exposes fantasies of infrastructural imperialism that both underestimate ecological and social realities and overestimate the power of innovative designs and engineered solutions.

Given that Southey devotes much energy to aesthetic critique and only footnotes the near failure of the work in terms of use–value, it is important to consider the sweeping aesthetic significance assigned to the bridge as a human-made part of the British landscape. Positioned between pronouncements of

---

[20] Gregory K. Dreicer, "Building Bridges and Boundaries: The Lattice and the Tube, 1820–1860," *Technology and Culture* 51, no. 1 (2010): 126–63.

[21] Dreicer, "Building Bridges and Boundaries," 157.

[22] The Sunderland Bridge is now known as the Wearmouth Bridge, which crosses the River Wear near the mouth of the North Sea. Wilson's bridge first underwent repair in 1805 (just under twenty years after its grand opening) and got a massive overhaul by famed civil engineer Robert Stephenson from 1857 to 1859.

Suspension Bridges, Modern Canals, and the Infrastructural Sublime

the structure's iron monstrosity or its confectionary frailty is a Kantian, universalizing judgment on the nature of bridges and the place of bridges in nature. Southey addresses the role of this technological artifact, this tribute to material and cultural boundaries tastefully negotiated, within its greater environment of the natural world. Each landscape "improvement," or what Southey's tourist chalks up to mere "novelty" within ongoing attempts at infrastructural innovation, takes a back seat to universalizing aesthetic taste, downplaying commercial, functional, or political ends. Whether "rude" or "magnificent," and assumedly whether one is from Spain or England, "there is not any [technology] which unites so well with natural scenery, and so heightens its beauty, as a bridge, if any taste, or rather if no bad taste, be displayed in its structure." This remark cannot be reduced to the simple formula of fashion over function. It instead marks the sweeping naturalism and universalizing logic Bruno Latour associates with constructions of the modern subject, a type of person which he postulates has always been only mythologically extant, but which theorists often argue emerges in the eighteenth century, post Enlightenment.[23] For Latour, "cultural differences" like those exhibited in Southey's text "shined so vividly" due to the unquestioned presumption of an overall "unity of nature, [that] provided the common denominator" upon which distinctions between cultures and civilizations relied.[24] If a presumed unity of nature undergirds cultural relativism, then grounding assumptions about "laws of nature" integral to prevailing discourses of natural sublimity underwrote nineteenth-century colonial ideologies and nationalized significances linked to great infrastructural undertakings.[25]

And yet, while according to this schema the nationalist may praise John Bull's ability to float a bridge proudly above a chasm, one cannot escape the

---

[23] See Bruno Latour, *We Have Never Been Modern* (Cambridge, MA: Harvard University Press, 1993).

[24] Bruno Latour, *War of the Worlds: What about Peace?* trans. Charlotte Bigg, ed. John Tresch (Cambridge and Chicago: Prickly Paradigm Press, 2002), 6. Latour critiques the idea that the modern subject is grounded by a representational and material divide. He suggests that a regularized denominator of abstract and homogenous nature "was even more indisputably common when one moved from the world of human nature to the world of non-human nature. The possibility of disagreement among specialists or disciplines certainly remained, but ultimately the world (in the singular) external nature would be enough to bring agreement among them all. Different cultures existed, with their many idiosyncrasies, but at least there was only one nature with its necessary laws. Conflicts between humans, no matter how far they went, remained limited to the representations, ideas and images that diverse cultures could have of a single biophysical nature" (6).

[25] Transatlantic colonial ideologies routinely justified maintaining or establishing socioeconomic hierarchies on the grounds of assumed laws of nature. See Eric J. Sundquist, "Melville, Delany, and New World Slavery," in *To Wake the Nations: Race in the Making of American Literature* (Cambridge, MA: Harvard University Press, 1994), 135–221.

The Romantic Sublime and Representations of Technology

fact that the structure occupies a uniquely fragile position in relation to a natural landscape not uniformly valued. This bridge is at once an overdetermined display of human ingenuity and a reminder of the particularized and precarious place of diverse British citizens and subjects among "nature's works." Such a rhetorical formulation bespeaks the condition of the infrastructural object and its relationship to the Romantic imagination and thought. In other words, Southey's text illuminates the relationship of monument to peoplehood and between building and thinking.[26] Bringing together two banks, wobbling and ever-decaying as it stretches from end to end, the bridge requires almost constant care and attention; like an "hollow, open, spider work"—the delicate web-work edifice of the arachnid—for Southey, British bridgework cannot but represent both foundation and ephemerality. Crucially, it straddles multiple realms: the particular, the universal, the natural, the national, and the technological.

II: Thomas Telford, Colossus of Roads, and "A Spider's Web in the Air"

For acclaimed British engineer and architect Thomas Telford, the Menai Bridge had seemed inevitable since the Act of Union in 1801, as he wanted to provide in the physical world a bond that had been forged in the legislative realm. Crossing the turbulent Menai Strait and reducing London to Dublin travel time by nine hours, it was to be the jewel of the Holyhead road project and indeed was heralded as a "most stupendous piece of work."[27] After completing other assignments, Telford began seriously planning this one in 1810. But progress halted in 1811 "when," as he put it enigmatically, "circumstances occurred which led to the postponement of my ... plans."[28] While the nature of these "circumstances" invite speculation, he would return to his "plans" post-Waterloo. A coupling of parliamentary Acts in 1818 and 1819 appropriated funds and vessels needed to secure sufficient laborers and building materials. Construction began with blasting in 1819, shortly before Telford would befriend Poet Laureate Robert Southey. The "first stone of this wonderful work was laid [discretely] (without the least appearance of

---

[26] For a foundational essay on the connection not only between building and thinking but also between building, dwelling [being with and within], and thinking, see Martin Heidegger, "Building Dwelling Thinking," in *Basic Writings*, 343–63.

[27] *Mirror of Literature, Amusement, and Instruction*, vol. 7, eds. Reuben Percy and John Timbs (London: J. Limbird, Strand, 1826), 381. Hereafter citations are noted in-text by page number.

[28] Thomas Telford, *Life of Thomas Telford, Civil Engineer, Written by Himself Containing a Descriptive Narrative of His Professional Labours: With a Folio Atlas of Copper Plates*, ed. John Rickman (London: Payne and Foss, 1838), 218.

148

Suspension Bridges, Modern Canals, and the Infrastructural Sublime

pageantry, and it may be added, with the utmost privacy)," perhaps due to the project's belated starting.[29] Following suit, many of the undertaking's more involved processes prompted little fanfare. These tasks included forging the iron frames and suspension chains, laying the stone-work necessary for the two main piers, and quarrying for and then constructing seven gray marble arches to support the bridge's framework and roadway. Ironically, upon completion and throughout the nineteenth century, authors deemed the bridge over the Menai Strait to be so wholly stunning that it appeared to belong to neither humankind nor nature—regardless of the earthly grounds that supported, anchored, and comprised each abutment, and regardless of the many human hands and minds that helped to bring the bridge into being.

To Britons, the iron chains and suspended passage of the bridge over the Menai Strait was the stuff of lore; the bridge was read as a sublime artifact for being both beyond nature and above the doing of mere mortals.[30] Despite it being described repeatedly in language and images, as the archive shows, in line with familiar scripts of sublime landscape aesthetics, viewers foregrounded such remarks with requisite evocations of the sublimely unpresentable and paradoxical. They stumbled over themselves as they cleared room in their minds and lexicons to reckon with what some called the "eighth wonder of the world."[31] Of course, Telford's acclaimed work is at once human-fabricated and earthborn, but as scores of laborers nudged the bridge toward completion, print representations of the artifact undermined its association with both the earth and the human hands that made it. In popular literature, the Menai Suspension Bridge became known as a thing sublime, a reified sublime aesthetic object, decontextualized, separate from the very nature and forms of labor from which it sprang. Its sublime status as an iconographic civil artifact effaced the necessarily aggregate efforts of the material world and human hands responsible for its existence.

The widely circulated periodical, *The Mirror*, stresses the structure as a sublime bridge beyond this world and its words, a structure confounding

---

[29] Joseph Pring, *Particulars of the grand suspension bridge, erected over the Straits of Menai by order of government; designed by, and built under the immediate direction of Thomas Telford, Esq. Civil engineer. Began in May, 1819, and opened, for the use of the public, on Monday, January 30, 1826* (London: J. Brown, 1826), 571. It is worth noting that placing the first stone did not take place until after the tide was effectively diverted from the Anglesey shore to fabricate a temporary causeway; the diverted waters carried away a number of cattle unaccustomed to the swifter, more concentrated stream created by this augmentation. See Pring, *Particulars of the grand suspension bridge*, 571.

[30] Douglas Nichol, "The Whita Hill Building Stone Quarries at Langholm, Scottish Borders–Environmental Geology and Historical Aspects," *Proceedings of the Institution of Civil Engineers – Municipal Engineer* 133, no. 4 (1999): 207.

[31] Pring, *Particulars of the grand suspension bridge*, 581.

The Romantic Sublime and Representations of Technology

human characterization, where "nothing but a sight of it can convey anything like an idea of its magnificence to the mind. Every representation of it, as a drawing, cannot fail to be paltry. It sets drawing at defiance!" (381). The bridge—unpresentable and unearthly, unique and quasi-godlike—is paradoxically both anomalous and ubiquitous: "The country round is bleak in the extreme, nor are there any features in the landscape to render it at all picturesque. It is nothing but the bridge itself; but that is everything! It is a creation in the clouds, and appears to be above the power of mortals either to erect or control; it almost forms part of the creation!" (381). Printed almost immediately following the project's completion (1826) and for *The Mirror*, a publication known for spectacle, not substance, this particular article no doubt sought to capitalize on popular thought linking sublime discourses to unprecedented unveilings of large-scale civil infrastructural projects.

In sublime accounts, such as those of the popular press detailing the opening of the largest suspension bridge the world had yet to see, the engineer's masterpiece appears both independent and autopoietic. It is nothing but the bridge itself, and yet it is everything. These narratives liken the vast civil artifact to a quasi-supernatural totality, in turn conferring such force to the Crown. As the periodical puts it, this expansive infrastructural artifact appears as if it had been fashioned in mid-air, seems a creation of the clouds and at once surpasses them by also seeming to form a central part of creation itself. It is as if the bridge by its very nature activates elements of some larger vital and creative force operative within the naturescape at large. Dissolving the bridge's well-documented origins, *The Mirror* pointedly does not evoke the work of those who built it, nor does it explicitly refer to even Telford's part in proposing its general outline. Sensationalizing the bridge to the greatest possible extent, the article is at pains to exhibit what is most apt to pique the minds of its readers: the *je ne sais quoi* of the bridge that suggests that it has a life of its own, separate from the hands of its creators and disaffiliated from those substances and tools with which it was created.

The Mirror then deploys another recurrent trope of sublime infrastructural discourse by fancifully imagining that any built environs as daunting as these must surely belong to the terrain of giants. Seemingly innocent references to would-be suprahuman giants implicitly make humans into something more magical, larger, and fantastic than they really are. The bridge is for, belongs to, and is now in service to the metaphorical giants Britons have become, in light of a technological prowess perhaps matched only by whatever natural powers they have yet to overcome. The author writes: "At the first view that is obtained of Menai Bridge, on the road from Bangor, *one pier* only is visible; it then looks as if a giant had passed by, and carelessly dropped a silken thread over a rocky fragment; but when you closely examine it, its massy abutments and ponderous chains, the globe itself appears too weak and frail to support the

150

Suspension Bridges, Modern Canals, and the Infrastructural Sublime

burden!" (381, original emphasis). With this description, the structure seems a by-product effortlessly established—a naturalized thing of casual waste more than ponderous craft, insofar as a giant might have relaxed his hand, casually discarding a gossamer thread.

Next, the narrative effectually zooms in on the bridge; it now looks to be massive, almost extraterrestrial, alien to earth, with "the globe itself appear(ing) too weak and frail to support the burden." Such phrasing begs the question of earthly carrying capacity, of whether such sublime, alien-seeming transformations of the earth's surface are sustainable or not. At the same time, these oppositional, paradoxical analogues (bridge to silken thread and technological work to supernatural weight) make light of the structure's apparent density while also hyperbolizing it, neither allowing for nor grappling with the bridge in its complexity.

It is important to note that wherever this account describes a bridge materializing at will or coming into being supernaturally via the hand of a giant, appearing suddenly as some unearthly mass, it takes a page from the trope of the sublime at its most material. This is the more material than immaterial or metaphysical valence derived from the verb *sublimate*, a valence denoting exceedingly rapid transformations between material states such as when artic ice sublimates or sublimes off into the air without ever first becoming liquid. *Sublimate*'s material connotations recurrently surface throughout poetic and popular narratives dedicated to Telford's infrastructural technologies, particularly as authors depict jarring, surprising, or disjunctive material transformations. But there is an additional fixture of the language of the natural sublime that is of some salience here—that of flouting established or imagined laws of nature. The article from *The Mirror* closes by once again emphasizing how the bridge defies representation and by foregrounding Telford's use of chain and rod to counter the more lawless seeming turns of "natural law:"

> In this part of the country, the features of nature are all great; it seems as if nature was sporting with mankind, and showing her superiority. All the erections of man are small and insignificant, whilst nature luxuriates in her creations, without law or bounds. But Telford has almost entered into a competition with nature.—What, though mountain is piled on mountain;—what, though sea roars in unrestrained fury at their bases; what, though the mountains and the sea are exposed to all the thundering of the lawless winds;—yet has Telford set them at defiance! He has chained mountain to mountain, by a bridge hung in the clouds. Though the storms roll above it, and the sea roars beneath it, it stands firm in unmoved magnificence, defying their united powers, and *there* it appears likely to remain, until that time when "the foundations of the earth shall be shaken!" (381, original emphasis)

The Romantic Sublime and Representations of Technology

The "firm" and "unmoved" bridge becomes a metonym for Britannia. While this narrative rehearses the biblical story of the end of days as well as the well-trod, reductive story pitting humanity against the terraqueous globe, it does so in a manner predicated upon sublime states of material transformation. Such narratives, like stories casting earthen structures as something somehow extraterrestrial, do not draw currency from truth, and even less from fact, but from immaterial aesthetic value and poetic, or rather, linguistic license and play. Just as the bridge does not hang from the clouds, it has never stood "firm." In truth, even on the work's opening day, "[t]he wind, due south, blew fresh throughout the day, which caused a trifling, though scarcely perceptible, undulatory motion about the centre of the bridge."[32] The author's appeal to fixity and suggestion that mortal ingenuity might yield the creation of perfectly secure bearings are tantamount to wishful thinking. Narratives of the infrastructural sublime underscore a powerful human desire to augment the landscape into the shape of a more predictable external world. But, of course, the bridge would never be an "unmoved magnificence;" its material realities could never match up with an impossible immaterial aesthetic.

Over the top sublime stylings of the Menai Suspension Bridge composed by the periodical press resonate with words drafted by the Poet Laureate to be carved into stone. In Scottish Inverness, a marble slab stands before the eastern end of the Caledonian Canal (also famously planned by Telford), bearing the following lines from an inscription authored by Southey:

> Telford, - who, o'er the vale of Cambrian Dee,
> Aloft in air, at giddy height upborne,
> Carried his navigable road: and hung
> High o'er Menai's Strait the bending bridge!
> Structures of more ambitious enterprise
> Than minstrels, in the age of old romance,
> To their own Merlin's magic lore ascribed.
> Nor hath he for his native land performed
> Less, in this proud design;[33]

As Southey's verse suggests, the "bending" suspension bridge over the Menai Strait (1819–1826), jewel of the larger London to Holyhead road project to which the bridge belonged, cemented the fabled status of Telford the civil architect and engineer regardless of any ill-fated bridges or ineffective canals. Once rivaled in the British popular imagination perhaps only by John

---

[32] Pring, *Particulars of the grand suspension bridge*, 580.
[33] Robert Southey, *Robert Southey: Later Poetical Works, 1811–1838*, vol. 1, eds. Tim Fulford and Lynda Pratt (London: Pickering and Chatto, 2012), 257–8, lines 9–17.

Suspension Bridges, Modern Canals, and the Infrastructural Sublime

Rennie (1761–1821), Telford today is known the world over as the father of civil engineering.[34] Fascinatingly, the reception history of Telford's works—mediated both by his friend Southey, the national poet, and the nation's growing popular press—reinforce how common yet reductive readings of vast infrastructural projects as national emblems unfold in tandem with aestheti-cized notions of the architect as *the* technological author, *the* Romantic or even Merlin-esque genius *qua* poet, *the* prime subjective agent.[35] Repeatedly in the literature of the latter half of the Romantic era, grand undertakings like canals and bridges mark the work of "astonishing" nationalized genius and "stupendous" human prowess precisely because texts figure them as the human-fabricated counterparts or rivals to sublime works of nature.[36] The literary lives of such trademark structures, along with that of the larger, famed Holyhead road, provide compelling instances of how the language of the sublime dialectically informs the popular reception of remarkable works of both nature and humanity. Though the Romantic sublime quite familiarly allows for reductive characterizations of stunning works of nature, it also routinely masks the complex nature of technological and cultural work home to infrastructural projects as well as imperial politics.

In Southey's dedicatory lines, made physically manifest beside the Caledonian Canal—ostensibly in perpetuity—sublime tropes of transport and of suspended or arrested movement converge. Southey's reductive infrastructural figurations downplay the long duration of the building process and obscure various material and cross-cultural collaborations. For instance, his depiction of the bridge over the Menai imagines Telford—not the banks of the earth—shouldering the entire load of the bridge, and its burdensome construction is prepared for without difficulty by the hands—not of laborers—but of the "immortal" architect: "Telford, - who, o'er the vale of Cambrian Dee, / Aloft in air, at giddy height upborne, / Carried his navigable road: and hung / High o'er Menai's Strait the bending bridge!" Southey decorates Telford's "navigable road" and bridge with the language of the sublime which disproportion-ately touts presentist product over enduring process. These civil artifacts are metaphorically "hung" "aloft" by the engineer seemingly in an instant. Further

---

[34] For British historians, Rennie's name is unlikely to pale in comparison to Telford, since Rennie designed not only the Lancaster Canal (1792–1803), the Kennet & Avon Canal (1794–1810), the Royal Military Canal (1804–1809), but also Kelso Bridge (1800–1804), Waterloo Bridge (1811–1817), and London Bridge (1824–1831).

[35] This persistent single author model, or better myth, obscures actual networks of collaboration. The Caledonian Canal endeavor lends just such an example; Telford worked jointly on that project with another engineer, William Jessop, until 1812. See Skempton, *A Biographical Dictionary of Civil Engineers*, 684.

[36] Joseph Priestley, *A Course of Lectures on Oratory and Criticism* (London: J. Johnson, 1777), vii, 503.

153

The Romantic Sublime and Representations of Technology

aggrandizing Telford's infrastructural works, Southey weds celebratory lines applauding Telford's unique "structures" to inventions praised in some remote, more Romantic and magic time, expanding the temporal reach of Telford the engineer here cast as instantaneously effective magician, and in turn diminishing slower material processes and labor practices integral to infrastructural works. In this case, Southey's poem rehearses a mythologized historical account of these nationalized civil artifacts, with the Menai Suspension Bridge becoming an "ambitious enterprise" surpassing those to which "Merlin's magic lore [was] ascribed." Blurring the bounds of various natural supernaturalisms built into the rhetoric of Romantic-era sublime aesthetics, these poetic lines project assumedly universalized powers of nature onto quite particularized men and assumedly singular, monolithic cultural traditions. The poet's dedicatory remarks appropriate nationalized misunderstandings of technological invention, fueling myths of solitary (if not poetic) genius and human authorship that gain much of their rhetorical force by disavowing complex realities of nature and culture, or otherwise ignoring what Donna Haraway would call the collaborative forces of necessarily conjoined naturecultures.[37]

Contrastingly, in his most detailed treatment of the Highland canal works, Southey's journals leave behind the sublime's reductive tropes of material and temporal paradox to foreground how Telford's intellectual labor must work alongside the mason's physical labor to negotiate mud, earth, and stone. It is also here that the poet comes nearest to presenting the engineer's locks as instruments operating alongside the riverbed as opposed to effortlessly occupying it. An entry dated 12 September accounts for both the agential richness of the sea's floor and the much-involved processes necessary to form "Telford's" locks:

> The masonry at the mouth is about ten feet above high water mark: the locks large enough to admit a 32 gun frigate, the largest which has ever been made. There was a difficulty at the mouth from the nature of the bottom, being a mud so soft that it was pierced with an iron rod to the depth of sixty feet. A foundation was made by compressing it with an enormous weight of earth and stones, which were left during twelve months to settle, after which a pit was sunk in it, and the sea lock therein founded and built. This was a conception of Telford's, and had it not been for this bold thought the design of the canal must have been abandoned. The length of the basin is 800 yards, the breadth 150. Already the Sea has, as it were, adopted the outworks, and clothed the embankment and the walls with sea-weed.[38]

---

[37] See Haraway, *Manifestly Haraway*.
[38] Robert Southey, *Journal of a Tour in Scotland in 1819* (London: J. Murray, 1929), 167–8.

Suspension Bridges, Modern Canals, and the Infrastructural Sublime

This passage comes precariously close to adopting the logic of the egotistical sublime long married to anthropocentric notions of the individuated Romantic genius. But there is in fact a good dose of subtlety here as Southey details how Telford had to change his thinking, his plans, and his projections to think with and of the shifting earth that necessarily forms the basis for the canal. In contrast to the more reductive characterizations of landscape improvement at times surfacing in both his poetry and prose, here Southey foregrounds process over product while recognizing some of the project's numerous contingencies—in particular the project's wider material agencies—in place of solely highlighting individualistic accounts of hyperbolic human (engineer) or cultural (British) agency. Although twenty-first century readers could and should hope for more, at least here the liminal environment between land and sea is beginning to be given its due, as is the long duration entailed in effecting the engineer's always-adapting and ever-evolving projections.

Though in general, the structure itself, the engineered earth mined to make it, and the local environment it altered, tended to garner little regard in public-facing documents. But a modern bridge suspended captured readers' and viewers' imaginations, seeming as it did to grant humanity the dream of "build[ing] castles in the air."[39] Southey dubbed Telford "Pontifex Maximus" for his architectural brilliance especially in regard to bridgework and, as we have seen, at times he compared assembling these "floating" technological artifacts to feats of magicianship, to some Merlin-esque spell. Writing in similar regard, William Roscoe notes how "in the clear light of an autumnal sunset ... [with] the bright sun, the rocky picturesque foreground, villas, spires, and towers here and there enlivening the prospect—the Menai Bridge appeared more like the work of some great magician than the mere result of man's skill and industry."[40] With this common rhetorical gesture, ramifying representations of nature and technology render the scene sublime, while ironically the hard work of each, and that of humankind, is at risk of being edited out. When Barry Allen suggests that a "bridge may be" just as suitable an example "of knowledge as any true scientific proposition or theory," he "define[s] the quality that marks an artifact as a work of knowledge as superlative artifactual performance."[41] Activating such logic, two performative acts would cement how the Menai Bridge came to be known, understood, and celebrated: placing the final bolt in the first suspension chain; and then successfully fixing the

---

[39] Pring, *Particulars of the grand suspension bridge*, 569; for a similar treatment of the bridge as "'a castle in the air,'" see Samuel Smiles, *The Life of Thomas Telford, Civil Engineer: With an Introductory History of Roads and Travelling in Great Britain* (London: J. Murray, 1867), 275.

[40] William Roscoe quoted in Smiles, *The Life of Thomas Telford*, 276.

[41] Barry Allen, "Turning Back the Linguistic Turn in the Theory of Knowledge," *Thesis Eleven* 89, no. 6, (2007): 6.

The Romantic Sublime and Representations of Technology

final chain itself. Similar to a debutante at her ball, the artifact is celebrated when it is at last fit to be enjoyed, is put on display when it is deemed close enough to being "finished," now ready for social use—not a thing of process but a reified object of cultural appropriation.

Just two points in the bridge's arduous construction elicited any fanfare— the work's starting and its stopping—each celebration revolving around suspension, each hoisting up not quite a castle, but a bridge into the air. One marked when the first suspension chain "was thrown over the straits of Menai," the other announced the fateful day when workers fixed the last bolt for the final suspension chain. Finishing what started back in May of 1819 with an explosive first strike, "removing the inequalities of the rock called Ynys-y-moch," the "Opening of the BRIDGE" commenced on 30 January 1826.[42] The latter gala event honored the public opening of "this stupendous, pre-eminent and singularly unique structure," marrying infrastructural pursuit with techno-logical spectacle (579). The symbolic entity selected to first journey above the Menai Strait was the Royal London and Holyhead mail-coach set for Dublin. Included in its cargo was the resident engineer, the mail-coach superintendent, the director of the iron and timber work done on the bridge, the sons of the contractor for the masonry, and "as many more as could find room to sit or stand, or even procure a place to hang by" (579). After the mail-coach success-fully crossed the toll booth, passing the "glare of lamps" lighted all along the structure, a procession of notables followed: first, the private carriage of one of the "Commissioners, drawn by beautiful greys;" Telford's own vehicle; the "first stage-coach," belonging to the "Pilot, Bangor and Carnarvon" company; the first "London stage-coach," the Oxonian; the carriage of Sir Erskine, "late proprietor of the [local] ferry, drawn by four elegant greys, decorated with ribbons, followed by numerous gentlemen's carriages, landaus, gigs, cars, poney-sociables, &c. &c., upwards of one hundred and thirty in number, and horsemen innumerable" (579). Thousands were in attendance and spirits were high, with "numerous pedestrians, among whom were several persons of the first distinction ... parading along the beautiful platform roadway for several hours" (579). Then there were the national flags, cannons on either side of the bridge, "which continued firing at intervals the whole day," musicians trumpeted the opening of the suspension bridge by playing the National Anthem (580).[43] Pring closes his review of the day's events with the following declaration couched in sublime discourse: "When we reflect on the varied appearance of the numerous persons and objects present, the elegance of the equipages, the bold and sublime scenery of the country adjacent, and though

---

[42] Pring, *Particulars of the grand suspension bridge*, 570, 579. Hereafter citations are noted in-text by page number.

[43] See also Smiles, *The Life of Thomas Telford*, 277.

156

Suspension Bridges, Modern Canals, and the Infrastructural Sublime

not least, of the general public utility of this grand national work, it must be allowed that the *cowp-d'ail* [sic] was most enchanting;" (580).[44] The resulting scene is a study of how to conjure the infrastructural sublime, replete with its attendant nationalist charge and *demos ex machina* logic. Britons unite to behold not a just a bridge but a "grand national work," rendered sublime not in itself but in its contingent relationship to the "bold and sublime scenery of the country adjacent." The resulting aesthetic is that of a sublimely British scene, made all the more exceptional for its mass of Britons in their "elegant equipages" and its tasteful, infrastructurally engineered management of British bodies and boundaries.

Contravening conventional sublime narratives painting the bridge as the stuff of fanfare or giant's play, Telford's writing, like Southey's journaling (whether in jest or earnest, whether produced for public consumption or private reflection), evokes a thread of sublime discourse less like an infrastructural sublime fostering dreams of national aggrandizement and mastery and more akin to a material sublime puzzling over earthly agency and unsurmountable mystery. Indeed, the material sublime, with its swift and often sudden or discordant physical transformations (as in the aforementioned jump from ice to vapor), grounds any iteration of the technological or infrastructural sublime, whether we recognize it or not. It is simply that the infrastructural sublime emphasizes beginnings and endings, forsaking stories of painstaking process. Then nations and their most inventive members seem just as able to swiftly and effortlessly transform the earth as forceful nature appears to do in well-known narratives of the material sublime reaching back to biblical floods, classical myth, epic traditions, and so on.

But Telford's more materially sensitive sublime aesthetic interweaves sought-after human securities with the natural world's more insecure and volatile features. Telford's take on the very bridge he helped to run above the Menai Strait acknowledges it as a thing of process and of fear. He writes in a mode that eschews epiphanic registers of sublime discourse privileging either the heightened moment of inception and/or arrested moment of completion or their opposite, the ever-enduring and everlasting—or more oddly yet, some paradoxical mixture of both. The engineer here feels particularly anxious with regard to his uniquely designed suspension chain since "[i]ts failure had been predicted; and, ... [the work entire] had been freely spoken of as a 'castle in the air.'"[45] Also, remembering weak pillars of the past, in his memoir

---

[44] *"cowp-d'ail"*: "VIEW, n. 1 1 § *vue* (portée des yeux), f.; 2. 1 *vue* (etendue de ce qu'on peut voir), f.; 3. 1 *vue* (manière don't les objets se presentment à la vue), f.; 4. 1 *vue*, f.; *point de vue*, m.; *coup d'œil*, m.; *perspective*, f.; 5. 1 *vue*, (tableau, dessin, estampe), f.; 6. § *coup d'œil*; *regard* m." Alexander Spiers. *Spiers and Surenne's French and English Pronouncing Dictionary*, vol. 1 (London: D. Appleton & Co., 1861), 611.

[45] Smiles, *The Life of Thomas Telford*, 275.

The Romantic Sublime and Representations of Technology

he expresses concern over right materials and labor protocols. Bearing in mind "the example of the pillars of St. Chad's church (Shrewsbury), [and] when that edifice fell in the year 1788," he explains that "one of the most important improvements [was] to introduce into masonry ... the preference of cross walls to rubble, in the structure of the pier, or any other edifice requiring strength."[46] Adding that the rubble fills used in buildings like St. Chad's church were no better than "a heap of rubbish confined by side-walls," he reveals the fallen church "was ever fixed in [his] memory" (221). Fixed in his memory, too, was the need for repair and revision, not any myth of national exclusivity.

And yet, even as Telford turns his gaze earthward, celebrating facets of the bridge that buttress, support, or ground the structure, as opposed to heralding vainglorious promenades leading to sublime vistas from above, there exists a tension in his writing about his work, just as there is across Southey's writings. While Telford is able to put at arm's length the seductive pull of aerial castles not reducible to rubble, he still reaches for an almost superhuman agency, a sublime or godlike semblance of control ushered in by technological ingenuity. In his autobiographical narrative he delights chiefly in putting fear at bay, and relishes recounting moments like those of the year 1823 when

> the first iron-plate in the main-chain tunnel was fixed ... the mode of fixing the main-chains in the rock being an important operation, and worthy of inspection by every visitor of the bridge, who feels no dread at entering by a side-drain (on the Anglesey side) into a cavern in the rock, containing gigantic iron-work, and productive of feelings of superhuman agency. No precautions were spared to render every part perfectly true, and therefore secure; (224–5)

The engineer is here quite invested in the tale of sublime romance—the heroic quest for strength, security, and control—while the greater populace rides the tide of proliferating sublime discourses grounded in reductive material imaginings and collapsed temporalities, all wistfully homogenized under the aegis of so-called natural law.

While Telford looks down, surveying joints, cross-walls, and the interiors of caves and tunnels, he nonetheless is well acquainted with the experience of his supporters, of those reveling in a patina of technology, mankind, and landscape offered in the view from above, from atop the bridge. The engineer's remarks on the bridge's opening day reveal again that he was not wholly immune to the pull of the infrastructural sublime that would script structures

---

[46] Thomas Telford, *Life of Thomas Telford, Written by Himself,* 221. Hereafter citations are noted in-text by page number.

Suspension Bridges, Modern Canals, and the Infrastructural Sublime

as novelties and cast the completion of bold designs as exemplars of a national imagination fully realized:

> Upon my report to the state of the works, the Commissioners determined that the passage over the bridge should be opened on the 30th of January 1826. The weather, about that time, proved very stormy; and previously to the opening day, Sir Henry Parnell and myself examined the entire structure, and found all necessary arrangements made. On Monday morning, at half-past one o'clock, the London mail-coach, occupied by W.A. Provis, W. Hazledine, the two junior Wilsons, Thomas Rhodes and the mail-coach superintendent, was the first that passed across the estuary, at the level of 100 feet above that tideway which heretofore, had presented a decisive obstruction to travelers. The Chester mail passed at half-past three o'clock, and Sir Henry Parnell, with myself, drove repeatedly over; about nine o'clock, and during the whole day, was an uninterrupted succession of passing carriages, horsemen and pedestrians, who had assembled to enjoy the novelty; and in the evening all the workmen were regaled with a joyous festival.
>
> Thus was successfully accomplished a complicated and useful bridge of unexampled dimensions, which has now, for the last eight years, converted what was formerly a disagreeable and sometimes dangerous part of the journey to and from Ireland, into an object of national curiousity and delight. (228–9)

Worthy of note is how workers enter into Telford's account, whereas and as we have seen, for those reading the bridge wholly through an untempered lens of infrastructural sublimity, and as no more than a reified "object of national curiousity and delight," laborers garner little to no mention. Though what the engineer fails to note are the four deaths incurred by men laboring on this project. While he might valorize realities of material and labor processes more than his bridge's viewing audience, it is interesting to find that he does not record the deaths of those who passed away while under his employment. Instead, it is Pring's account that charts not only a national achievement in the creation of an infrastructural artifact that drew an "inconceivable number of foreigners, of the highest distinction and celebrity ... which seem(ed) to have excited the surprise and attention of the most scientific men in every quarter of the globe,"[47] it also commemorates the deaths of J. Read, David Roberts, Robert Roberts, and John Key, without failing to note the representative nature of the constitutively "singular coincidence" affiliated with the birth origins of each of the departed, being Scottish, Irish, Welsh, and English, respectively.

---

[47] Pring, *Particulars of the grand suspension bridge*, 580.

The Romantic Sublime and Representations of Technology

But here, the attention bestowed upon the deceased, like that of the emphasis put upon the final bolt, or final chain, points less to human frailty in the face of natural and technological obstacles as it adds for Pring a nationalized and imperial dimension both to how the bridge is viewed and how it is written and read. Telford, while sometimes taking recourse to the language of the sublime, never forgets the material; while the periodical press, and, at times, Southey adopt a more nationally inflected technological sublime, that is, they promote a misleading and misguided aesthetic—the infrastructural sublime—spinning paradoxical stories of singular genius and infrastructural mastery that mask difficulties of work, cost, loss, and threat. Sublime infrastructure, when cast against a backdrop of sublime nature, dialectically informs a façade where Britain appears uniquely authorized to assume control of land, sea, and myriad laboring human beings.

Infrastructures of empire fuel colonial, nationalist thought not by embodying and thus signaling a knowledge of making that is bereft of natural wonder or any kind of magic apparently inherent in the material world. Instead, technologies, when appearing sublime, seem able to inspire a similar wonder, power, magic, and (material) mystery—an almost poetic alchemy of fiat-like invention. As anthropologist Brian Larkin observes, "infrastructures [can] exist as forms separate from their purely technical functioning, and they need to be analyzed as concrete semiotic and aesthetic vehicles oriented to addressees. They emerge out of and store within them forms of desire and fantasy."[48] When marked by the language of the sublime, civil artifacts betray a key iteration of sublime discourse, the infrastructural sublime, which appropriates and redirects the allure of material transformation and swift kinesthetic transmutation drawn from the verb *sublimate* and linked first off to the material sublime. In lieu of channeling the enigma of the innumerable or the pull of the infinite on the one hand, or fantasies of subjective agency on the other, the branch of sublime discourse known as the material sublime originally and more simply championed wonders of material agency, often elevating arresting states of suspension and transport above all else. Yet, in being overwritten by tales of national and individual agency, the infrastructural sublime ultimately undercuts any radical dimensions of the material sublime that might frustrate fictions of subjective or imperial agency through the material sublime's grounding suggestion of an inherent limit to human or national agency or autonomy. Within sometimes coordinating and sometimes competing sublime discourses, all too often the humbling logic of a pervading material sublime beyond human knowing and beyond human control is impressed into political service by being reframed in the more exclusive,

---

[48] Brian Larkin, "The Politics and Poetics of Infrastructure," *Annual Review of Anthropology* 42 (2013): 329.

Suspension Bridges, Modern Canals, and the Infrastructural Sublime

individuating terms of human invention and national achievement. Both the bridge and the canal experienced an industrial and figurative renaissance in the Romantic era.[49] Heretofore untenable but now manifest, unprecedented skyward or watery structures counterpoise the apparent futility connoted by a poetic castle in the air, feeding autopoietic fantasies that moved off the page and took form as seemingly realizable infrastructural if not imperial dreams. By these lights, the material sublime is leveraged to advance national and imperial iterations of the infrastructural sublime. Ironically, steeped as it is in the logic of *demos ex machina* that downplays the aggregate work of landscape and laborer alike, the rhetorical force propping up the infrastructural sublime is none other than the material sublime, Romanticism's shared figurative tool for evoking unconquerable powers and mysteries of the natural world.

---

[49] For instance, spanning from his first major appointment as the general agent of the Ellesmere Canal in 1793 to his final station as lead engineer for the Broomielaw Bridge over the River Clyde in Glasgow, Telford helped to plan and supervise the construction of over 1,200 bridges, at least 7 canals, 920 miles of roads in the Highlands, and numerous harbors in England, Scotland, Wales, and Ireland. These numbers become all the more impressive considering that at this time Telford was only one of a cadre of celebrated British architect-engineers working both in and out of Albion's isles. As noted previously, William Jessop (1745–1814), John Rennie (1761–1821), and Thomas Wilson (1751–1820) were also famously active during the Romantic period. Jessop's notable achievements include his part in establishing the Grand Canal of Ireland (1753–1805), the West India Docks (1800–1802), England's Surrey Iron Railway (1801–1802), and the Kilmarnock and Troon Railway in Scotland (1807–1812). Among other projects, Rennie won renown for his work on the Lune Aqueduct (1793–1797), and Waterloo Bridge (1811–1817). Wilson assumed major advisory or lead engineering roles in the production of the Wearmouth or Sunderland Bridge (1792–1796), Spanish Town Bridge in Jamaica (1800–1801), Staines Bridge (1803–1806), Yarm Bridge (1803–1806), Boston Bridge (1800–1807), and Newport Pagnell Bridge (1808–1810). It is also important to acknowledge the fact that Jessop and Rennie worked collaboratively on a number of Telford's assignments; in fact, all of the infrastructural civil artifacts mentioned here required the overlapping work of many hands and many minds. For a more detailed catalogue of Telford's various undertakings, see Keith Ellis, *Thomas Telford: Father of Civil Engineering* (Dunstable: Priory Press, 1974) and Skempton, *A Biographical Dictionary of Civil Engineers*.

Conclusion

An Aesthetic of Intimate Relations: Romanticism's Child of Sublime Nature and Technology—the Material Sublime

the role of technology here is ambiguous

—Eric B. White, *Reading Machines in the Modernist Transatlantic: Avant-Gardes, Technology and the Everyday* (2020)

Nature is not now, nor ever has been, a pure category.

—Robert Macfarlane, *Landmarks* (2016)

The stories we tell about technology contour and fundamentally reroute how we imagine humanity and nature. This is especially true for sublime, wonder-driven tales of technology because such narratives frame and shape how we understand the more creative, destructive, and transformative agencies of humankind and nature. Such cross fertilization between representations and understandings of nature and culture became possible during the Romantic period because "in the early nineteenth century, the distinction between a machine, as that which is moved by an external force, and an organism, as a system whose motive force is internal, often broke down."[1] Sublime representations of technology informed by narratives of sublime nature appear in accounts of extraordinary infrastructural works and unprecedented inventions discussed in this book's chapters on British suspension bridges, steam engines, and even far-flung seismographic tools. Furthermore, during the Romantic period, everyday technological artifacts also acquired a sublime

[1] Tresch, *The Romantic Machine*, 12.

The Romantic Sublime and Representations of Technology

status. In literature and on the stage, tools and inventions both metaphorical and literal were presented as being worthy of the great esteem and reverence typically conferred by sublime discourse. Rudimentary instruments, ancient tools, and more complicated technologies were routinely presented as eliciting the sublime's signature emotive response, triggering highly charged mixed feelings ranging from a Kantian attraction and repulsion to a Burkean astonishment laced with terror.

Sublime accounts of technology matter because they address the high stakes of invention while simultaneously marking a profound ambivalence surrounding processes of creation and destruction, surrounding what comes of the worlds we build and unbuild. The sublime's potent cocktail of wonder and fear points to the heightened tensions that swirl around great feats of human ingenuity or cultural creativity and expose a profound undercurrent of unease felt toward great transformative powers held by the natural world. As Timothy Morton musingly put it, "In a splendid irony, the theorist of technological development par excellence supplies thinking with resources for ecological critique."[2] Taking seriously Morton's tangential remark—wherein he registers an irony at work in how ecocriticism would owe much to the theorist of technology—we can begin to grasp how the study of Romanticism's technological sublime proves vital to any thorough assessment of our shared moment of environmental crisis.

The Romantic century (1750–1850) and its preoccupation with the aesthetic of the sublime coincided with wave upon wave of industrialization within Britain. Across the eighteenth century, steam engines would accelerate coal mining and iron productions. The last quarter of the eighteenth century witnessed a rise of factories with fast-moving machinery, which generally drove working conditions down while ramping up textile production. During the last half of the eighteenth century and running well into the first third of the nineteenth, dizzying resources and energies were poured into updating the British transport system, with modern canals, bridges, and roads growing into a sprawling network of roadways and waterways. Yet until recently, in secondary literature, Romantic representations of technology all but fade into the background or else become selectively remembered as wholly negative, as undermining the heights of humanity and sullying pristine nature. William Blake's proto-Marxist rendering of Britain's "Satanic Mills" and William Wordsworth's misgivings about expanding railways still drive the stories we tell about Romanticism's modern elevation if not sacralization of humanity and nature, a development which was fueled by sublime discourse. Such misremembered histories of literature come at the expense of working to reconcile

---

[2] Timothy Morton, *Ecology Without Nature: Rethinking Environmental Aesthetics* (Cambridge, MA and London: Harvard University Press, 2007), 164.

164

Conclusion

the figurative and political overlap between technology and poetry during an age of rapid industrial growth.

Throughout each industrializing wave, the sublime was in the air and on the tip of the tongue. Discourses of the sublime functioned as a sort of common tongue or *lingua franca* used by those chronicling harrowing stories of human and natural invention, of making and creation, as well as destruction. From the lofty technē of elevated literary works to sprawling technics of vast infrastructural systems defying so-called laws of nature, tales of sublime technologies index how authors conceptualize humanity's relationship with the natural world. Sublime aesthetics reveal judgments made and assumptions felt about the power of technology and these judgments and assumptions tacitly authorize divergent definitions of humanity and nature. On one end of the spectrum, stories of sublime technologies script a world where technology stands in for a humanity diametrically opposed to nature. These are the type of representations of sublime technologies that so troubled Leo Marx in the late twentieth century, spurring him to remark upon how "the awe and reverence once reserved for the Deity and later bestowed upon the visible landscape is [in American literature] directed toward technology or, rather, the technological conquest of matter."[3] Then on the other end of this continuum, tales of technological wonder outline a world that operates not by way of combative dyads but instead by collective human and natural agencies. The latter iterations of the Romantic technological sublime "resemble[e] a Keatsian material sublime, echoing sublime word histories, where the ambivalent, transformative, and uncontrollable aggregate agencies of nature are always all around us–building us up and breaking us down like everything else in the natural world."[4]

The more room a given story makes for sublime representations of human inventions built from co-determining natural and cultural factors, fates, and futures, the less room a given portrait of sublime technology leaves for fueling fantasies of human exceptionalism or for stoking misguided thinking that would reduce the natural world to little more than human resource, a repository of materials and energies harbored within the earth to use at our disposal. As each chapter in this book demonstrates, sublime rhetoric would become inseparable from much more than mythological tellings of the power of the pen, the tongue, and poetry (as with ancient Longinus's well-known treatise, *On the Sublime*). Sublime rhetoric comes to likewise scaffold mythologies of great technological change and invention that then go on to shape how the natural world is imagined, understood, valued, and handled.

As British Romanticism emerged in dialogue with great industrial changes such as those mentioned above, its stories of pronounced technological agency

---

[3] Marx, *The Machine in the Garden*, 197.
[4] Speitz, "The Sublime," 175.

The Romantic Sublime and Representations of Technology

found a fitting home with the era's existing spate of sublime tropes and plotlines. Long prior to the eighteenth century, the sublime stood as western philosophy's most privileged aesthetic category treating transformative forces of invention, creation, and destruction.[5] In the Romantic period, standard sublime fare included plotlines featuring naturalized destructive forces and disasters (e.g. the Terror; war; earthquakes; floods) and awe-inspiring humanized creative forces (e.g. the much-vaunted written work of a Milton or Shakespeare; renditions of a monotheistic humanoid god's sudden and single-handed creation of the earth).[6] Narrative representations of a humanized technological sublime run along the lines of the latter sublime script, tending to play out a logic known to some as the egotistical sublime. Under this rubric, humanity begins to diverge from nature. Humanity's creative agency transcends or rises above nature by means of a kind of exceptional innovation or ingenuity driven to excess via humanity's unique tools of imagination and invention. Put simply, here humanity sets itself apart from the natural world. Any immaterial (mental, ideological, spiritual) and material (physical, kinesthetic, visceral) worlds built by humanity are assumed to be uniquely distinct from nature's feats of worldbuilding and unbuilding. According to this narrative formula, Romanticism's sublime technologies endorse overblown estimations of human inventive agencies at the cost of grossly downplaying humanity's dependence upon nature.

But, as alluded to earlier, there are tales of a different stripe, of a kind that might include shadings of the egotistical sublime and so may tend toward human exceptionalism as they rehearse stories of technological wonder, but which ultimately bear an overriding logic grounded first and foremost by the thinking of the material sublime. An aesthetic of the material sublime appears in works of Romantic literature that espouse a tempered program of technological ethics where agency doesn't neatly belong to this or that source and where the verb form of the word *sublime*, referring to swift and unexpected transformations between states of matter, remains in play when not reigning supreme. Crucially, these sublime stories authorize a kind of thinking about

---

[5] Ancient Longinian thought (c. 1st century CE) considers the invention of verse powerful enough to move readers, to transport them out of themselves via a lofty or high style deployed in literature that often describes destructive or violent scenes and scenery. Throughout the seventeenth and eighteenth centuries British thinkers increasingly turned to sublime aesthetics to note the mysterious allure of matter in continuous motion, matter that, as Keats would put it, is "unsettled" and assumedly ripe for transformation (into something more or less) both because it is unsettled and thus not static and also because human thought was nowhere close to being settled regarding the state of matter, what it is or does, what it could do or could be. See, for example, Joseph Addison, *The Spectator*, no. 412 (Monday 23 June 1712) and Anthony Ashley Cooper, the third Earl of Shaftesbury, *Characteristics of Men, Manners, Opinions, Times*, 3 vols. (London: John Darby, 1714).

[6] See Ashfield and de Bolla, *The Sublime: A Reader*; Samuel Johnson, *Dictionary of the English Language* (London: J. & P. Knapton, 1755).

Conclusion

technological agency not premised upon a universal schism between nature and culture where one ultimately overpowers the other. These narratives largely evade the individualistic logic of the exceptional egotistical sublime, and instead activate the everyday aggregating logics of the material sublime.

Both terms—*egotistical sublime* and *material sublime*—are from Keats. While I discuss the material sublime across the preceding chapters, to fully fathom the egotistical sublime's relation to the material sublime requires a turn to Keats's famed letter to Richard Woodhouse (27 October 1818) on the chameleon poet, which outlines Keats's thinking about creative genius and human ambition. Keats's "camelion Poet" embraces traditional facets of sublime aesthetics, with mystery, paradox, ambivalence, destruction and creation forming a basis for poetic taste and right action.[7] The "camelion Poet" "enjoys light and shade," relishes not just the "bright" and the luminous but also "the dark side of things" because each "end in speculation."[8] Aligning with a Burkean sublime and working against a Kantian version of sublime experience that ultimately resolves the tensions it provokes, Keats's sublime bears out a radical realism as its tensions carry on without any promise of resolution.

Keats's key contribution in this discussion entails how his rendition of sublime creative process exacts intimate costs which other sublime narratives of invention or inventors disallow, disavow, or ignore as such accounts depend upon safe distance from danger, dread, and insecurity. Keats famously describes the "camelion Poet" as the kind of poet he hopes himself to be, as a "sort distinguished from the wordsworthian or egotistical sublime; which is a thing per se and stands alone."[9] What follows echoes his poetry on the material sublime, where sublimity is less about resolution or solitude, separateness, or individuation and more about unavoidable togetherness and myriad difficult relations. We find not individual genius nor unchecked power but disturbing, mysterious aggregates and a sea of limitations. This situation might not be what Keats would prefer to be the case, but importantly, it is what he indeed reads and feels to be true. He writes: "It is a wretched thing to confess: but is a very fact that not one word I ever utter can be taken for granted as an opinion growing out of my identical nature – how can it, when I have no nature?"[10] According to Keats, his words, his ideas, his arguments and opinions are not his own. They arrive as products of shared invention.

Here Keats's thinking anticipates Heidegger's discussion of poetry and other technics as being co-constituted by various co-responsible parties, inclusive

---

[7] Directly following discussion of the "camelion Poet," Keats states that he is "ambitious of doing the world some good." Keats, "Letter to Richard Woodhouse, 27 October 1818," 294–6.

[8] Keats, "Letter to Richard Woodhouse," 295.

[9] Keats, "Letter to Richard Woodhouse," 295.

[10] Keats, "Letter to Richard Woodhouse," 295.

The Romantic Sublime and Representations of Technology

of human laborers and inventors and whatever elements of the natural world might make possible any given technology and all technologies.[11] Because Keats's works are neither his own nor his to own, they overturn the model of the egotistical sublime where the poet and what the poet makes each exists apart from all others and "stands alone," not even standing with nature. In stark contrast to this, the Keatsian "camelion" poet participates in a human nature that is also of a piece with the larger natural world, importantly diverging from the egotistical poet who would exist apart from others including nature's others. For Keats, the presence of others presses upon him such that he is never alone. This model forecloses narrow dreams of individuated self-preservation or transcendent omnipotence. What appears in their place is a forthright acknowledgment of the loss and cost that comes with creative endeavor. "When I am in a room with People, if I ever am free from speculating on creations of my own brain," he writes "then not myself goes home to myself: but the identity of every one in the room begins to so press upon me that, I am in a very little time annihilated—not only among Men; it would be the same in a Nursery of children."[12]

Rather than the egotistical sublime type, rather than considering himself a poet or a creative "genius" that is separate, apart, or stands alone, the Keatsian "camelion poet" exists with others to such an extent that each word he creates also belongs to another, and while being with others might allow him to co-create words, doing so also annihilates no small part of himself. Connected to Keats's account of the poet as inescapably relational and vulnerable, Romantic literature bears accounts of technological invention grounded in the material sublime. Such narratives emerge wherever powerful technologies arise and operate by way of aggregate natural and cultural forces manifested in intimate, unavoidable conjunction with one another, functioning beyond individuated control, where making or worldbuilding does not come easy and comes at great cost, with some degree of unmaking being part of the creative process. Ambivalent feelings long home to sublime discourse on creation, destruction, and invention, here edge readers toward admitting human contingency and limitedness rather than imagining that we might circumvent limits and transcend boundaries, or that we could ever exist apart from them.

Sublime tropes, as well as sublime narrative frameworks and forms, shape Romanticism's mythologized accounts of technology (as I discuss in Chapter 1), with Romantic versions of the Prometheus myth often foregrounding combative dyads embroiled in sublime contests, individualized heroics, and epic antagonisms. In contrast, the then well-known but now forgotten Trophonius

---

[11] Heidegger, "The Question Concerning Technology," 315–18.
[12] Keats, "Letter to Richard Woodhouse," 295.

Conclusion

myth showcases related parties working out how to lift one another up in the face of sublime material contingency, ambivalence, and uncertainty. Popular Romantic-era renditions of the Prometheus and Trophonius myths throw into stark relief the different worlds these sublime myths authorize, and what's at stake in embracing them. British Romanticism's historical moment was awash in sociopolitical and natural events that were commonly represented via sublime discourse. Authors drew on the sublime as an elevated platform for expressing conflicted feelings often generated by high-stakes events. To name a significant few, such events included continuous warfare in Europe interrupted only briefly by the peace achieved by the Treaty of Amiens (25 March 1802–18 May 1803), growing British imperialism across the Romantic period, the American Revolution (1775–1783), the Haitian Revolution (1791–1804), the French Revolutionary Wars (1792–1802), the so-called Industrial Revolution (1760–1840), the Lisbon quake (1755) and Calabrian earthquakes (1783), and the eruption of Mount Tambora (1815) that triggered what Britons would call the year without a summer (1816). Beyond showcasing mixed, conflicting emotions of the highest order, the aesthetic of the sublime everywhere marks uncertainty and worlds of sudden change, and depending on what strand of sublime story telling you got, you might be encouraged to imagine safe distance and individuated freedoms as with the egotistical sublime, or you might be invited to imagine frightening proximity and joint constraint as with the material sublime. By these lights, it prompts little wonder which version of Romanticism's mythic technological sublimity we have been inclined to reiterate and remember most.

The Material Sublime: An Aesthetic of Inexorable Intimacy

Percy Shelley writing to dear friends about a steam engine dreaming, being born, falling in love. Robert Southey and Thomas Telford journaling private notes about bridges, roads, and canals—all dizzying the mind for being more than mere imaginings, for being tantamount to human dreams intermixed with iron and earth; the work of many hands, many forces. John Keats penning couplets to a sick friend as he dreams of all worldbuilding arising from a "material sublime."[13] Erasmus Darwin's unpublished philosophical poem tacitly suggesting that in the long run the case of humanity follows most closely not from the myth of Prometheus but Trophonius: human invention is not first about independence, protection, or competition but interdependence, uncertainty, and care.

This book has been arguing that we need to take better notice of the sublime stories we tell about technology, making, and invention. Its chapters chart

---

[13] John Keats, "[Dear Reynolds, as last night I lay in bed]," lines 1, 69.

169

The Romantic Sublime and Representations of Technology

how sublime narratives of human invention, from works of poetry to works of industry, from seismometers to suspension bridges, can cast human agency as all powerful, eliding humanity's many dependencies. Yet the preceding chapters do even more to demonstrate how sublime narratives of human technē and technics can authorize important counternarratives stressing not self-reliance or unfettered agency but inescapable interdependence and anything but mastery. As we find with the examples numbered above, the most crucial tales of the technological sublime that we can borrow from the Romantic century first began as private songs borne out by intimate relations and close connections with others.

That British Romanticism's anti-Promethean narratives of sublime poetics and technics seemed to require a precondition of intimacy is both telling and troubling. I'll get right to the troubling part. Why should it be that Shelley had to be writing to the Gisbornes, had to have his guard down to pick up his pen to author his compelling disfiguration and disarticulation of Prometheus?[14] Why was it that Keats offered only to his close friend, Reynolds, his most useful thinking on the sublime? That is, why did he keep his thoughts on the material sublime so close to the vest? After all, contemporary aesthetic theorist Sianne Ngai notes how even today the sublime is "still western philosophy's most prestigious example of an aesthetic category that derives its specificity from mixed or conflicting feelings."[15] Along these lines, "'Ngai recognizes that, in the case of the material sublime, 'we don't make it sublime via judgement but the judgement reflects sublime being.'"[16]

In the realms of western philosophy, the stakes could not be higher. In terms of the material sublime, Keats could be said to be risking very little by sharing far and wide verses detailing the world as he sees it, and then in light of that, the worlds we ought to make within it. But then again, the world he navigates in his poem to Reynolds is as wonderous as it is fearsome, leading him to account not simply for the "colours of the sunset" but also animals at prey, humanity included, that his mind just cannot shake.[17] Such questions are all the more readily answerable if we ask them of Southey. We do not have to take too many guesses as to why his personal ledgers chronicle conjoined wonders of mud and man, noting the insecure and materially sublime infrastructures that naturecultures yield; meanwhile his

---

[14] Here I echo Paul de Man's influential work on Shelleyan poetics of disfiguration; see Paul de Man, "Shelley Disfigured," in Harold Bloom et al., *Deconstruction and Criticism* (New York, Continuum: 1979).

[15] Jasper and Ngai, "Our Aesthetic Categories: An Interview with Sianne Ngai."

[16] Michele Speitz, "Affect and Air: The Speculative Spirit of the Age," *Romanticism and Speculative Realism*, eds. Chris Washington and Anne C. McCarthy (New York: Bloomsbury, 2019), 39.

[17] Keats, "[Dear Reynolds, as last night I lay in bed]," lines 68, 86–110.

Conclusion

public-facing poetry written while serving as British Poet Laureate props up a singularly sublime engineer and an imperial nation of highest exception.[18] If only Darwin had not revised his poetry on Trophonius as he had, then in the ensuing alternate future maybe Hoare's play, *Cave of Trophonius*, could have enjoyed a longer run. And perhaps then stonemason Trophonius, nourisher of others' minds, might have had a better shot at returning to the cultural forefront as often as does Mary Godwin Shelley's self-serving modern Prometheus, Victor Frankenstein. If only.

Of course, it is fitting that intimacy makes or breaks the value and verisimilitude of Romanticism's technological sublime. Akin to sublime aesthetics, intimacy trades in paradox. As Nancy Yousef makes clear, "intimacy is the condition for the possibility of being alone."[19] Yousef's *Romantic Intimacy* highlights how the "paradoxical senses of the term 'intimacy'—most private, most shared—need not be fixed in opposition to one another but held together as coexisting inflections of time spent with one another."[20] Extending Yousef, key in this case is how these Romantic authors' "most private" missives to intimate others or "most private" writings penned in personal ledgers document their "most shared" ideas on the sublime. These personal papers house their most revealing, most telling, most honest grapplings with the politics and ethics of sublime worldbuilding and unbuilding, where sublime aesthetics mark not any exceptional transcendence or supernatural agency, but relations and uncertainties that cannot be outdone in mind or matter. These private thoughts on the sublime convey each author's ideas about inescapable human dependencies and open-ended relations with others, the natural world, the things humans build. They also expose another layer of intimacy: our intimate relationship with technology that inevitably remakes us—just as the myth of Trophonius would have it. If Yousef is correct to say that "intimacy is the condition for the possibility of being alone," as with a child being able to fall asleep because of its intimate ties to a mother, such aloneness is never without an enduring sense of connection inspired itself from a real connection.[21] Then it is precisely these kinds of deep and abiding—and ultimately uncontrollable—links to the poetics and technics we make that underpin each author's turn to the logic and language of the sublime, with its signature figurations of ambivalent forces, its hallmark expressions of vexed feelings.

To close, I offer one final example of British Romanticism's sublime representations of technology where intimacy resides at the core of a less private

---

[18] Donna Haraway coins the term "naturecultures" to denote the inseparable union of works of nature and works of art. See *Manifestly Haraway*, 123.

[19] Nancy Yousef, *Romantic Intimacy* (Stanford, CA: Stanford University Press, 2013), 122.

[20] Yousef, *Romantic Intimacy*, 119.

[21] Yousef, *Romantic Intimacy*, 122.

The Romantic Sublime and Representations of Technology

iteration of technology's indebtedness to nature. Percy Shelley's philosophical poem, *Queen Mab*, was first published in 1813 but appeared in four different editions by 1822. In that poem, Shelley's technologies recall the sublime legacy of poetry as technē, suggesting in the end that the sublimity of human technics is intimately bound up with a sublime material world. In the first section of *On the Sublime* [*Perì Hýpsous*], Longinus offers that the sublime in literature ought "not to persuade the audience but rather to transport them out of themselves."[22] Longinus's classic essay figuratively refers to moving audiences, to metaphorically transporting if not transforming them in light of sublime aesthetics. Working along similar lines, Shelley's radical poem, *Queen Mab*, literalizes the Longinian metaphor. Technologies of sublime transport spring into action, carting characters off to the heavens and delivering them to the loftiest of heights. Dramatizing the effect of sublime aesthetic experience, the dreaming babe Ianathe takes new shape, sheds her earthbound body, and traverses the cosmos while alighted atop Queen Mab's celestial car. By the close of the poem's opening canto, Ianathe and her consort, the eponymous fairy queen, have been conveyed at last to Nature's "fitting temple," which amounts to no less than the vast reaches of space, that "plurality of worlds,--the indefinite immensity of the universe."[23] The second canto goes on to describe an "aërial mansion," the colossal perch which grants Ianthe and Mab two stunning views: the Earth in miniature; and a vast system of suns, worlds, and sublunary spheres (2.92). First, therefore, the duo finds support in an ethereal chariot, and later, they rest upon an airborne edifice that yields unparalleled sublime vistas. In each case, Shelley's characters depend upon technologies of the sublime in order to see the earth for the first time, again.

Put another way, Shelley could not tell the story of sublime transformative experience without including technology. His is not simply a tale of the natural supernatural and the dizzied spectator.[24] It is a narrative of the work of art in the age of technological and material sublimity, wherein to be sublime is to be cooperative and constitutive, dependent and interconnected.[25] In the poem, tropes of the mechanical supernatural—and not simply the natural supernatural—loom large even as Shelley casts the Romantic machine in a supporting role to nature. For, just as celestial technologies elevate Shelley's

[22] Longinus, *On the Sublime*, in *The Loeb Classical Library*, 2nd ed. (Cambridge, MA and London: Harvard University Press, 1995), 163.

[23] Shelley, "Queen Mab; A Philosophical Poem," in *Shelley's Poetry and Prose*, eds. Donald H. Reiman and Neil Fraistat (New York and London: Norton, 2002), 16–71, line 1.268, n. 4. Hereafter citations are noted in-text by line number.

[24] See M. H. Abrams, *Natural Supernaturalism*.

[25] Here I gesture toward Walter Benjamin's influential essay, "The Work of Art in the Age of Mechanical Reproduction," in *Illuminations*, ed. Hannah Arendt (New York: Schocken Books, 1968), 217–51.

Conclusion

characters, a wondrous materiality of air propels Mab's sublime vessel. Vitally, respired air animates the technē that is poetry. Since what counts as the pinnacle of the sublime in the poem is not rooted to the earth but paradoxically grounded in the air, operative in aerial bodies that scatter throughout the universe or transit through space—like words carried by breath and air—the poem instantiates a Shelleyan typology of sublimity.[26] *Queen Mab* brings to life a material sublime that binds the wonders of nature to the wondrous machine, that weds the eloquent force of poetry to the transformative potential of technology.

Since Longinus connected the rhetorical force of oral poetry to the sublime so long ago, it may seem of little consequence that the technē of language first mediates sublime experience in *Queen Mab*.[27] But whereas the Longinian sublime celebrates the oral delivery of genius-derived words, trumpeting the "heat and spontaneity of [technē's] successful delivery," Shelley's technologies foreground the prowess and primacy of air itself. For Longinus, the technē of sublime poetry transports the reader in part because "what inspires wonder casts a spell upon us."[28] In effect reactivating another page from the Longinian formula, Shelley's poem enlists an enchanted fairy queen. But prior to any description of this spell-casting character, the poem lavishes attention upon the astonishing arrival of a "rushing sound" produced not by Mab but by her magical car. The chariot first heralds the fairy's appearance, ushering forth a "wondrous strain" that is "softer than the west wind's sigh" (1.45, 1.46, 1.50). It harkens back to the symbolic technology of lyric poetry. Its strain is in

---

[26] See Angela Leighton, *Shelley and the Sublime: An Interpretation of the Major Poems* (Cambridge, Cambridge University Press, 1984). "As an aesthetic of the vast in nature, and of an equivalent largeness of soul in the spectator, the eighteenth-century sublime may be seen to offer a challenge to the principle of representative perception which is the basis of English empiricism. It protects from the evidence of mere sense perception the ideas of original genius, imagination and inspiration, and thus protects an element of the mystical and inexplicable in the work of art" (vii).

[27] Jonathan Lamb's searching consideration of the Longinian sublime highlights this very point. He reminds us how "The most remarkable effects of the Longinian sublime thrive here, in the imbrication of orality and literacy. If ... Plato developed an oral form that obeyed the laws proper to writing, Longinus does just the reverse, which is why he admired Demosthenes so ardently. Although they write, they use their ink to be heard, and to reproduce in their texts not just the bare outlines of a *techne*'s exemplary fragment, but also the heat and spontaneity of its successful delivery ... The slanted, associative structuring of Longinus's fragments on the theme of light, for example, has a lot in common with what Havelock calls the 'principle of the echo' in recited poetry, 'a kind of binding principle which ties bundles of recited situations together ... The formulas used in the first instance are repeated with necessary variation for the second and a physical scene once used is reflected in its counterpart.'" Jonathan Lamb, "Longinus, the Dialectic, and the Practice of Mastery," *ELH* 60, no. 3 (Autumn 1993): 545–67, 562–3.

[28] Longinus, in *The Loeb Classical Library*, 2nd ed., 164.

The Romantic Sublime and Representations of Technology

keeping with the unpredictable songs of the wind lyre or Aeolian harp. But the quickening sound of the fairy's charioted arrival reads all the more sublime. It is indeed "wilder than the unmeasured note of that strange lyre whose strings / The genii of breezes sweep" (1.51–2). Mab's car owes much to the plastic medium that makes possible the oral delivery of eloquent force. Resembling poetry's songs and the lyre's notes, the chariot's sublimity is nothing without the air. Nonetheless, all of this begs the question: why champion the chariot and not just the lyre of sublime poetry?

The extraordinary being that is Mab arrives in a likewise fantastic vessel, a chariot that speaks to the reader as sublime poetry might. Like the "lines of rainbow light" that visually announce Queen Mab's appearance, which Shelley compares to the technologically mediated beams of the moon "when they fall / Through some cathedral window," what might be sublime, what "may not find / Comparison on earth," does in fact find some sort of oblique, poetic analogy in what is spectacular in nature (such as a rainbow's prismatic light) and what registers fantastic because of technology (such as decorated moonlight pouring through a stained glass window). Sublime natural and technological sounds and sights make Shelley's "Fairy Queen" and her vessel.

Aggregate natural and cultural sublimities shape the Shelleyan figure who later rewrites the story of humanity by relying on technologies to help her reconceive the natural world. Unlike the strings of the lyre here seemingly played only by the "breezes," the mythopoeic chariot makes known its aggregate, collective, though uneven operators. The poem's lyre accrues much of its charge by eliding human presence, particularly that of *homo faber*, the hands that built it. As with conventional understandings of Romanticism's Aeolian harp, the wind alone reads as the instrument's rightful player with the lyre symbolizing the genius poet and his unmediated connection with the natural world. The traditional story of the Romantic wind harp works to mythologize and naturalize the output of the rare poetic genius. Read in this way, lyre and wind harp cast the typical musician, artist, or inventor as an unfortunate if not impure intermediary—an intruder not belonging to the natural world and not truly a part of its songs. The majority of inventive, creative humanity become interlopers not to be trusted with—and more importantly, not responsible for—either the music or the instruments we make.

But the car comes in tandem with its horses or "coursers," its drivers, and its riders (1.60). And where the Aeolian harp is stationary, passive, touched by nature's sweeping breezes, the chariot and its company work together—after a fashion, they resemble the work of so many sweeping breezes—and more. Channeled through the air, they collectively yet heterogeneously produce their sublime, "rushing" sound. Contingent natural and cultural sublimities inform the fancifully appointed characters (Mab and her team of coursers) and airborne machine (chariot) who jointly stand in for the vehicle of Shelley's

Conclusion

poetic imagination.[29] Christopher R. Miller likewise takes Mab for "a figure of the imagination," a "personif[ication of] the 'Intellectual Beauty' that Shelley would celebrate in 1816," and a character who also "prefigures the Witch of Atlas." However, my analysis departs from Miller's when he suggests that Mab "is utterly alone."[30] Shelley's recurrent references to the beings who pull her chariot and to the car itself make it difficult to qualify her as being thus alone. She can only be counted in a wholly solitary manner if Shelley's celestial chariot and its courses do not count, as it were. In other words, she is only alone in the strictest anthropocentric sense, a sense that is destabilized by the terms of Shelley's poem. The interlinked narrative trajectories shared between Mab, her chariot, and the horses that lead them fuse the potentiality of imagination to that of poetry, of human thought to technology. The car's prominence prefigures that of the harp, or more broadly, of the work of art. Shelley's celestial chariot foregrounds the technological, material, and imaginative preconditions necessary for poetry.

Framing the history of the work of art in terms of its technological precursors, its material relations, and their contingent imaginings aligns with Shelley's larger project, which involved no less than radically recasting the history of the earth and the cosmos. The literary lineage of the poem's chariot illuminates various tensions pertaining to natural, technological, and human agencies, which Shelley's poem revises by way of its deployment of sublime aesthetics. An enduring doublet of divine agency and technological salvation prefigures the sublimity of *Queen Mab*'s "ethereal car," (1.65) which of course risks a tacit endorsement of the kind of naïve techno-determinism or techno-salvationism I have been arguing the Romantic technological sublime undoes when it espouses an underlying logic of the material sublime. Indeed, Shelley's celestial car echoes Milton, just as Milton reactivates sublime imagery of biblical prophecy. Mythic means of conveyance signal Mab's supernatural status, heightening her significance as they carry her above all earthly wonders.[31] As such, to begin to know her is to first meet her car:

[29] See Christopher R. Miller, "Happily Ever After? The Necessity of Fairytale in *Queen Mab*," in *The Unfamiliar Shelley*, eds. Alan M. Weinberg and Timothy Webb (Hampshire and Burlington, VT: Ashgate, 2008), 69–84.

[30] Miller, "The Necessity of Fairytale in *Queen Mab*," 74.

[31] Here Mab's sublime status is reinforced by her "queenly" elevation. Shelley's early poem repatterns landscape ideologies wherein high or low geographical positioning directly corresponds with one's social standing. In *Queen Mab*, the chariot plays a key role in raising Mab physically and symbolically, which begs important questions about technology's relationship to status and class. This kind of social stratification trope would later frame Shelley's biography and literary legacy, but without the same technological valence. As Neil Fraistat reminds us, Mary Shelley deployed such patterns of thought in order "to produce a powerful rhetoric of Shelley" in *Posthumous Poems* by emphasizing "the master tropes of … 'unearthliness' and 'elevation'—that is to say, purity inscribed by upper-class

175

The Romantic Sublime and Representations of Technology

Behold the chariot of the Fairy Queen!
Celestial coursers paw the unyielding air;
Their filmy pennons at her word they furl,
And stop obedient to the reins of light:

These the Queen of spells drew in,
She spread a charm around the spot,
And leaning from the ethereal car,
Long did she gaze, and silently,
Upon the slumbering maid. (lines 1.59–67)

Seemingly elevating her to the ranks of the sublime, meaning the ranks of the otherworldly, the "Queen of spells" commands a Shelleyan version of the Miltonic Chariot of Paternal Deitie. In contrast to Mab, however, Milton's charioteer is the belligerent Son of God in *Paradise Lost* who wages war against Satan and his army of fallen angels. The much-discussed Chariot of Paternal Deitie, which the Son rides into battle, takes inspiration from biblical angels arrayed with fiery wheels and blazing horse-drawn chariots. With each of these sublime figures (the Son or an angel, and thanks to Shelley, a fairy), so-called supernatural force is carried out only after technologies carry them in. No longer driven by a bellicose god, the car becomes all the more sublime by its own lights in Shelley's lines. Closely following comparisons that link the chariot's "burning wheels," which once belonged to prophetic angels and punishing gods but which now recall as well the "flaming sparkles" of the steam carriage, the fairy's car "moved on ... Eddied above the mountain's loftiest peak ... [and] traced a line of lightning" (Shelley, "Queen Mab," 1.215, 1.212, 1.216, 1.217). No longer a tool or a possession of omnipotent gods, Shelley's celestial chariot is commandeered by a less potent and more pagan earthly deity.

These revisions are important because Shelley's account of the material agencies of the celestial car underpinning Mab's sublimity and aerial authority arrive at a moment when the aesthetic of the sublime had become the running category for thinking about matter, especially unruly matter that seemed to flout nature's laws. First heard ("Hark!" [Shelley, "Queen Mab," 1.45]), now seen ("Behold"), the chariot's perplexing physicality is rife with disjunctive markers of the "material sublime," markers which would later be defined by implication in Keats's "Epistle to Reynolds."[32] In the eighteenth century, the

---

status, the rhetoric of high culture." See Neil Fraistat, "Shelley Left and Right," in *Shelley: Poet and Legislator of the World*, eds. Betty T. Bennet and Stuart Curran (Baltimore, MD: Johns Hopkins University Press, 1996), 105–13, 107.

[32] John Keats, "[Dear Reynolds, as last night I lay in bed,]" 132–5.

Conclusion

discourse of the sublime was key to how people made sense of experience—to how they considered what it was that moved the human spirit. Increasingly often what moved these "sensitive" subjects was physical motion itself. For instance, Adam Smith addresses sublime aesthetics in numerous places in his *Essays on Philosophical Subjects* (1758), underscoring a "surprised admiration" born of a "succession of objects" in an "uncommon train or order." Amidst his discussion of the sublimity located in bizarre disharmony, Smith numbers the befuddling "motion of iron" as one such example taken from a broader catalog of "fluctuation[s]" that move "the spirit."[33] Smith aligns a wondrous sublimity not solely with nature's more profound movements but more simply with stunning instances of physical mutability. Significantly, Dr. Johnson's famous dictionary, also drafted in the mid-eighteenth century, refers to both movements of the sublime: the rhetorical and the physical. Whereas he initially notes the Longinian strain of a *sublime* or *high literary style* then typified by Miltonic verse, he later attends to *sublime* in its verb form—meaning not simply to raise in stature but also to change in a very real material and chemical sense. Citing both Donne and Newton, Johnson first exhibits the term's association with rapidly varying material states as rendered by fire in the poet's lines and then turns to Newton's *Optics* to note the process of sublimation, where substances transmute directly from a solid into a vapor, never becoming liquid in between.[34]

It bears noting that while the adjective *sublime* and the noun *the sublime* have long enjoyed an association with the unknowable or the mythical, the verb also signals realms of the indescribable or the mystifying. In the latter case, the verb forms *to sublime* or *to sublimate* mark physical wonders, grounded in a "missing" state or stage of transformation. Keeping this active and kinesthetic valence of the sublime in mind, a materially informed etymological and figurative interplay is hard to miss in Smith's example of uncharacteristically molten iron, or in Keats's parade of the incongruous from his poem on the "material sublime." The verb *sublimate* denotes sudden or surprising physical alteration. It evokes cognitively challenging morphologies of matter as opposed to descriptors of the metaphysically transcendent. *Sublimate* captures something of the stupendous, the overwhelming, and the confounding, derived from an altogether marvelous materiality. As Keats knew, the sublime, often thought of as rising above the natural, was intimately tied to the material.

In *Queen Mab*, otherwise impossible feats of sublime transport and transformation routinely come about by mechanical means, informing a sublime

---

[33] Adam Smith, *Essays on Philosophical Subjects*, eds. Joseph Black and James Hutton (London, 1795), 237, 239.
[34] Johnson, *Dictionary of the English Language*, 111–12.

The Romantic Sublime and Representations of Technology

aesthetic grounded in powerful forces of materiality. Astonishing technologies allow the poet to replace divine transcendence with diffuse sublimity and to trade tyrannical dominance for collective contingency. Illuminating the place of sublime technologies within the poem's larger imaginings, Shelley revises the story of the sublime so as to include more than Romanticism's traditionally held trinity of humanity, nature, and divinity. Shelleyan sublime technologies assume a pronounced force of their own and yet can never be wholly independent in themselves or for themselves. Like sublime poetry, which combines eloquent force and latent power, Shelley's sublime technologies are works that rely upon both humanity and nature. In this sense, Shelleyan technological sublimity embeds a model of interactive dependence and interdependence not usually espoused in more well-rehearsed models of the sublime which would finally champion one entity alone. Shelley's celestial machines are Romantic not for trumpeting humbling powers of nature or humanity alone. Rather they remind us that what is most terrifying and awe-inspiring may not be any one dominating entity residing in the clouds but rather the overwhelming dependencies that pertain to all persons, all planets, all made things. Like the transformative technē of poetry and Shelley's celestial machine, both of which depend, at the very least, upon the wondrous materiality of air—we are not alone, and never could be. We abide in intimate relations; we cannot help but reside within sublime relations shaped only in part by our own ambivalent makings, undoings, and inventions.

At their best, Romanticism's sublime technologies make legible an inescapable intimacy at the core of human worldbuilding and unbuilding, revealing not just unavoidable intimacies but also inexorable realities, reinforcing that what we might feel or what we might believe to be most private, most individual, most independent, turns out to be most shared. Enduring accounts of Romantic sublimity pit humanity against nature in an epic transcendental battle, with the powers of mind or forces of nature finally dethroning the other. For Immanuel Kant and William Wordsworth, pinnacles of human thought, intellect, and imagination would overshadow Edmund Burke's "howling wilderness" or Percy Shelley's "primæval mountains."[35] But another sublime populates the pages of Romantic literature, one that cuts against simplistic binaries painting nature as humanity's ultimate other: a technological sublime intermingled with the material sublime, a technological sublime itself indebted to a material sublime that both precedes it and makes it possible. Steam engines and their makers channel the ethereal forces of the heavens echoing Keats's "material sublime." Modern suspension bridges make real the poet's dream of building castles in the air. A vast section of a canalworks spanning a geological rift in Caledonia,

---

[35] Edmund Burke, *A Philosophical Enquiry*, 97; Percy Shelley, "Mont Blanc: Lines Written in the Vale of Chamouni," in *Shelley's Poetry and Prose*, line 99.

178

Conclusion

built in part by human hands, becomes "Neptune's Staircase."[36] These are not antagonistic, oppositional stories of human and natural forces working and worldbuilding against one another. They are stories of sublime uncertainty and relationality, featuring overlapping fates, puzzles, and constitutive agencies of humanity, nature, and technology.

---

[36] Robert Southey, "Inscription for a Tablet at Banavie, on the Caledonian Canal," in *Robert Southey: Later Poetical Works, 1811–1838*, eds. Tim Fulford, Lynda Pratt, and Carol Bolton (Abingdon: Taylor & Francis Group, 2012), 257–8, 257.

Bibliography

A Greek–English Lexicon, edited by Henry George Liddell and Robert Scott; revised and augmented throughout by Sir Henry Stuart Jones with the assistance of Roderick McKenzie. Oxford: Clarendon Press, 1940.

Abrams, M. H. "The Correspondent Breeze: A Romantic Metaphor." In *The Correspondent Breeze: Essays on English Romanticism*, 25–43. New York: Norton & Co., 1981.

—. *Natural Supernaturalism: Tradition and Revolution in Romantic Literature*. New York and London: Norton, 1971.

Addison, Joseph. *The Spectator*, no. 412. Monday 23 June 1712.

Albrecht, W. P. "The Tragic Sublime of Hazlitt and Keats." *Studies in Romanticism* 20, no. 2 (1981): 185–201.

Alcock, Mary. "The Air Balloon." In *Poems, &c. &c. by the Late Mrs. Mary Alcock*, 107–11. London: Printed for C. Dilly, Poultry, 1799.

Allen, Barbara T. "Poetry and Machinery in Shelley's 'Letter to Maria Gisborne.'" *Nineteenth Century Studies* 2 (1988): 53–61.

Allen, Barry. "Turning Back the Linguistic Turn in the Theory of Knowledge." *Thesis Eleven* 89, no. 6 (2007): 6–22.

"An Account of an Earthquake Felt at Lisbon, December 26, 1764: In a Letter to the Rev. Samuel Chandler, D.D.F.R.S." *Philosophical Transactions of the Royal Society of London* 55 (1765): 43–4.

Arendt, Hannah. *The Human Condition*. Chicago, IL: University of Chicago Press, 1958.

Ashfield, Andrew and Peter de Bolla. *The Sublime: A Reader in British Eighteenth-Century Aesthetic Theory*. Cambridge: Cambridge University Press, 1996.

Aubin, Robert Arnold. *Topographical Poetry in XVIII-Century England*. New York: Modern Language Association of America, 1936.

Baillie, Joanna. "Address to a Steam Vessel." In *Fugitive* Verses, 248–54. London: Edward Moxon, Dover Street, 1840.

Barad, Karen. *Meeting the Universe Halfway: Quantum Physics and the Entanglement of Matter and Meaning*. Durham, NC: Duke University Press, 2007.

Barbauld, Anna Letitia Aikin, "Eighteen Hundred and Eleven, A Poem." London: J. Johnson 1812. https://quod.lib.umich.edu/b/bwrp/barbaeight.

Barnett, Suzanne L. "Romantic Prometheis and the Molding of Frankenstein." In *Frankenstein and Its Classics: The Modern Prometheus from Antiquity to Science Fiction*. Edited by Jesse Weiner, Benjamin Eldon Stevens, and Brett M. Rogers, 76–90. London: Bloomsbury, 2018.

Benjamin, Walter. "The Work of Art in the Age of Mechanical Reproduction." In *Illuminations*, edited by Hannah Arendt, 217–51. New York: Schocken Books, 1968.

Bennett, Jane. *Vibrant Matter: A Political Ecology of Things*. Durham, NC: Duke University Press, 2010.

Bermingham, Ann. *Landscape and Ideology: The English Rustic Tradition 1740–1860*. London: Thames and Hudson, 1987.

Bewell, Alan. *Romanticism and Colonial Disease*. Baltimore, MD: Johns Hopkins University Press, 2000.

Black, J. David. *The Politics of Enchantment: Romanticism, Media, and Cultural Studies*. Waterloo, Canada: Wilfrid Laurier University Press, 2002.

Bolton, Carol, ed. *Letters from England: By Don Manuel Alvarez Espriella*. New York: Routledge, 2016.

Bullock, William et al. "An Account of the Earthquake, Novem. 1, 1755, as Felt in the Lead Mines in Derbyshire; In a Letter from the Reverend Mr. Bullock to Lewis Crusius, D.D.F.R.S. *Philosophical Transactions of the Royal Society of London* 49 (1755–1756): 398–444.

Burgess, Miranda. "Transport: Mobility, Anxiety, and the Romantic Poetics of Feeling." *Studies in Romanticism* 49, no. 2 (2010): 229–60. http://www.jstor.org/stable/41059287.

Burke, Edmund. *A Philosophical Enquiry into the Origin of Our Ideas of the Sublime and the Beautiful*, edited by Adam Phillips. Oxford World's Classics. Oxford: Oxford University Press, 1990.

—. *Two letters addressed to a member of the present Parliament, on the proposals for peace with the regicide directory of France*. Dublin: William Porter, for P. Wogan, P. Byrne, H. Colbert, W. Porter, J. Moore, J. Rice, H. Fitzpatrick, and G. Folingsby, 1796.

Byron, George Gordon. *The Complete Poetical Works*, edited by Jerome J. McGann, and Barry Weller. Oxford: Clarendon Press, 1980.

Caldcleugh, Alexander. "An Account of the Great Earthquake Experience in Chile on the 20th of February, 1835; With a Map. By Alexander Caldcleugh, Esq. F.R.S. F.G.S. &c." *Philosophical Transactions of the Royal Society of London* 126 (1836): 21–6.

Callaghan, Madeleine. "'Any thing human or earthly': Shelley's Letters and Poetry." In *Letter Writing Among Poets: From William Wordsworth to Elizabeth Bishop*, edited by Jonathan Ellis, 111–25. Edinburgh: Edinburgh University Press, 2015.

Bibliography

Chakrabarty, Dipesh. "The Climate of History: Four Theses." *Critical Inquiry* 35, no. 2 (2009): 197–222.

Chandler, James. *England in 1819: The Politics of Literary Culture and the Case of Romantic Historicism*. Chicago and London: University of Chicago Press, 1998.

Chico, Tita. *Designing Women: The Dressing Room in Eighteenth-Century Literature and Culture*. Lewisburg, PA: Bucknell University Press, 1999.

Cladis, Mark S. "Romantic Nature." In *Nature and Literary Studies*, edited by Peter Remien and Scott Slovic, 141–60. Cambridge: Cambridge University Press, 2002.

Clark, Charles Edwin. "Science, Reason, and an Angry God: The Literature of an Earthquake." *New England Quarterly* 38, no. 3 (1965): 340–62.

Coeckelbergh, Mark. *New Romantic Cyborgs: Romanticism, Information Technology, and the End of the Machine*. Cambridge, MA: The MIT Press, 2017.

Coffey, Donna. "Protecting the Botanic Garden: Seward, Darwin, and Colebrookdale." *Women's Studies* 31, no. 2 (2002): 141–64.

Connelly, Joan. *The Parthenon Enigma*. New York: Knopf, 2014.

Cooper, Anthony Ashley, the third Earl of Shaftesbury. *Characteristics of Men, Manners, Opinions, Times*. 3 vols. London: John Darby, 1714.

Corcoran, Clinton DeBevoise. *Topography and Deep Structure in Plato: The Construction of Place in the Dialogues*. Albany, NY: SUNY Press, 2016.

Cox, Jeffrey N. *Poetry and Politics in the Cockney School: Keats, Shelley, Hunt and Their Circle*. Cambridge: Cambridge University Press, 1998.

Cull, Ryan, "Interrogating the 'Egotistical Sublime': Keats and Dickinson Near the Dawn of Lyricization?" *The Emily Dickinson Journal* 22, no. 1 (2013): 55–73.

Curran, Stuart. *Shelley's Annus Mirabilis: The Maturing of an Epic Vision*. Pasadena, CA: Huntington Library Press, 1975.

Darwin, Erasmus. *The Temple of Nature; Or, The Origin of Society: A Poem. With Philosophical Notes*. London: J. Johnson, T. Bensley, 1803.

—. *The Progress of Society by Erasmus Darwin. Romantic Circles Scholarly Editions*. 2006. https://romantic-circles.org/editions/darwin_temple/progress/progress. html.

de Bolla, Peter. *The Discourse of the Sublime: Readings in History, Aesthetics and the Subject*. Oxford: Basil Blackwell, 1989.

de Man, Paul. "Shelley Disfigured," in Harold Bloom et al., *Deconstruction and Criticism*. New York, Continuum: 1979.

Demson, Michael. "Percy Shelley's Radical Agrarian Politics." *Romanticism* 16, no. 3 (2010): 279–92.

Dreicer, Gregory K. "Building Bridges and Boundaries: The Lattice and the Tube, 1820–1860." *Technology and Culture* 51, no. 1 (2010): 126–63.

Duffy, Cian. *Shelley and the Revolutionary Sublime*. Cambridge: Cambridge University Press, 2009.

183

Duffy, Cian and Peter Howell. *Cultures of the Sublime: Selected Readings, 1750–1830*. London and New York: Palgrave Macmillan, 2011.

d'Ulloa, Don Antonio. "An Account of the Earthquake at Cadiz, in a Letter to the Spanish Ambassador at the Hague, from Don Antonio d'Ulloa, F.R.S." *Philosophical Transactions of the Royal Society of London* 49 (1755–1756): 427–32.

"The Earth Speaks: Scientific Notes." *Friends' Review; a Religious, Literary and Miscellaneous Journal* 32, issue 22 (11 January 1879): 351.

Economides, Louise. *The Ecology of Wonder in Romantic and Postmodern Literature*. New York: Palgrave Macmillan, 2016.

Ellis, Keith. *Thomas Telford: Father of Civil Engineering*. Dunstable: Priory Press, 1974.

Ende, Stuart A. *Keats and the Sublime*. New Haven, CT: Yale University Press, 1976.

Fairer, David. "Eighteenth-Century Poetic Landscapes." *The Coleridge Bulletin*, New Series 13 (Spring 1999): 1–18.

Ferguson, Frances. *Solitude and the Sublime: Romanticism and the Aesthetics of Individuation*. New York: Routledge, 1992.

Fraistat, Neil. "Shelley Left and Right." In *Shelley: Poet and Legislator of the World*, edited by Betty T. Bennet and Stuart Curran, 105–13. Baltimore, MD: Johns Hopkins University Press, 1996.

Fraistat, Neil and Donald H. Reiman, eds. *Shelley's Poetry and Prose*. 2nd ed. New York: W. W. Norton & Co., 2002.

Gandy, Matthew. "Cyborg Urbanization: Complexity and Monstrosity in the Contemporary City." *International Journal of Urban and Regional Research* 29, no. 1 (2005): 26–49.

Green, Henry. "Extract of a Letter from Mr. Henry Green to Mr. James Ayfchough, Optician, in Ludgate-Street, relating to the Earthquake felt Sept. 30. 1750." *Philosophical Transactions of the Royal Society of London* 46 (1750): 723–4.

Groom, Nick. "Introduction" to Mary Shelley, *Frankenstein: Or, the Modern Prometheus*, 1818 Text, xxx–xxxii. Oxford: Oxford University Press, 2018.

Guthrie, William. "A New Geographical, Historical, and Commercial Grammar; and present state of several kingdoms of the world." Vol. 2. *History and Geography*. London, 1790.

Halberstam, Jack. "Public Thinker: Jack Halberstam on Wildness, Anarchy, and Growing Up Punk." Interview by Damon Ross Young. *Public Books*, 26 March 2009. https://www.publicbooks.org/public-thinker-jack-halberstam-on-wildness-anarchy-and-growing-up-punk.

Hall, James H. "The Spider and the Silkworm: Shelley's 'Letter to Maria Gisborne.'" *Keats-Shelley Memorial Bulletin* 20 (1969): 1–10.

Hamblyn, Richard. "Introduction" to *Literature and Science, 1660–1834*. Vol. 3, ix–xviii. London: Pickering and Chatto, 2003.

—. "Notes from Underground: The Lisbon Earthquake," *Romanticism* 14, no. 2 (2008): 108–18.

Bibliography

Hamilton, William Sir. *An Account of the Earthquakes in Calabria, Sicily, etc. As communicated to the Royal Society.* Colchester: J. Fenno, 1783.

—. "An Account of the Earthquakes Which Happened in Italy, from February to May 1783. By Sir William Hamilton, Knight of the Bath, F. R. S.; in a Letter to Sir Joseph Banks, Bart. P. R. S." *Philosophical Transactions of the Royal Society of London* 73 (1783): 169–208.

Haraway, Donna J. *The Companion Species Manifesto: Dogs, People, and Significant Otherness.* Cambridge and Chicago: Prickly Paradigm Press, 2003.

—. *Manifestly Haraway.* Minneapolis, MN: University of Minnesota Press, 2016.

Hartman, Geoffrey H. *The Unremarkable Wordsworth.* Minneapolis, MN: University of Minnesota Press, 1987.

Hartman, Saidiya V. *Scenes of Subjection: Terror, Slavery, and Self-Making in Nineteenth-Century America.* Oxford and New York: Oxford University Press, 1997.

Heidegger, Martin. "Building Dwelling Thinking." In *Basic Writings: From "Being and Time" [1927] to "The Task of Thinking" [1964],* translated by David Farrell Krell, 343–63. Rev. ed. San Francisco, CA: Harper Collins, 1993.

—. "The Origin of the Work of Art." In *Basic Writings: From "Being and Time" [1927] to "The Task of Thinking" [1964],* translated by David Farrell Krell, 139–212. Rev. ed. San Francisco, CA: Harper Collins, 1993.

—. "The Question Concerning Technology." In *Basic Writings: From "Being and Time" [1927] to "The Task of Thinking" [1964],* translated by David Farrell Krell, 307–41. Rev. ed. San Francisco, CA: Harper Collins, 1993.

Hirst, William. "An Account of an Earthquake in the East Indies, of Two Eclipses of the Sun and Moon, Observed at Calcutta: In a Letter to the Reverend Thomas Birch, D.D. Secret. R.S. from the Reverend William Hirst, M.A.F.R.S." *Philosophical Transactions of the Royal Society of London* 53 (1763): 256–62.

Hoare, Prince. *The Cave of Trophonius.* Manuscript held in the Larpent Collection, Huntington Library, LA899.

Hogan, Charles Beecher, ed. *The London Stage, 1660–1800: A Calendar of Plays, Entertainments & Afterpieces Together with Casts, Box-Receipts and Contemporary Comment.* Carbondale, SI: Southern Illinois University Press, 1968.

Holland, Jocelyn. "From Romantic Tools to Technics: Heideggerian Questions in Novalis's Anthropology." *Configurations* 18, no. 3 (Fall 2010): 291–307. https://doi.org/10.1353/con.2010.0021.

—. *The Lever as Instrument of Reason: Technological Constructions of Knowledge around 1800.* London: Bloomsbury, 2019.

Holland, Jocelyn and Susanne Strätling. "Introduction: Aesthetics of the Tool— Technologies, Figures, and Instruments of Literature and Art." *Configurations* 18, no. 3 (2010): 203–9.

Holmes, Richard. *The Age of Wonder: How the Romantic Generation Discovered the Beauty and Terror of Science.* New York: Pantheon, 2009.

Horkheimer, Max and Theodor W. Adorno. *Dialectic of Enlightenment: Philosophical Fragment*, edited by Gunzelin Schmid Noerr. Translated by Edmund Jephcott. Redwood City, CA: Stanford University Press, 2002.

Hough, Susan Elizabeth and Roger G. Bilham. *After the Earth Quakes: Elastic Rebound on an Urban Planet*. New York: Oxford University Press, 2006.

Hughes, D. J. "Potentiality in Prometheus Unbound." In *Shelley's Poetry and Prose*, edited by Neil Fraistat and Donald H. Reiman, 603–20. 1st ed. New York: W. W. Norton & Co., 1977.

Hyde, John. "An Account of the Earthquake felt at Boston in New-England, Novem. 18, 1755. Communicated by John Hyde, Esq. F.R.S.," *Philosophical Transactions of the Royal Society of London* 49 (1755–1756): 439–42.

Jackson, Steven J. "Rethinking Repair." In *Media Technologies: Essays on Communication, Materiality, and Society*, edited by Tarleton Gillespie, Pablo J. Boczkowski, and Kirsten A. Foot, 221–39. Oxford: Oxford University Press, 2014.

Jasper, Adam and Sianne Ngai. "Our Aesthetic Categories: An Interview with Sianne Ngai." *Cabinet*, Issue 43: Forensics (Fall 2011). Accessed 1 May 2018. http://cabinetmagazine.org/issues/43/jasper_ngai.php.

Jennings, Humphrey. *Pandæmonium 1660–1886: The Coming of the Machine as Seen by Contemporary Observers*, edited by Marie-Louise Jennings and Charles Madge. Forward by Frank Cottrell Boyce. London: Icon Books, 2012.

Johnson, Samuel. *Dictionary of the English Language*. London: J. & P. Knapton, 1755.

Jones, Steven E. "Shelley's 'Letter to Maria Gisborne' as Workshop Poetry." *The European Legacy* 24, Issue 3–4 (2019): 380–96.

Kant, Immanuel. *Critique of Judgment*, translated by Werner S. Pluhar. Indianapolis and Cambridge: Hackett Publishing, 1987.

—. "History and Physiography of the Most Remarkable Cases of the Earthquake Which Towards the End of 1755 Shook a Great Part of the Earth." 1799.

Keach, William. *Shelley's Style*. New York: Methuen, 1984.

Keats, John. "[Dear Reynolds, as last night I lay in bed]." In *Keats's Poetry and Prose*, edited by Jeffrey N. Cox, 132–5. New York and London: W. W. Norton & Company, 2008.

—. "Letter to George and Tom Keats, 21, 27? December 1817." In *Keats's Poetry and Prose*, edited by Jeffrey N. Cox, 107–9. New York and London: W. W. Norton & Company, 2008.

—. "Letter to Richard Woodhouse, 27 October 1818." In *Keats's Poetry and Prose*, edited by Jeffrey N. Cox, 294–5. New York and London: W. W. Norton & Company, 2008.

Kelley, Theresa M. *Reinventing Allegory*. Cambridge: Cambridge University Press, 1997.

Klancher, Jon. "Scale and Skill in British Print Culture: Reading the Technologies, 1680–1820." *Studies in Eighteenth-Century Culture* 47 (2018): 89–106. https://doi.org/10.1353/sec.2018.0008.

Bibliography

Lamb, Jonathan. "Longinus, the Dialectic, and the Practice of Mastery." *ELH* 60, no. 3 (Autumn 1993): 545–67.

Larkin, Brian. "The Politics and Poetics of Infrastructure." *Annual Review of Anthropology* 42 (2013): 327–43.

Latour, Bruno. *Reassembling the Social: An Introduction to Actor-Network-Theory.* Oxford: Oxford University Press, 2007.

—. *War of the Worlds: What about Peace?*, translated by Charlotte Bigg. Edited by John Tresch. Cambridge and Chicago: Prickly Paradigm Press, 2002.

—. *We Have Never Been Modern.* Cambridge, MA: Harvard University Press, 1993.

Lazarus, Micha. "Sublimity by *fiat*: New Light on the English Longinus." In *The Places of Early Modern Criticism*, edited by Gavin Alexander, Emma Gilby, and Alexander Marr, 192–205. Oxford: Oxford University Press, 2021.

Leighton, Angela. *Shelley and the Sublime: An Interpretation of the Major Poems.* Cambridge: Cambridge University Press, 1984.

Lindstrom, Eric Reid. *Romantic Fiat: Demystification and Enchantment in Lyric Poetry.* Basingstoke: Palgrave, 2011.

Longinus. *On the Sublime.* In *The Loeb Classical Library*, 159–307. 2nd ed. Cambridge, MA and London: Harvard University Press, 1995.

Lopes, Dominic McIver. *Being for Beauty: Aesthetic Agency and Value.* Oxford University Press, 2018.

Lyotard, Jean-François. "Philosophy, Politics, and the Sublime." *Continental Philosophy* 8 (2002): 1–30.

McFarland, Thomas. *Romanticism and the Forms of Ruin: Wordsworth, Coleridge, and Modalities of Fragmentation.* Princeton, NJ: Princeton University Press, 1981.

Macfarlane, Robert. *Landmarks.* London: Penguin Random House, 2016.

McGann, Jerome. *The Romantic Ideology: A Critical Investigation.* Chicago, IL: University of Chicago Press, 1983.

MacLeod, Christine. *Heroes of Invention: Technology, Liberalism and British Identity, 1750–1914.* Cambridge: Cambridge University Press, 2007.

Mallet, Robert. "Account of Experiments Made at Holyhead (North Wales) to Ascertain the Transit-Velocity of Waves, Analogous to Earthquake Waves, through the Local Rock Formations." *Philosophical Transactions of the Royal Society of London* 151 (1861): 655–79.

—. "Appendix to the Account of the Earthquake-Wave Experiments made at Holyhead." *Philosophical Transactions of the Royal Society of London* 152 (1862): 663–76.

Marx, Leo. *The Machine in the Garden: Technology and the Pastoral Ideal in America.* Oxford: Oxford University Press, 2000 (1964).

May, Tim. "Coleridge's Slave Trade Lecture: Southey's Contribution and the Debt to Thomas Cooper." *Notes and Queries* (2008): 425–9.

Mellor, Anne. "Promethean Politics." In *Mary Shelley: Her Life, Her Fiction, Her Monsters*, 70–88. New York: Methuen, 1988.

The Romantic Sublime and Representations of Technology

Michell, John. *Conjectures concerning the cause, and observations upon the Phaenomena, of earthquakes; Particularly of That great Earthquake of the first of November 1755, which proved so fatal to the City of Lisbon, and whose Effects were felt as far as Africa, and more or less throughout almost all Europe. By the Reverend John Michell, M. A. Fellow of Queen's-College, Cambridge.* London, 1760.

Miller, Christopher R. "Happily Ever After? The Necessity of Fairytale in Queen Mab." In *The Unfamiliar Shelley*, edited by Alan M. Weinberg and Timothy Webb, 69–84. Hampshire and Burlington, VT: Ashgate, 2008.

Miller, Perry. *The Life of the Mind in America: From the Revolution to the Civil War Books One to Three.* Foreword by Elizabeth W. Miller. London: Victor Gollancz Ltd, 1966.

Mirror of Literature, Amusement, and Instruction, edited by Reuben Percy and John Timbs. Vol. 7. London: J. Limbird, Strand, 1826.

Monk, Samuel H. *The Sublime: A Study of Critical Theories in Eighteenth-Century England.* Ann Arbor, MI: University of Michigan Press, 1960.

Morton, Timothy. *Ecology Without Nature: Rethinking Environmental Aesthetics.* Cambridge, MA and London: Harvard University Press, 2007.

—. "Nature and Culture." In *The Cambridge Companion to Shelley*, edited by Timothy Morton, 185–207. Cambridge: Cambridge University Press, 2006.

—. "Romantic Disaster Ecology: Blake, Shelley, Wordsworth." In *Romantic Circles Praxis Volume: Romanticism and Disaster*, edited by Jacques Khalip and David Collings, paras. 1–32. 2012. https://romantic-circles.org/praxis/disaster/HTML/praxis.2012.morton.html.

—. "Sublime Objects." *Speculations II* (2011): 207–27.

Moten, Fred. "Resistance of the Object: Aunt Hester's Scream." In *In the Break: The Aesthetics of the Black Radical Tradition*, 1–24. Minneapolis and London: University of Minnesota Press, 2003.

Muri, Allison. *The Enlightenment Cyborg: A History of Communications and Control in the Human Machine, 1660–1830.* Toronto: University of Toronto Press, 2007.

Nersessian, Anahid. "Romantic Difficulty." *New Literary History* 49, no. 4 (Autumn 2018): 451–66.

Nesfield, William. *An oration, delivered at the opening of the iron bridge at Wearmouth, August 9, 1796. By William Nesfield, M. A. Provincial Grand Chaplain, Durham. And a sermon, preached in the chapel at Sunderland, on the same occasion, by John Brewster, M. A. Chaplain of the Lodge of Philanthropy, Stockton, No. 19. To which is added, an Appendix, Containing an Account of the Order of the Procession, Ceremonies, Used on that Occasion, &c.* London: Christopher and Jennett, 1796.

Nichol, Douglas. "The Whita Hill Building Stone Quarries at Langholm, Scottish Borders – Environmental Geology and Historical Aspects." *Proceedings of the Institution of Civil Engineers – Municipal Engineer* 133, no. 4 (1999): 207–10.

Nicolson, Marjorie Hope. *Mountain Gloom and Mountain Glory: The Development of the Aesthetics of the Infinite.* Ithaca, NY: Cornell University Press, 1959.

Bibliography

Nye, David E. *American Technological Sublime*. Cambridge, MA: MIT Press, 1994.

OED Online. Oxford University Press. www.oed.com.

Oeser, Erhard. "Historical Earthquake Theories from Aristotle to Kant." In *Historical Earthquakes in Central Europe*, edited by Rudolf Geutdeutsch, Gottfried Grunthal, and Roger Musson, 11–31. Vienna: Geologische Bundesanstalt, 1992.

O'Neill, Michael. *Romanticism and the Self-Conscious Poem*. Oxford: Oxford University Press, 1997.

Ong, Walter J. *Orality and Literature: The Technologizing of the Word*. London: Routledge, 2000 (1982).

—. "Romantic Difference and the Poetics of Technology." In *Rhetoric, Romance, and Technology: Studies in the Interaction of Expression and Culture*, 255–83. Ithaca, NY: Cornell University Press, 2013.

Parry, J. P. "Steam Power and British Influence in Baghdad, 1820–1860." *The Historical Journal* 56, no. 1 (2013): 145–73.

Pausanias. *Description of Greece*, translated by W. H. S. Jones and H. A. Ormerod, M.A. 4 Vols. London: William Heinemann Ltd., 1918; Cambridge, MA: Harvard University Press, 1966.

Pennie, John Fitzgerald. *The Royal Minstrel; Or, The Witcheries of Endor, An Epic Poem, In Eleven Books*. Dorchester and London: G. Clark; Longman, 1817.

Perry, Mr. and William Stukely, "An Account of the Earthquake Felt in the Island of Sumatra, in the East-Indies, in November and December 1756. In a Letter from Mr. Perry to the Rev. Dr. Stukeley, Dated at Fort Marlborough, in the Island of Sumatra, Feb 20. 1757. Communicated by the Rev. Wm. Stukeley, M.D.F.R.S.," *Philosophical Transactions of the Royal Society of London* 50 (1757–1758): 491–2.

Peters, Tom F. *Transitions in Engineering: Guillaume Henri Dufour and the Early 19th Century Cable Suspension Bridges*. Basel: Birkhäuser, 1987.

Peyssonel, John Andrew. "Observations upon a Slight Earthquake, Tho' Very Particular, Which May Lead to the Knowledge of the Cause of Great and Violent Ones, That Ravage Whole Countries, and Overturn Cities. By John Andrew Peyssonel, M.D.F.R.S. Translated from the French." *Philosophical Transactions of the Royal Society of London* 50 (1755–1756): 645–8.

Plato. *Phaedrus*. In *Five Dialogues: Euthyphro, Apology, Crito, Meno, Phaedo*, translated by G. M. A. Grube. 2nd ed. Cambridge: Hackett Publishing, 2002.

Pratt, Lynda. *Robert Southey and the Contexts of English Romanticism*. Aldershot: Ashgate, 2006.

Pratt, Lynda, Tim Fulford, and Ian Packer. "General Introduction: Southey as a Letter Writer," *The Collected Letters of Robert Southey, A Romantic Circles Electronic Edition*. Accessed 23 April 2019. https://romantic-circles.org/editions/southey_letters/letterEEd.26.genIntro.html.

Priestley, Joseph. *A Course of Lectures on Oratory and Criticism*. London: J. Johnson, 1777.

Priestman, Martin. "Introduction" to *The Progress of Society by Erasmus Darwin*. *Romantic Circles Scholarly Editions*. 2006. https://romantic-circles.org/editions/darwin_temple/progress/progress.html.

—. "Introduction" to *The Temple of Nature by Erasmus Darwin*. *Romantic Circles Electronic Editions*. 2003. http://romantic-circles.org/editions/darwin_temple.

—. *The Poetry of Erasmus Darwin: Enlightened Spaces, Romantic Times*. Abingdon and New York: Ashgate, 2016.

—. "Prometheus and Dr. Darwin's Vermicelli: Another Stir to the *Frankenstein* Broth." In *Frankenstein and Its Classics: The Modern Prometheus from Antiquity to Science Fiction*, edited by Jesse Weiner, Benjamin Eldon Stevens, and Brett M. Rogers, 42–58. London: Bloomsbury, 2018.

Pring, Joseph. *Particulars of the grand suspension bridge, erected over the Straits of Menai by order of government; designed by, and built under the immediate direction of Thomas Telford, Esq. Civil engineer. Began in May, 1819, and opened, for the use of the public, on Monday, January 30, 1826*. London: J. Brown, 1826.

Radcliffe, David Hill. "Genre and Social Order in Country House Poems of the Eighteenth Century: Four Views of Percy Lodge." *Studies in English Literature, 1500–1900, Restoration and Eighteenth Century* 30, no. 3 (Summer 1990): 445–65.

Regier, Alexander. *Fracture and Fragmentation in British Romanticism*. Cambridge: Cambridge University Press, 2010.

Reveley, Henry to Percy Shelley, 17 November 1819, note 3. In *The Letters of Percy Bysshe Shelley, Volume II: Shelley in Italy*, edited by Frederick L. Jones, 157–8. Oxford: Oxford University Press, 1964.

Reynolds, Nicole. *Building Romanticism: Literature and Architecture in Nineteenth-Century Britain*. Ann Arbor, MI: University of Michigan Press, 2010.

Richardson, Alan. *The Neural Sublime: Cognitive Theory and Romantic Texts*. Baltimore, MD: Johns Hopkins University Press, 2010.

Rigby, Kate. "Writing After Nature." *Ecological Humanities* 39–40 (2006), https://australianhumanitiesreview.org/2006/09/01/writing-after-nature/.

Rogers, Brett M. and Benjamin Eldon Stevens. "Classical Receptions in Science Fiction." *Classical Receptions Journal* 4, no. 1 (May 2012): 127–47.

Rogers, Neville. *Shelley at Work: A Critical Inquiry*. Oxford: Clarendon Press, 1956.

Rolt, L.T.C. *Thomas Telford*. New York: Penguin, 1985.

Schachter, Albert. "Trophonius." In *The Oxford Classical Dictionary*, edited by Simon Hornblower and Antony Spawforth. 3rd rev. ed. Oxford: Oxford University Press, 2005.

Scott, Grant F. *The Sculpted Word: Keats, Ekphrasis, and the Visual Arts*. Hanover and London: University Press of New England, 1994.

Scott, Walter. *Guy Mannering: or The Astrologer*. 2 Vols. Connoisseur Edition. Boston: Estes and Lauriat, 1893.

Bibliography

Setzer, Sharon. "'Pondr'ous Engines' in 'Outraged Groves': The Environmental Argument of Anna Seward's 'Colebrook Dale.'" *European Romantic Review* 18, no. 1 (2007): 69–81.

Seward, Anna. "Colebrooke Dale" in *Eighteenth-Century Poetry: An Annotated Anthology*, edited by David Fairer and Christine Gerrard, 582–5. 3rd ed. Hoboken, NJ: Wiley-Blackwell, 2014.

Shaw, Philip. *The Sublime*. New York and London: Routledge, 2006.

Shelley, Mary Godwin. *Frankenstein: Or, the Modern Prometheus*. 3 vols. London: Lackington, Hughes, Harding, Mavor, & Jones, 1818.

Shelley, Percy Bysshe. *Alastor; or, The Spirit of Solitude*. In *The Poems of Shelley, Volume 1: 1804–1817*, edited by Geoffrey Matthews and Kelvin Everest, 458–89. London: Longman, 1989.

—. "The Cloud." In *The Poems of Shelley, Volume 3: 1819–1820*, edited by Jack Donovan, Cian Duffy, Kelvin Everest, and Michael Rossington, 355–64. London: Longman, 2011.

—. *A Defence of Poetry*. In *Shelley's Poetry and Prose*, edited by Neil Fraistat and Donald H. Reiman, 509–35. 2nd ed. New York and London: W. W. Norton & Company, 2002.

—. *Letter to Maria Gisborne*. In *The Poems of Shelley, Volume 3: 1819–1820*, edited by Jack Donovan, Cian Duffy, Kelvin Everest, and Michael Rossington, 425–61. London: Longman, 2011.

—. "Mont Blanc: Lines Written in the Vale of Chamouni." In *Shelley's Poetry and Prose*, edited by Donald H. Reiman and Neil Fraistat, 96–101. 2nd ed. New York: W. W. Norton & Co., 2002.

—. *Ode to the West Wind*. In *The Poems of Shelley, Volume 3: 1819–1820*, edited by Jack Donovan, Cian Duffy, Kelvin Everest, and Michael Rossington, 211–12. London: Longman, 2011.

—. "Queen Mab." In *Shelley's Poetry and Prose*, edited by Neil Fraistat and Donald H. Reiman, 15–71. 2nd ed. New York and London: W. W. Norton & Company, 2002.

Shelley to Henry Reveley, 17 November 1819, note 3. In *The Letters of Percy Bysshe Shelley, Volume II: Shelley in Italy*, edited by Frederick L. Jones, 157–8. Oxford: Oxford University Press, 1964.

Shelley to John and Maria Gisborne, 26 May 1820. In *The Letters of Percy Bysshe Shelley, Volume II: Shelley in Italy*, edited by Frederick L. Jones, 201–3. Oxford: Oxford University Press, 1964.

Shelley to Maria Gisborne, 13 or 14 October 1819. In *The Letters of Percy Bysshe Shelley, Volume II: Shelley in Italy*, edited by Frederick L. Jones, 123–6. Oxford: Oxford University Press, 1964.

Shelley to Maria Gisborne, 16 November 1819. In *The Letters of Percy Bysshe Shelley, Volume II: Shelley in Italy*, edited by Frederick L. Jones, 154–6. Oxford: Oxford University Press, 1964.

Shelley to Thomas Love Peacock, 12 July 1820. In *The Letters of Percy Bysshe Shelley, Volume II: Shelley in Italy*, edited by Frederick L. Jones, 212–14. Oxford: Oxford University Press, 1964.

Skempton, A. W. *A Biographical Dictionary of Civil Engineers in Great Britain and Ireland: 1500–1830*. London: ICE Publishing, 2002.

Smiles, Samuel. *The Life of Thomas Telford, Civil Engineer: With an Introductory History of Roads and Travelling in Great Britain*. London: J. Murray, 1867.

Smith, Adam. *Essays on Philosophical Subjects*, edited by Joseph Black and James Hutton. London, 1795.

Smith, Louise Z. "The Material Sublime: Keats and 'Isabella,'" *Studies in Romanticism* 13, no. 4 (Fall 1974): 299–311.

Solomonescu, Yasmin. "Percy Shelley's Revolutionary Periods." *ELH* 83, no. 4 (2016): 1105–33.

Southey, Robert. *Journal of a Tour in Scotland in 1819*. London: J. Murray, 1929.

—. *New Letters of Robert Southey*, edited by Kenneth Curry. Columbia, NY: University Press, 1965.

—. *Robert Southey: Later Poetical Works, 1811–1838*, edited by Tim Fulford and Lynda Pratt. London: Pickering and Chatto, 2012.

Sperry, Stuart. "The Epistle to John Hamilton Reynolds." In *Keats's Poetry and Prose*, edited by Jeffrey N. Cox, 583–92. New York and London: W. W. Norton & Company, 2008.

Speitz, Michele. "Affect and Air: The Speculative Spirit of the Age." *Romanticism and Speculative Realism*, edited by Chris Washington and Anne C. McCarthy, 37–55. New York: Bloomsbury, 2019.

—. "The Sublime." In *Nature and Literary Studies*, edited by Peter Remien and Scott Slovic. Cambridge: Cambridge University Press, 2002.

Spiers, Alexander. *Spiers and Surenne's French and English Pronouncing Dictionary*. Vol. 1. London: D. Appleton & Co., 1861.

Stanback, Emily B. *The Wordsworth-Coleridge Circle and the Aesthetics of Disability*. London: Palgrave Macmillan, 2016.

Steward, Mr. "An Account of the Earthquake Which Happen'd about a Quarter before One O'Clock, on Sunday, September 30. 1750. By Mr. – Steward to the Earl of Cardigan." *Philosophical Transactions of the Royal Society of London* 46 (1750): 721–3.

Stiegler, Bernard. *Technics and Time, 1: The Fault of Epimetheus*, translated by Richard Beardsworth and George Collins. Stanford, CA: Stanford University Press, 1998.

Stillinger, Jack. "Keats and Romance." *Studies in English Literature, 1500–1900* 8, no. 4, Nineteenth Century (Autumn 1968): 593–605.

Sundquist, Eric J. "Melville, Delany, and New World Slavery." In *To Wake the Nations: Race in the Making of American* Literature, 135–221. Cambridge, MA: Harvard University Press, 1994.

Bibliography

Swann, Mandy. "Shelley's Utopian Seascapes." *Studies in Romanticism* 52, no. 3 (Fall 2013): 389–414.

Telford, Thomas, and John Rickman. *Life of Thomas Telford, Civil Engineer, Written by Himself Containing a Descriptive Narrative of His Professional Labours: With a Folio Atlas of Copper Plates.* London: Payne and Foss, 1838.

Thomas, Sophie. *Romanticism and Visuality: Fragments, History, Spectacle.* London and New York: Routledge, 2008.

Thompson, Ann. "Shelley's 'Letter to Maria Gisborne': Tact and Clutter." In *Essays on Shelley*, edited by Miriam Allott, 144–59. Liverpool: Liverpool University Press, 1982.

Tresch, John. "The Machine Awakens: The Science and Politics of the Fantastic Automaton." *French Historical Studies* 34, no. 1 (Winter 2011): 87–123.

—. *The Romantic Machine: Utopian Science and Technology after Napoleon.* Chicago, IL: University of Chicago Press, 2012.

Trifunac, Mihalio D. "75th Anniversary of Strong Motion Observation: A Historical View." *Soil Dynamics and Earthquake Engineering* 29, no. 4 (April 2009): 591–606.

Trumpener, Katie. *Bardic Nationalism: The Romantic Novel and the British Empire.* Princeton, NJ: Princeton University Press, 1997.

Varey, Simon. *Space and the Eighteenth-Century English Novel.* Cambridge: Cambridge University Press, 1990.

Webb, Timothy. "'Cutting Figures': Rhetorical Strategies in Keats's Letters." In *Keats: Bicentenary Readings*, edited by Michael O'Neill, 144–69. Edinburgh: Edinburgh University Press, 1997.

—. "Scratching at the Door of Absence: Writing and Reading 'Letter to Maria Gisborne.'" In *The Unfamiliar Shelley*, edited by Alan M. Weinberg and Timothy Webb, 119–36. Surrey, England: Ashgate, 2009.

Weinberg, Alan. "Freedom from the Stranglehold of Time: Shelley's Visionary Conception in *Queen Mab*." *Romanticism* 22, no. 1 (2016): 90–106.

Weiskel, Thomas. *The Romantic Sublime: Studies in the Psychology of Transcendence.* Baltimore, MD: Johns Hopkins University Press, 1976.

Weymarn, W. W., "An Account of an Earthquake in Siberia: In a Letter from Mons. Weymarn to Dr. Mounsey, Principal Physician of the Emperor of Russia, F.R.S. Translated from the French. Communicated by Mr. Henry Baker." *Philosophical Transactions of the Royal Society of London* 53 (1763): 201–10.

Whitaker Gray, Edward. "Account of Earthquake Felt in Various Parts of England, November 18, 1795; With Some Observations Thereon. By Edward Whitaker Gray, M.D.F.R.S," *Philosophical Transactions of the Royal Society of London* 86 (1796): 353–81.

White, Eric B. *Reading Machines in the Modernist Transatlantic: Avant-Gardes, Technology and the Everyday.* Edinburgh: Edinburgh University Press, 2020.

Whytt, Robert. "An Account of the Earthquake Felt at Glasgow and Dumbarton; Also of a Shower of Dust Falling on a Ship between Shetland and Iceland; in a Letter from Dr. Robert Whytt, Professor of Medicine in the University of Edinburgh, to John Pringle, M.D.F.R.S." *Philosophical Transactions of the Royal Society of London* 49 (1755–1756): 509–11.

Williams, Raymond. *The Country and the City.* Oxford: Oxford University Press, 1973.

Willmoth, Frances. "John Flamsteed's Letter Concerning the Natural Causes of Earthquakes." *Annals of Science* 44, no. 1 (1987): 23–70.

Winner, Langdon. "Technologies as Forms of Life." In *Readings in the Philosophy of Technology*, edited by David M. Kaplan, 103–13. Oxford: Rowman and Littlefield, 2004.

Winterson, Jeanette. *The Passion.* London: Bloomsbury, 1987.

Winthrop, John. "An Account of the Earthquake Felt in New England, and the Neighbouring Parts of America, on the 18th of November 1755. In a Letter to Tho. Birch, D.D. Secret. R.S. by Mr. Professor Winthrop, of Cambridge in New England." *Philosophical Transactions of the Royal Society of London* 50 (1757–1758): 1–18.

Wolfall, Richard. "An Account of the Earthquake at Lisbon, Nov. I. 1755, in Two Letters from Mr. Wolfall, Surgeon, to James Parsons, M.D.F.R.S." *Philosophical Transactions of the Royal Society of London* 49 (1755–1756): 403–8.

Wolfson, Susan J. "'*This* is *my* Lightning' or; Sparks in the Air." *SEL Studies in English Literature 1500–1900* 55, no. 4 (Autumn 2015): 751–86.

Wollstonecraft, Mary. *The Works of Mary Wollstonecraft*, edited by Janet Todd and Marilyn Butler. London: William Pickering, 1989.

Wordsworth, William. "Steamboats, Viaducts, and Railways." In *The Poetical Works of William Wordsworth*. Vol. 7, edited by William Knight, 389–90. London and New York: Macmillan, 1896.

Yousef, Nancy. *Romantic Intimacy.* Stanford, CA: Stanford University Press, 2013.

Index

Abrams, M. H., *The Correspondent Breeze* 119
Adorno, Theodor W. 78
   Dialectic of Enlightenment 36–7, 138n5
Aeolian lyre/harp 20–1, 109, 110, 119, 174
aesthetic categories 28, 29, 60
aesthetic distance 70, 125n60
aesthetic judgments 5–6
Agamedes 39, 43–4, 57
agential sublime aesthetic 92
Allen, Barry 155
ambivalent logic 25, 47, 60, 67–8, 90, 104, 136, 168
American authors 9–10n23, 35–6
Apollo 43–5, 46, 57
apostrophic mode 97
arch bridges 142n13, 145–6
Archimedes 109–10, 115, 123, 125
Arendt, Hannah 84
artificial–natural landscapes, meeting points 138
arts 86
   see also technē
asyndeton 16n42
attraction–repulsion response 77

Bacon, Francis 37
Baillie, Joanna, "Address to a Steam Vessel" 117
Barad, Karen 105n4
beauty–sublime counterpoint 49
Bennett, Jane 53
Bentham, Jeremy 52
Bewell, Alan 88, 104n1
   Natures in Translation 6
Black, J. David 10
Blackwell, Christopher W. 46n47
Blake, William 164
boats 111n21
   see also sailboats; steamships
Boileau, Nicolas 30
Bolton, Carol 144n18
Boston earthquake 73–4
bridges 21–2, 137–9, 178
British Empire 135–62
"British" style engineering 141–8
building–thinking relationship 148
Burdon, Rowland 142
Burke, Edmund 5, 7, 45, 49, 53, 66, 70, 90, 139, 164, 167, 178
   A Philosophical Enquiry 125n60, 135
   Reflections on the Revolution in France 8n19

Byron, Lord 32–3
  Childe Harold's Pilgrimage 59

Cain, Tubal 126
Caledonian Canal 152–3, 178–9
canals 138, 152–4, 161, 178–9
Catherine of Braganza 72n18
Cavalleri, Giovanni Maria 79, 85
cave, co-construction of 50–1
Chakrabarty, Dipesh, "The Climate of
  History" 126
Chandler, James 110
chariots 173–5, 176
Charles II 72n18
children 108–10, 114, 119
chronographs 81–2n46
civil engineering 136–62
Cladis, Mark S. 6
Clarkson, Thomas 21n43
clouds 103–4
coal 87
Coeckelbergh, Mark, *New Romantic
  Cyborgs* 10–11, 63–4
Coffey, Donna 54
Coleridge, Samuel Taylor 9n21
colonial ideologies 141, 147, 160
comedy 120n44
"compressed air" hypothesis 76
Connelly, Joan 43
consumption 98
Corcoran, Clinton DeBevoise 43
coterie poems 120n44
couplet form
  house poems 121
  ideological implications 126
Cox, Jeffrey N. 120n44
craft 52
  see also technē
creativity
  inventions and 87
  sublime scripts of 27–63
"cultural differences" 147
culture 8–9
Curran, Stuart 111

cyborgs 11
Cyclops figure 53–4

Darwin, Charles 38, 52
Darwin, Erasmus 1, 42, 51–2, 169
  Botanic Garden 120
  Progress of Society 17, 52, 55
  Temple of Nature 17, 52–61
Davy, Sir Humphry 117
de Man, Paul 100
death 45, 103
demos ex machina 141, 146, 161
Demosthenes 173n27
deus ex machina 141
Devil's Bridge 139–40n9
Donne, John 177
dreaming 119
Dreicer, Gregory K. 146
Duca della Torre 78
Duffy, Cian 6–7, 86–7
  Cultures of the Sublime 68
dwelling–building connection 148n26

earth
  human condition relationship 84
  narrative space and 126
  as place of repair 59
earthquakes 19–20, 69–85, 90, 92
ecocritics 23–4, 164
ecological technological sublime
  42–52
Economides, Louise 65
egotistical sublime 109, 155, 167–9
electricity 32
Emerson, Ralph Waldo 35
engineers, godlike control 114–15,
  158
England
  earthquakes 72–4
  Portuguese trade relationship
    72n18
Enlightenment 11, 110
entanglement 105n4, 109
entrapment 124–5

Index

environment, human relationship to 63

Epicureus 56

Epimetheus 37–9, 44

estate poems *see* house poem genre

ethical–aesthetic rubric 88–91, 98

Fairer, David, "Eighteenth-Century Poetic Landscapes" 53n57

Ferguson, Frances 145

Solitude and the Sublime 68

fire 87, 113

flower/woman analogy 54

Fraistat, Neil 175–6n31

Frankenstein, Victor (character) 4, 18, 28, 30–1, 33–4, 39, 51, 171

Franklin, Benjamin 18, 28, 32, 33

Gandy, Matthew 135

Gegenes 43

gender binaries 53–4

genius 4, 14, 22

German Romantic nature philosophy 23

giants 150–1

gin 125

Gisborne, John 112, 117, 170

Gisborne, Maria 112, 117–18, 120n43, 123, 133, 170

godlike control, engineers 114–15, 158

Godwin, William 118

Enquiry Concerning Political Justice 106n8

Halberstam, Jack 100–101

Hamblyn, Richard 72n18

Hamilton, Sir William 77–8

Haraway, Donna 53, 56, 154

harps 107, 109, 110

see also lyres

Hartman, Geoffrey 139

Hartman, Saidiya 54n62

Hawthorne, Nathaniel 35

Haydon, B. R. 12–13

Hazeldine, William 142n13

Heidegger, Martin 31, 37, 48, 52, 65, 67, 82, 167–8

Herschel, William 55

Highland canal works 154

Hoare, Prince 42

The Cave of Trophonius 18, 47–52, 58, 171

Holland, Jocelyn 3, 47, 78, 86, 109

Holmes, Richard 12–14

The Age of Wonder 11, 14

Holyhead road project 148, 152–3

Horkheimer, Max, *Dialectic of Enlightenment* 36–7, 138n5

house poem genre 120–3

Howell, Peter 7

Cultures of the Sublime 68

Hughes, D. J. 111n21

humanity-nature, battle of 178

hyperbaton 16n42

imperialism 135–62

industrialization 60, 164–5

industry, sublime scripts of 27–3

"inequality of mankind" 85–91

infrastructural sublime 69–85, 135–62

insects 121–3, 129

intimacy 163–80

inventions/inventors 4, 27, 37–8, 85–91, 164

genius discourse 4–5

sublime status 12, 36

iron bridges 142, 144, 146

Ironbridge, Coalbrookdale 142

Jackson, Steven J. 101

Jena School 23

Jennings, Humphrey 12–13

Pandæmonium 1660–1886 11

Jessop, William 153n35, 161n49

Johnson, Dr. 177

Jones, Steven E. 85–6, 117, 125

197

Kant, Immanuel 5–7, 18–20, 28–9, 35–6, 49, 65–70, 72, 84–5, 87, 89, 91, 99–100, 139–41, 147, 164, 167, 178
  Critique of Judgement 5, 70
Keach, William 120n44, 130
Kean, Edmund 95
Keats, John 1, 7, 18–20, 63–102, 109, 122, 166n5, 168, 169–70
  "Epistle to Reynolds" 91–8, 170, 176
Kelley, Theresa M., *Reinventing Allegory* 139–40n9
Klancher, Jon 1n1
knowledge 138n5, 155

Lamb, Jonathan 173n27
language as tool 47–8
Latour, Bruno 53, 147
  War of the Worlds 147n24
"laws of nature" 147, 151, 158
Lazarus, Micha 30
Leighton, Angela, *Shelley and the Sublime* 173n26
levers 106, 109–10
lightning 32–3, 93, 109
limin 41
liminal space 141, 155
limis 41
liquefaction process 79
Lisbon earthquake, 1755 19, 69, 72, 74–7, 84, 90
literal terms 18, 164
literary devices, typology of 16n42
locks, canals 154–5
Longinus 5, 16, 28, 32–3, 35, 106, 166n5, 173, 177
  On the Sublime 16n42, 27, 29–30, 172
Lopes, Dominic McIver 2
Lorrain, Claude, "Enchanted Castle" 92
Lucretius 56
  De Rerum Natura 59

Lyotard, Jean-François 49, 139
lyres 105–9, 114, 130, 133, 174

McGill, Scott 42n36
machinery–poetry relationship 104, 116
machines
  image of 119n41
  motive force 63–4
MacLeod, Christine, *Heroes of Invention* 4
magicianship 155
Mallet, Robert 80–5
Mammon 90–1
man-machine concept 11
Marx, Leo 66, 165
  The Machine in the Garden 2, 9–10n23
Marxism 110
material sublime 18–19, 39–40, 42, 51–3, 55–58, 63–102
  counternarratives 83, 125
  egotistical sublime relation 167
  infrastructural sublime and 157, 160–1
  intimate relations 163–80
  relational politics of 46
  sublime nature relationship 68
  technological sublime dialogue 138, 157
  will and 91–101
matter, "unsettled" form 166n5
mechanical arts–poetry relationship 88–9
mechanical supernatural 172
mechanists 125n59
Mellor, Anne K., *Mary Shelley* 33
Melville, Herman 35
memory 131
Menai Bridge 142n13, 148–61
metal 113–14
metaphorical terms 18, 164
Michell, John 76–7
Miller, Christopher R. 175
Miller, Perry 9–10n23, 35–6

Index

Milton, John 166, 175, 177
Paradise Lost 176
The Mirror periodical 149–50
Mississippi Valley earthquake
1811–1812 78–9
"monstrousness" 82
Morton, Timothy 23, 105n3, 106n7,
107n11, 110, 164
Moten, Fred 54n62
mountain ranges 8, 151
Muñoz, José 100
Muri, Allison 11
myths 17–18, 71, 119, 129, 175
see also Prometheus myth;
Trophonius myth

nationalist views 140–1, 145–6,
153–4, 157, 159–61
natural–artificial landscapes, meeting
points 138
"natural laws" 147, 151, 158
nature
co-constitution of 17
humanity, battle with 178
sublime in 5, 7–9
technology connection 59
Nersessian, Anahid 60
Nesfield, William 138–41, 143–5
New England earthquakes 73–4, 75
Newton, Sir Isaac, *Optics* 177
Ngai, Sianne 5, 8, 104n2, 170
Nicolson, Marjorie Hope, *Mountain
Gloom and Mountain Glory* 8
normative sublime tropes 72–5, 78, 83
Nye, David E. 66, 78
The American Technological Sublime
9–10n23, 36

Oblivion figure 57
oikos 57, 59
Old Testament narratives 30
O'Neill, Michael 122n47
Ong, Walter J., "Romantic
Difference" 10

oracles 44–5
organicism 110
"ornament" 140
overconsumption 98
Owen, Robert 106n8

Paine, Thomas 21, 106, 110n16, 142,
145
Palmieri, Luigi 80, 85
Pandora 38
Parnell, Sir Henry 159
the pastoral 8, 53
Pausanias 50
Description of Greece 43, 44–5, 57
Peacock, Thomas Love 107n10
pendulums 78, 79
Pennie, John Fitzgerald, *The Royal
Minstrel* 34–5
periphrasis 16n42
Peterloo massacre 107
Petrarchan love poetry 116
*Philosophical Transactions of the Royal
Society of London* 71, 80, 84n54
the picturesque 8
Plato 173n27
Phaedrus 122, 131–3
Plato's cave 97
Plutarch 43
poetry
as co-constituted 167–8
communal nature of 58
as creative force 18
dimensions of 17
machinery relationship 104, 116
mechanical arts relationship 88–9
technē alignment 20
poiesis 65, 67
polish 93
ponderous, use of term 52–8
"ponderous metal" 17, 53–4
Pope, Alexander 122
Portugal–England trade relationship
72n18
praxis 63–4

199

Priestman, Martin 52, 54, 59
Pring, Joseph 159–60
privacy 171
prometheans 38
Prometheus myth 18, 27–63, 87, 93, 124–5, 168–70
protagonist-contra-antagonist plotlines 51
Pythagoras 115n29

queer theory 100

Read, J. 159
Regier, Alexander 75, 90
Rennie, John 152–3, 161n49
repair 49–50, 59
Reveley, Henry 85, 112–15, 117–18, 119, 123–5, 126
Reynolds, J. H. 19, 91–8, 170
rhetoric 75, 165
Rigby, Kate 23–4
roads 148–61, 161n49
Roberts, David 159
Roberts, Robert 159
'romantic machine' 109–10, 119n41
Roscoe, William 155
ruins 137

sailboats 106, 111–12
St. Chad's church 158
Salsano, D. Domemico 78
scientific genius 14
Scott, Grant F. 92–3
Scott, Walter, *Guy Mannering* 59
Sedgwick, Eve K. 100
seismographic sublime 63–102
seismographo-electro-magnetico 80
seismology 18–19, 20
seismoscopes 80, 81n46
sensationalism 71, 75, 77, 150
Seward, Anna 1
   "Colebrook Dale" 53–5
Shakespeare, William 125, 166
   Richard III 95

Shaw, Philip 9
   The Sublime 68
Shelley, Mary Godwin 1, 4, 8, 112, 117
   Frankenstein 4, 18, 27–8, 30–4, 39, 51, 171
   Posthumous Poems 175n31
Shelley, Percy Bysshe 1, 18–21, 33, 65, 67, 69, 72, 85–91, 97–100, 103–36, 169–70, 178
   Alastor 103
   "The Cloud" 103–4
   A Defence of Poetry 19, 85–87, 98, 105, 107–8, 124
   Laon and Cythna 109
   Letter to Maria Gisborne 20, 85, 111, 119–20, 125, 130
   "Mont Blanc" 83, 85, 87
   Ode to the West Wind 105, 107, 133
   Queen Mab 104n1, 109, 172–8
silkworms 121
Skempton, A. W. 142
Smith, Adam, *Essays on Philosophical Subjects* 177
Smith, Louise Z. 91n74
Socrates 131–2
solitariness 115
Solomonescu, Yasmin 115n29
Sophocles 119
sound 108, 129
Southey, Robert 1, 4, 8, 21, 136–7, 141–8, 152–5, 158, 160, 169
   Letters from England 22, 141, 143–5
Sperry, Stuart 93–5
spiders 121–3
steam engines 86, 124, 178
steamships 85–6, 106, 111–13, 115–16, 117–18, 119, 124–6, 128
Stephenson, Robert 146n22
Stiegler, Bernard 17, 37
Stillinger, Jack 91–2n74
stone 58

Index

Strätling, Susanne 47, 78
sub condition 41
sublimation 79–80, 151, 160, 177
sublime
  applications 9, 29
  paradoxical logic of 139–40,
    143–4, 145
  roots of term 15–16, 40–1
  technology as 60
  use of term 3
  in verb form 40–1, 79, 166, 177
sublime-experience-induced aphasia 49
sublime–material nature relationship 68
sublime rhetoric 75, 165
sublime tools 48, 78
sublime-tool-as-tongue metaphor 48
Sunderland Bridge *see* Wearmouth
  Bridge
supernatural narratives 138n5, 154,
  172, 175
suspension bridges 21–2, 142n13,
  148–61, 178
sweeping aesthetics 146–7
Swift, Jonathan 122
  The Battle of the Books 122n47
syntax 16, 99, 109, 121

technē 3, 20, 67, 86
  contemporary thinking 52
  counternarratives 170
  see also poetry
technological determinism 67, 175
technological salvation 67, 77, 175
technological sublime 9–10n23, 136
  applications 29
  logic of 28, 34
  material sublime dialogue 138, 157
technology
  communal nature of 58
  as repair location 59
Telford, Thomas 4, 8, 21, 136–7,
  148–61, 161n49, 169
  Memoirs 22
temporalities 37–8, 142–3

thinking–building relationship 148
Thompson, Ann 120n43
Thoreau, Henry David 35
tools 47–8, 78, 86, 164
transportation technologies 21–2, 164
  see also bridges; canals;
    steamships
Tresch, John 65, 75, 119n41
  The Romantic Machine 10, 63–4
trophonian 39
Trophonius myth 18, 27–63, 168–9,
  171

uncertainty 18–19, 24–25, 29, 40,
  45–51, 60, 66, 73, 83, 88, 92–96,
  104, 123, 133, 169, 179

volcanic eruptions 76, 78, 79
Voltaire 84, 93

Walker, James 142n13
Watt, James 117
Wearmouth Bridge 138, 140
Webb, Timothy 125n59
Weiskel, Thomas, *The Romantic
  Sublime* 68
Whitman, Walt 35
Wilson, Thomas 142, 146, 161n49
wind 119, 174
Winner, Langdon 128–9
Winthrop, John 76
Wolfson, Susan 32–3
Wollstonecraft, Mary 83
Woodhouse, Richard 167
Wordsworth, Dorothy 9n21, 15
  *Recollections of a Tour made in
    Scotland* 12–13
Wordsworth, William 7, 9n21, 116,
  131, 164, 178
worldbuilding 63–102
worms 122–3
writing tools 78

Yousef, Nancy, *Romantic Intimacy* 171

Printed in the USA
CPSIA information can be obtained
at www.ICGtesting.com
CBHW051520021224
18316CB00004B/142